"A remarkable tale of passion, endurance and icy nerve."

Ted Simon

"An unquestionably gutsy journey … told with the courage, integrity and raw energy that you'd expect of a person prepared to tackle the vast frozen wastes on a bicycle."

Benedict Allen

"Cycling through Siberia in winter is a frightening, dangerous and painful undertaking. It is also a magical and enchanting experience that encapsulates the best of extreme adventure travel. Helen has proved herself to be a voracious traveller, a tough adventurer, and a fine writer."

Alastair Humphreys

"True grit. An inspirational woman whose open-minded curiosity takes her beneath the snow and ice to the warmth of the Siberian people."

Sam Manicom

A Siberian Winter's Tale

Cycling to the Edge of Insanity
and the End of the World

Helen Lloyd

Take On Creative

When not stated explicitly, distances are given in kilometres and temperatures in degrees Celsius.

For the purposes of anonymity and to protect privacy, some names have been changed.

First published in 2015
by Take On Creative

Cover design by Helen Lloyd

ISBN 978-0-9576606-2-5

www.takeoncreative.com

The Author

Helen Lloyd grew up in Norfolk, England. She studied Engineering and has worked in industry. Travelling has been a part of her life since she was sixteen. In 2009, she quit her job to embark on her first long journey by bicycle, from England to Cape Town. *Desert Snow* is her debut book about the journey through Africa. As well as cycling 45,000 kilometres through forty-five countries on four continents, she has also made remote journeys by river and on horseback. Between journeys, she spends her time in Norfolk and Buckinghamshire.

Photography

Helen Lloyd is an avid photographer and strives to capture the journeys she makes through photography.

Photographs from her journey through Siberia are available to view on her website:

www.helenstakeon.com/a-siberian-winters-tale/

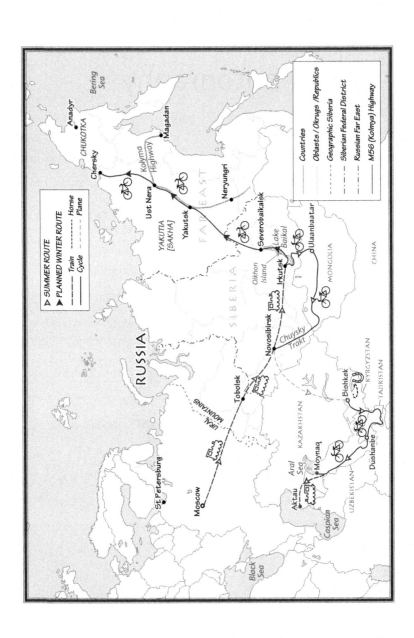

Preface

The idea for a winter trip began with my reading *Ten Thousand Miles with a Dog Sled – A Narrative of Winter Travel in Interior Alaska* by Hudson Stuck. Published in 1916, it made winter in the northern latitudes sound harsh, yet captivating and beautiful. It sounded so foreign from what I knew and had experienced before. I read Jack London and the winter became more intoxicating. It was the call of the wild. I cannot explain it, but if you have heard it you will know what I mean. It is not an audible sound. It is a primeval feeling. It rouses from the pit of the stomach. It gently rumbles from within and gradually becomes more violent; it shakes your whole body and that feeling, which you've been struggling to repress, builds in pressure until you can contain it no longer. Then it gushes up through your belly and chest and squeezes your heart so tight that you hold your breath until, finally, it rushes to your head. And there it simmers, steaming away, always whispering to you. The only way to quieten and calm it is to follow the call. You will never know peace until you do.

Books can be dangerous things in the hands of people who not only dare to dream, but to turn their ideas into reality. When I read *Tent Life in Siberia* by George Kennan, I knew exactly from where the call came.

Helen Lloyd
August 2015

O.

Silence. I have stopped breathing.

I am listening for a sound. Anything to break through this white wall of nothingness. Just my heart is beating, a bass drum booming. The shock waves blast out of my chest and explode in my ears, the muffled echo reverberating around my two-hat-covered head.

Every boom shouts, 'You're still alive!'

And the echo repeats, 'You're crazy'.

Hell, I never felt more alive. I am seriously beginning to wonder about the crazy part.

For hours now – days even, weeks perhaps, for time is frozen here like the rivers – my world has been evaporating into nothing. Now, there is no sound except the beating of my heart, heavy breathing and the crackle of my bike tyres over the packed snow. Earlier, it was a monochrome land of white snow and the dark Siberian forest against a solid blue sky. Then the trees thinned out and the mountains receded leaving only a barren land flattened out, and the sky clouded over so that all the colour and contrast have faded to white.

I feel nothing through these layers, wrapped up against the winter chill. And I smell nothing, not a single faint scent in the air. Winter is a clean and sterile operating theatre. Everything is gone. Even the wind.

Everything, except me.

This is how I imagine the end of the world will be. It won't be pitch black like the spaces between the stars or the utter darkness of a windowless room after the light has been switched off. There is something fearful about the dark. We imagine we are not alone with things lurking in the shadows. No, the end of the world will be all white – pure and untouched – seeing everything; seeing nothing. We'll each stand alone, in peace, surrounded by a blank canvas that can be transformed into any image our mind desires.

But when you hear or see something emerge from this white nothingness, how will you know if it's real or in your head?

I take a deep breath. A rush of icy air shoots into my lungs, and the cold burns through the back of my throat and forks like lightning through my veins. It's a reality check. I must move. Or freeze. I choose to move forward. The only other way is to go back. You see, I cannot leave the road; the snow is too deep. I tried it before and sank. Sank deep enough to scare myself; another time I may not be able to drag my body out.

Now, I stay on the road and simply keep moving forward. I pedal on along the Road of Bones – a narrow ridge bounded by the vast expanse of the endless Siberian wilderness. And I will keep going until there is nowhere left to go – to the end of the world.

'The end of the road, you mean.'

'No, I mean the end of the world. I keep telling you,' I insist.

There's no one there.

I am riding on the edge of insanity to the end of the world.

And the bass drum boom beats on and on.

1.

If you had asked me a year ago where I thought this journey would lead me, I could never have guessed it would be here – contemplating reality, contemplating my sanity.

It seemed obvious that the fight, the struggle, the challenge would be physical. If I didn't make it to Chersky, as I'd planned, way up on the north coast of Russia, well beyond the Arctic Circle and where there are no real roads, I figured it'd be because I met my end with a wolf's kiss or a fall through the ice of a frozen river. I was sure I had the sense to turn around or make another plan if the risks of continuing became too great. When you set off on an adventure, you must assume you will achieve what you set out to do. If you are always thinking about the back-up plan or escape route, then you'll most likely end up taking it. So, if I didn't make it, I hoped it would be because I met my end while putting up a fight. But wolves and frozen rivers only scared me a bit.

I had conjured up all manner of ends in a fear-driven risk assessment and safety analysis. Plenty of friends were willing to provide scenarios for my demise too, out of genuine concern, I think. It was the same when I had said I was going to cycle through Africa. Everyone knew of some danger that might befall me – usually ill-founded fears. It's funny how those who know least about a subject are often the ones most likely to impart advice on it. They always sound so sure of themselves, as if sounding assertive and authoritative will compensate for the fact they don't have a clue. On the contrary, it's the people who don't say much that often have the best advice.

Before I went to Africa, the talk was of lions and rhinos, mosquitoes and malaria, tribal wars and mass rape, death-by-machete with lots of blood and guts and death-by-cholera or some other hideous water-borne disease with lots of diarrhoea and vomiting. Well, none of that happened. Apart from malaria, a little vomiting and one lion encounter. I survived Africa despite other people's fears. All of it was worth it, that I know; I had an incredible time out there, living.

You'd think that tales of Africa and stories of a Siberian winter would have little in common, but that's where you're wrong. There are more similarities between these two regions than their distance apart and extremes of temperature might initially imply.

The fact that I knew so little about Russia, and especially Siberia, was part of its initial appeal. On the map of the world I pored over, it represented a vast unknown space begging to be explored and understood. 'Siberia', like 'Timbuktu', is a word I had long known, but I had never known exactly what or where it was, even whether it really existed. In the vaguest sense, it seemed a distant, vast frozen wasteland of snow and trees. But Siberia, I suspected, was much more than just the tundra and taiga.

The geographical territory defined by the term 'Siberia' has changed over time. Historically, Siberia spanned six time zones in Russia from the Ural mountains to the Bering Strait. Today, the geographical region of Siberia is split into two federal districts: Siberia in the west and the Far East. These federal districts are divided further into oblasts, okrugs and republics. It was Yakutia and Chukotka in the Far East that I especially wanted to cycle through.

Yakutia as the locals call it, and Sakha Republic as it's known officially, covers over three million square kilometres – a land area similar to India – but with a population of less than a million. Chukotka – a region whose principal town, Anadyr, is three times further from Moscow than Anchorage in Alaska – can only be reached overland in the winter when the ground and rivers freeze over, so that ice roads can be driven on. To say the whole area is remote and sparsely populated is an understatement. That was the appeal.

Before I plunged into Siberia, the talk was mainly of bears and mosquitoes. But these are only a problem in the summertime, when those few people who visit usually go. Winter's different – the bears are hibernating and the mosquitoes are dead. That's two fewer problems to worry about.

Unlike bears or wolves, falling through the ice of a lake or river was a genuine concern. Plenty of people who venture onto frozen lakes and rivers die this way. My planned route involved first cycling north over frozen Lake Baikal; I'd be spending a lot of time on the ice. I researched what to do if I did fall through. I set up my equipment to maximise my chances of getting out and getting help. I did not go to Siberia unprepared. I had even spent three weeks cycling and camping in northern Scandinavia the previous winter as a trial.

There was also an invisible threat. What scared me the most – and it wasn't until I was actually there with the silent killer staring me in the face that I realised this – was the Cold. I did not want to go to sleep one night and never wake up, only to be discovered some time later as a frozen blue body mummified in my sleeping bag. That would be a shit way to go. Bring on the wolves, I say.

Don't watch the film *The Grey* shortly before camping out in the Siberian taiga in midwinter. Same goes if you're headed for Alaska, I suppose. In case you don't know the film, it's about a group of oil workers who are flying out of Alaska when their plane crashes in the wilderness. The survivors, facing starvation and the cold, choose to walk out rather than await their fate. Over the coming days, they are hunted down by a pack of wolves, who no doubt can smell easy prey and hopelessness. The men are methodically picked off one by one, the weakest first, as they trek through the forest, fumbling through the snow and fighting against the cold. The wolves are depicted as monstrous beasts – natural born killers – perfectly evolved to survive in this harsh environment. Man, on the other hand, is not.

The first night I camped out in the taiga, down a little-travelled road with not a living soul for miles, I had one downright scary dream. I sometimes have those dreams where you wake with a start and sweat, sometimes a scream, and a heart beating like you're trying to outrun a wolf; and if you try to go back to sleep too soon you head straight back into the dream you thought you'd escaped from. It hadn't happened in a long time. Usually, it happens when I'm stressed, which is not a condition I'm prone to. This time I really was trying to outrun a wolf. The hellish nightmare shocked me back into reality so fast I only remember how it ended: when the wolf attacked and the pack leapt on me to rip my body apart. God, the pain!

It jerked me bolt upright in my tent. The pain instantly vanished, leaving me breathless with a pounding heart. Trust me, you do not want dreams like that when you're winter camping alone in the Siberian taiga. That was one cruel joke my mind played on me that night. Not only because there really might be wolves outside the tent, but when you sit bolt upright, you get a face-full of ice crystals, the frozen condensation that you've dislodged from the tent ceiling. That's bad enough every morning, but in the middle of the night when it's least expected is just another shock too much.

By the time I had fumbled around in my sleeping bag, found the toggle to loosen the seal around my neck and unzipped the bag enough to extricate an arm to brush off all the ice from my sleeping bag and out of my eyes, I was fully awake and boiler-room warm. I lay there in the darkness feeling my heart-rate slow to normal.

It was an eerily quiet night. Any noise was muffled as I lay cocooned in my sleeping bag with headband and woolly hat pulled down and neck-scarf pulled up over my ears. Would I even hear a wolf outside my tent? I doubted it. They are too stealthy and clever for that. The reality was that wolves weren't usually in this region. Then again, neither were English girls.

I couldn't get back to sleep after that. Nothing to do with the wolf dream; I was busting for the loo. Believe me, you've got to be really desperate to expend all the energy required to extract yourself from a polar-rated sleeping bag, put on sufficient clothing so you won't freeze some extremity, and then head out into the winter's night. The distance from the tent you're prepared to go before peeing is definitely related to the temperature. I took a few steps. Relieved, with my body still giving out heat from the exertion of extracting myself from the sleeping bag, I pulled up my thermals over my fat white backside and looked up at the other full moon.

The stars sparkled between the silhouetted trees, the snow glittered underfoot, and the icy, still air touched my cheeks and turned them rosy red. It was beautiful standing in the midst of the forest on that winter's night. I felt alive. It was like everything good in the world was expanding to fill every space and my heart was filled with a longing that the moment would never end. I stood, vulnerable, arms wide open, accepting it all, absorbing everything, humbled and fortified simultaneously by the universe.

As the cold from the ground seeped through my boots until the soles of my feet hurt, I rushed back into the tent and struggled into my sleeping bag where I would be warm and content until morning.

Fear of wolves was largely unfounded. Yes, the previous year there had been a massive cull because their numbers were growing too large and they were killing too many reindeer, which locals rely on for their livelihood. Never, though, was there a report of an attack on a human. That's not to say they weren't capable, but there are other, easier prey that don't go around carrying guns. Wolves stay away from the roads because they associate the smell of petrol with people. I'd be lucky to see a wolf, I was told by those quiet few who know what they're on about.

At the end of the film *The Grey*, there is only one man left on the run. He comes face to face with the alpha of the wolf pack. He has two choices: to give in or fight. There is a motto he remembers from his grandfather, a riff on Shakespeare's *Henry V* about going once more into the fight, to 'live or die' for one last day.

You see, I didn't go to Siberia in the winter because I want to die. I went because I choose to live.

2.

This three-month cycle ride across Siberia was part of a larger journey across Asia.

A linear journey, cycling across the continent from the Black Sea to the Bering Sea would have been the neatest solution. Logistically, considering the equipment required for the changing seasons, this was impractical. Red tape, namely visa restrictions, made this almost impossible. Instead, I split the journey into two: a summer and a winter part.

In the summer, I flew to Moscow and took the Trans-Siberian train to Irkutsk in Siberia. From there, I went west – cycling through Russia and Mongolia, travelling on horseback through Kyrgyzstan, continuing by bicycle via the Silk Road cities of Central Asia, and finishing with a train ride through Kazakhstan to Aqtau on the Caspian Sea. Then I flew home for Christmas. This gave me time to collect my winter equipment and prepare for the second part of the journey.

I had already booked my flight back out to Irkutsk. My timescale for the winter journey was tight. My plan was to cycle over frozen Lake Baikal, then make my way to Yakutsk and cycle along part of the Kolyma Highway before turning off the road and heading north to Chersky. I wanted to leave behind the vast swathes of taiga, go up and over the mountains and emerge on the windswept, snow-covered tundra and follow the Kolyma River that meandered ever northwards until the coast beyond the Arctic Circle.

I would have to begin the ride as soon as I arrived in the country since Russian visa restrictions meant I had only three months. The timing was crucial. If I left too early, Lake Baikal would not be frozen thick enough to cycle on. I researched when the lake usually freezes over – early January – and added a couple of weeks for margin. The reason I didn't leave until later was that if I left too late, I'd be travelling along the ice roads in the north as spring came when the rivers begin to thaw. That scared me more. By then, far north, it would be too late to turn back; I'd be far from help. I couldn't afford to take any risks if they could be avoided. If I had problems on Lake Baikal, at least I could get help relatively quickly. If the lake was not frozen – I didn't want to entertain the possibility – the only risk was to my plan, not my life.

I had discounted the idea of taking a satellite phone in favour of carrying an emergency SPOT device, a GPS tracker with functionality to send pre-determined messages, which would allow my family and friends to find out where I was and that I was OK. It also had an SOS button to notify international search and rescue services in the event of an emergency requiring immediate evacuation.

I considered this sufficient backup for Lake Baikal and along the road. Once I turned off the road and began the remote journey north to Chersky, 'immediate' rescue could take days. In the extreme cold, survival is measured in hours; days would be too late. Essentially, I would be alone and without backup. My only other support would be from passing trucks; I'd been told to expect one every few days. However, I was well-prepared and equipped for this journey. I was ready. And nervous.

Ever since I had selected a start date and booked my flight, I had wished for the lake to freeze in time and feared that it wouldn't. As the New Year dawned, I finally plucked up the courage to find out. My fears were confirmed. The real winter had not kicked in yet; temperatures were unseasonably warm. The lake had not frozen.

Every day I checked the online satellite image, updated every twenty-four hours. Some days the lake was not visible beneath the cloud; most days it showed up deep green with the northern tip white with ice cover. The ice line edged south slowly – too slowly – as the days passed.

Having to wait until the lake ice was thick enough to ride on safely would lose me valuable days. Every day spent waiting would be a day I'd have to make up later – one less rest day; one less day to shelter from bad weather; one less day to say sod it, I'm not going anywhere today, I just don't feel like it; one less day to say yes when someone invited me to go party or go fishing or visit friends. It's those spontaneous days I love most about the way I travel – when you wake up one morning thinking about the next hundred kilometres you'll be cycling that day, just like the day before, but by the end of the day you have not touched your bike and are setting foot on another path. Go with the flow. I prefer guidelines to plans. It would be a shame to turn down an opportunity because I had set myself a deadline to reach some arbitrary point on the map.

I was also aware that by putting myself under pressure to reach Chersky before my visa expired (because I definitely wanted to avoid a confrontation with Russian immigration), I would not rest when I should, would push on and cycle further when really I should stop and camp. That's when you start making the wrong decisions or bad judgement calls. But the cold doesn't give any margin for error.

Once the temperature drops and stays low, the lake freezes over in a week. Another week and the ice is thick enough to drive on. It

11

was easy to imagine the lake surface as a thin film of glassy ice that would gradually get thicker. *One girl and her bike weigh a lot less than a car. Maybe there'll be a few people walking on the ice already. Perhaps I can afford to wait a short time.* With these thoughts in my head, I flew to Siberia in January.

The flight from Moscow to Irkutsk was an overnight one. I have a habit of falling asleep when travelling by plane or bus or train. It comes from long car journeys visiting relatives in England as a back seat passenger when I was a child.

Sleep is the best way to spend time if you want it to pass quickly. As a child, you think you are going to live forever, and you carelessly wish away the less interesting hours. It's only with adulthood that it dawns on you that life is finite with not a moment to waste. It is a cruel irony that, with each passing year, you realise there is so much more to do and see and learn in life but, increasingly, less time to do it. Ultimately we have to accept and make peace with this reality. You cannot beat the inevitable. Still, I sometimes find myself thinking, what if I didn't have to spend so many hours a day sleeping? It's such a waste of precious time. Perhaps that is the reason why I travel under my own power now; I can't sleep while riding or walking.

At an altitude of 30,000 feet you get a rare bird's eye view of the earth. The first time I saw the world from that high up, I was wide-eyed with wonder. Now, it's as though my mind is so overwhelmed I can't fathom the grandeur of this big world view; my eyes glaze over and my eyelids become heavy, and then I rest my head upon the seat and drift off to sleep.

On this flight, I stayed awake a long time. Once the city lights of Moscow had disappeared from view and the immensity of the Siberian countryside lay ahead, the night was dark. Pinpricks of faint starlight broke through the deep black sky. Looking down at Russia, the only signs of life were clusters of street lights and houses, sparse and isolated, with faint glimmers of traffic on the road winding east across the vast expanse. The flight path must follow the unofficially-named trans-Siberian highway, the main artery across Russia besides the railway.

My introduction to Siberia had been very different in the summer when I'd travelled by train. Travelling fast between cities, it gives the illusion that the country is highly populated. Now, from the air, looking north beyond the road, there was darkness. Only occasionally did I spot another illumination, far out towards the horizon. Were they small settlements or, perhaps, oil flares or forest fires? Who lives out there on the edge of the inhabited world? To get a true impression as to the size of Russia, take a flight. It is incomprehensible from ground level.

As the hours passed and time-zones were crossed, the cities became smaller, the spread of lights more condensed. As the temperatures dropped further inland, the towns became masked by a smoky fog hanging above them. Out in the taiga, wood supplies are apparently endless. Homes are heated using this free source of energy. The smoke rises through the chimneys, but trapped beneath the inversion layer of heavy, cold air, it cannot escape. This is a common problem in towns, where traffic fumes and other forms of pollution mix with the woodsmoke. But from the plane, the woodsmoke looked like a protective cloak shielding the towns.

My first winter morning in Russia, I took the bus from Irkutsk to the lake. My first view of the lake that day was one of awe and disappointment. I had imagined and hoped for something utterly different.

The summer before, when I had cycled around the southern edge of the lake, I had expected to see dark blue stretching to the horizon like an ocean of unfathomable depth, under the clear skies of a hot

13

Siberian summer's day. Lake Baikal is, after all, the deepest and oldest lake in the world. Instead, the day was wet, grey and miserable with the cloud hanging low in the hills and the far side of the lake hidden behind mist and fog. Drenched, hungry and tired, I took one look at it and went in search of a hotel. My only comfort was that there were no mosquitoes when it rained.

The lake I saw now was as I had imagined it would be in the summer. It was beautiful. The problem was, it was now midwinter and I was hoping for a vast expanse of ice and snow. The deep blue rippling surface and waves gently lapping at the shore absolutely shattered my hopes of cycling to the other side.

Winter had only softly kissed the edges of the lake. The shore was glazed in ice where the water had lapped the stones and rocks and frozen over them. The rocky cliff faces were whitewashed from the waves that had crashed against them. The ice had been smoothed by the wind; the surface was pockmarked and the thick white icicles were slippery pillars reaching down to the water. The hillsides were covered in white trails where feet had compacted the snow, and the grass was dried to golden.

There was no point remaining disappointed. I could not change the weather any more than I could convince people I was not crazy for wanting to come to Siberia in the winter. I would not be cycling on the lake. Staring north, squinting from the sun and straining my eyes would not make the ice suddenly appear. It was there, somewhere beyond the horizon, inching southwards, I knew.

If I could not wait for winter's slow march here, I would have to go north to meet it. My revised plan was to cycle overland from Irkutsk towards Olkhon Island, the largest island of Lake Baikal, halfway up the western side of the lake. This would give me a few days to acclimatise and test my gear. It would also get me further north where the ice might be thick enough to cycle on. And if it wasn't, I'd just have to make a new plan.

14

I hoped the temperature would drop soon. I never imagined that thought would cross my mind while in Siberia in January. But be careful what you wish for ...

3.

It was minus seventeen degrees Celsius on the morning I set out from Irkutsk for Olkhon Island. From my experiences of cycling in northern Scandinavia the previous winter, that was the ideal temperature – not too cold, not too warm and wet.

The problem, however, was the smog – that same smog I had seen from the plane. Amidst the choking fumes, I felt at risk of suffocating from lack of oxygen. The smell of petrol was overwhelming. The biggest risk was not the pollution, but the poor visibility combined with the fact that many Russians are terrible drivers, with cars in dubious states of repair. When alcohol is added into the equation, Russian roads are some of the most dangerous in the world. Add snow, ice and fog and it's a cocktail for disaster.

I crawled slowly through rush hour, choking on the exhaust fumes that spread thickly amongst the traffic. Being hit by a car because the driver didn't see me until too late would be another shit way to go. I imagined screeching brakes and skidding tyres, then … nothing. Instead, I cycled on the sidewalks and risked ploughing over an unsuspecting pedestrian. The odds were in my favour then, even though it was much slower.

It took longer to reach Olkhon Island than expected. My alarm clock never woke me up. With two hats on and my head buried in the sleeping bag, I never heard it. With short days, I had wanted to be on the road with daylight, but I rarely woke up until the sun was shining.

Think it's difficult to get up on a Sunday morning at home because there's no urgent need to, and it's oh-so-cosy tucked up in the lovely warm bed? Just a few more minutes before you go put the kettle on and shuffle around your thermostat temperature-controlled home with slippers on ... Well, you should wake up outside in the Siberian winter when it's oh-so-cosy tucked up in the lovely thick arctic-rated sleeping bag. Just a few more minutes before you have to crawl out and shake off the snow, blindly struggle into your cold clothes inside a tent steaming with your hot breath, then plunge your feet into frozen boots, and fumble with the stove while your fingers get cold and then wait for the snow to melt before there's even any water to boil ... Trust me, it takes a mammoth amount of willpower to summon the energy required to get out of bed while winter camping. And then you've still got to take down the tent and somehow squeeze everything back into your panniers, which is much harder now they are frozen and stiff. That's to say nothing of the increased size and weight because no matter how much you shake and brush, there will be a significant amount of frost and ice stuck to everything. It is a depressing thought to know that with each day spent camping, you will be adding useless watery weight to your load. The one advantage of having to fight with your gear is that it gets the heart pumping and blood flowing to warm your extremities.

All you have to do then is get back to the road. That, at least, is easier in the morning, when you can retrace your steps through the snow from the night before; pushing and dragging your bike through partially trodden snow is marginally easier. If you inadvertently forgot to tighten up the bottoms of your trousers, you are guaranteed to have snow inside your boots by the time you reach the road. This must be removed, otherwise it will melt and soak your boot liners, which will then freeze your feet.

Now comes the second difficulty. On the main road, there are several cafes to cater for passing traffic. It takes a special kind of willpower to cycle past these cafes without stopping. I do not possess this willpower.

In order to feel less guilty about these indulgent stops, I fabricated a legitimate excuse to warrant entering these islands of warmth and caffeine and hot food. My excuse was water. Rather than spend time in the morning melting snow for the day's water supply, I would pop into a cafe and ask for my thermos to be filled with hot water. It saved me time and cold fingers.

I deluded myself that this was in the name of efficiency. Once I succeed in dragging my lazy self off the sofa or out of a sleeping bag, I can be very productive. Some people achieve this through perseverance, others are efficient. I prefer to be efficient. As with any skill, you will excel if you practise it enough.

That I then ordered a coffee and pancakes, a bowl of steaming ravioli that the Russians call *pelmeni*, or a pizza slice, and I spread my wet clothes along radiators and hot water pipes to dry, and wrote in my journal and checked emails and stared with loathing out of the window did rather undermine the legitimacy of my justification. The real excuse was that it was damn cold out and rather cosy in.

Those cafes were like black holes where time warped and shifted. Unwittingly, an hour or more would pass before I emerged. When there are only a few hours of daylight, it is understandable why my daily average distance was so pathetic: fifty kilometres was a good day. It wasn't because the cold made it harder to cover the distance – not when I was actually cycling. It was because I spent most of the day not cycling that I didn't get very far.

After three days on the road, my legs ached and I was tired. I had expected it to take three or four days to reach Khuzir, the main settlement on Olkhon Island, but at this rate it would take a week.

A disturbed sleep at the top of a hill was not conducive to a long ride to the lake, however. I knew it was a mistake to camp at the top of the hill; it means a cold ride downhill first thing, with the wind to freeze you and no effort required to warm you. It is much better to sleep in a valley, saving the big climb for the morning.

I had been riding with the rise and fall of the endlessly undulating road as it ran down to one frozen river and up to the next hill. It would have been easy to camp where the forest opened out by a river, but by the time I had freewheeled down the hill, I was cold with freezing hands. Instead, I pushed on up the next hill in an effort to get my heart pumping, blood flowing and body warm. Then the hillsides were tree-covered and the snow seemingly too deep for me to leave the road, so I continued down the other side.

Eventually, long after the sun had set, the pink dusk faded to a bruised purple, and I needed a torch to see beyond the road, I decided: enough. No moon or starlight shone through the forest. It was too dangerous to cycle fast and too cold to cycle slowly. It was time to camp – anywhere.

An old track running into the depths of the forest was faintly visible. Fresh snow had fallen since the last vehicle had used it, but beneath that sparkling white blanket, the snow would be compacted. Hopefully it would be a bit easier to push my bike across.

With the sun gone, the temperature had plummeted. My gloves did little to prevent the ice-cold metal tent poles from sapping life from my fingers. Once the tent was up and stove on, I ran and jumped and waved my arms to warm up until the food had cooked. I scoffed it so fast I burnt the roof of my mouth, but still the noodles were cold before I finished. Then I got into my sleeping bag. And slept. And dreamt about wolves.

When cycle-touring and looking for a place to camp, my thought process is always the same. Ideally, I like to be off the road well before dark, so I give myself an hour to find a place to camp. Within an hour you are almost guaranteed to find a suitable place. But it's never ideal. Since there's still an hour before dark, I hold out for a better spot – a better view, less risk of being seen, flatter ground, or easier to reach. Perhaps, I think, I'll just cycle a little further, there's plenty of time left. Each time I carry on, hoping the perfect place is just around the next bend. Yet whatever I find, it is never as good as one of the ones I've already passed. Then darkness descends; it is time to find any old place to sleep for the night. And that is the point when all accessible open ground vanishes. All this time I am cursing myself because I should have stopped at the first place I found. That's why I camped at the top of the hill that night. My options had run out.

As I knew it would be, it was a freezing downhill ride the next morning. And that's why, when I saw a cafe through the snow that was falling fast in thick, heavy flakes, I stopped to warm up. The lady serving food wondered why I hadn't stayed in the guesthouse in the next village. *Ah, so there's a guesthouse.*

When I looked out of the window of my cell-like room in the guesthouse the next morning, the sky was clear. What a change from the day before! Now the wind was howling. As I cycled across a wide river valley, the wind whipped across and cut through my jacket like a knife. When the road turned and wound upwards through the sheltered, gently rolling hills, however, it was a pleasant winter cycle. I pedalled through the final village on the mainland and came to the end of the road. Ahead was Olkhon Island.

In the summer, a ferry takes passengers across the short water crossing from the mainland. In the winter, once the lake is frozen and the ice is thick enough, vehicles drive over it. The water had only recently frozen and there were no vehicles on the lake. I could not see any tracks across it.

I stood, leaning over the handlebars, staring, pondering. *Is it really safe to cross yet?* There was no one to ask. No one would see me if I fell through the ice. I didn't even have the guts to take a few tentative steps onto it. Instead, I turned my bike around and sheepishly cycled back into the village.

At the local grocery store, the woman there was busy texting. I interrupted her. 'Do you know if there's a guesthouse here that's open?' *Hmm … thought I was gonna ask about the ice. Oh, well, that question can wait.* The lady looked up at me and said nothing. 'A guesthouse?' I persevered.

She locked up the shop without a word and started walking down the street in her slippers, never looking up from her mobile phone. 'Come,' she commanded, still on the phone. I hesitated. 'Come,' she repeated. *Oh, she means me. Right, OK then.* I followed.

The guesthouse she took me to looked closed. The lady knocked on the door through the metal grating, spoke a few words to someone and waited. A minute passed before the garage doors opened wide. A tall, young lad beckoned me in and showed me to a lakeside studio. I was the only guest, and this was the best room.

'Are you sure this will be OK? It's not very warm,' he asked as he rushed around turning on the heaters. I laughed. It was a hell of a lot warmer than camping out, which was my other option.

Once he had gone, I made a cup of tea and sat on the bed watching two children playing ice hockey on a small fenced section of the lake by the shore. They rushed round and round chasing the puck, skidding and sliding, wearing little more than tracksuits. The only signs that it was cold were their hats and gloves. With the hills softly lit by the setting sun reflected on the ice, it was a beautiful scene, especially when viewed from the warm indoors.

Later, the lad returned. 'Would you like to join us for dinner?'

'Thanks,' I replied, 'but I've just eaten.' He left. And two minutes later he returned.

'Will you join us for tea then? Or Russian whisky.'

'Russian whisky?'

21

'Yes. You know. Vodka. Come.'

On my summer journey from Moscow to Mongolia, I had been surprised by the lack of vodka I'd seen being drunk. The stereotype was not true, I concluded. I saw few youths drinking at all. When alcohol was involved, more often than not it was beer. I wondered whether young Russians today abstained because they had seen the effects of vodka on older generations; vodka intake is a major contributor in the low male life expectancy compared with female life expectancy in the country. But then I came to Siberia.

I followed the lad through the front door, took my boots off in the dark entranceway and entered into the tiny kitchen. I was introduced first to Yana and Viktor, the young lad's parents. Then I was introduced to Russian vodka.

I sat with Yana and Viktor at the side table, only table. It was already covered with plates of chicken, salami, cheese and fresh tomatoes, and glass jars of pickled gherkins and onions. The lad sat on a cushioned bench in the corner glued to his mobile phone. His sister, a young woman, sat crouched on the step of the doorway to another room. Close to the iron stove, she occasionally leant over, opened the small door and poked at the burning wood. Every time she did, I felt the heat fill the already warm, crowded room.

Behind Yana were some home-made painted wooden cupboards. Hanging on the wall was a clutter of utensils. Yana turned round and took out some glasses. Viktor took the vodka bottle from the pocket of his coat he still had on, unscrewed the lid and began pouring.

I told them about my plans and concerns about cycling on the ice to the island from here. They thought it was safe. Viktor phoned a friend who confirmed that vehicles were now driving to the island. It was safe to cycle; I had nothing to fear, Viktor said.

It was an enjoyable evening. Viktor, I think, would have liked it to last longer, but after the sixth vodka, I made my excuses, said I was very tired and needed an early night.

The next morning I waved goodbye to Viktor and his son and began to wheel my bike out of the garage.

'I'll give you a lift to the dock and see you get off safely,' Viktor said.

Viktor started up his truck while I wheeled my bike to the road. He was on the verge of lifting up my bike when I interrupted. 'I can take the bags off if it helps.'

'No need,' he replied as he took hold of the bike frame to lift it up. The wheels rose only slightly from the ground. 'It's heavy!' he exclaimed with a grunt.

'Yes. Shall I …?' But now Viktor had taken a proper grip with his giant hands, he hauled it up and over the truck side in one arcing move. It landed with a thud. *That was impressive.* Living out here, I guess you've got to be strong. Muscles are formed from years of manual labour, living off the land and a red meat-heavy diet. It's not the kind of sleek physique you get from frequenting the gym to look good.

At the dock, we sat in the truck and stared out to the island. 'You see the road on the other side? That's where the ferry usually goes.'

'I see,' I said.

'You could go that way, but then you have to get over the big hill. It would be better to cycle round to the next bay. There.' He pointed slightly to the left. 'It's further on the ice, about six kilometres, but then you can follow the track and join the road later.'

'Where exactly? There?' I pointed to the bay with an ice-bound, rusting boat jutting out. Viktor nodded and then explained in more detail the route over the island, of which I could only understand snippets. I was just happy for him to keep talking. If he was talking, I was still on solid ground inside a warm truck.

I wanted to say 'You'll wait to see that I get to the other side, won't you?' and 'You'll come get me if I fall through the ice, won't you?' But my Russian wasn't up to it. Although I'd learnt some basic Russian before I left home and had picked up more whilst travelling the previous summer, I could understand more than I could speak. All I could manage was, 'It is safe. Yes?' I wasn't worried about getting lost.

Viktor put one hand on my shoulder and smiled. 'Yes. I wouldn't let you go if not. Come on.' I guess he could see the anxiety I was trying to hide.

He waited while I sorted out my hat and jacket and gloves and got on the bike. Then he wished me a safe journey. I wobbled away. At the shoreline where the ice started, I stopped and turned back. Viktor was standing by the truck, waiting. I watched him waving his big bear hand at me. Then I turned and took my first nervous steps onto the ice.

Once I realised the bike tyres weren't going to slip out from under me, I pedalled harder. My heart was beating fast – not from the exertion, but from anxiety and fear and nerves like the kind you get before going up on centre stage to perform. I pedalled faster – less time on the ice that way. It was just like when I'd cycled through Botswana where there were known to be lions nearby. As if I could outrun a lion. As if I could dodge the thin ice.

The whole time I was pedalling, I was staring down at the black ice below. It was not a continuous sheet, but made up of many blocks where cracks had propagated and frozen again into myriad white scars. Some blocks of ice were thicker than others; some looked very thin.

It was mesmerising. And terrifying. But I was getting hot and needed to stop to take off a layer of clothing. I looked back to see if Viktor was still watching. He had gone, and the jetty was a distant speck.

I was alone. Stranded on a sea of ice.

The black ice was slippery underfoot; my rubber-soled boots

provided no grip, unlike the studs on my bike tyres. Gingerly, I began to lay the bike down, careful not to drop it. I envisaged the ice splintering … *Don't think about it.* As the handlebar touched the glassy surface, a cracking noise erupted. *Oh shit!* And in one continuous movement, I jumped at the noise and lifted the bike back up and shot off like a bullet out of a gun.

I was pedalling so fast, legs beating up and down like a sewing machine, and breathing so quickly, puffing like a locomotive; soon I was exhausted. Eventually I slowed the pace and started laughing at myself. The ice was solid; I had not fallen through. It was just a noise, nothing more. I stopped again. Now, without the noise of the crackling tyres, all was silent.

Nothing moved. An onlooker would have just seen a crazy chick standing and steaming like a turd in the middle of the lake; hot air rising from her head in the frigid atmosphere. There were no people around; only the sane survive in the cold, and they were all sensibly hidden away indoors. The Siberian dogs, though, are more hardy or foolish. I noticed one barking specimen making a dash for me. He slipped and scrabbled with legs flying out from underneath in all directions, then gained traction as his claws gripped the ice and eventually got close enough to hurl himself at my feet as a slobbering, panting ball of fur. I knelt down and gave him all my attention and affection and instantly felt a lot safer. I looked around wondering where the dog had come from and saw, by the shoreline of the island, a large log home with smoke trailing upwards from the chimney.

This time, when I heard a loud crack emanate from the ice, and noticed that the dog didn't flinch, I didn't worry. Now that I was still, I heard many more cracks and creaks as the ice moved and shifted from the pressure created by the moving water underneath and the wind over the top of this frozen shield.

My pannier soon became the sole object of the dog's attention. He could smell the salami. I heard a whistling sound coming from near the log home, presumably made by his owner. The dog stood alert, ears pricked for an instant and then turned his attention straight back to the salami. Again, the whistle sounded and this time the dog started to run off. Barely ten metres from me, he turned back. The smell of meat was too tempting. When a voice boomed out from the hillside, the dog ran towards it, struggling to stay on his feet. He looked at me, then from where the noise came, and back to me. The poor puppy just couldn't decide which way to go. But eventually he ran back home, leaving me alone once more.

In the mosaic of clear ice and crack lines, tiny white bubbles snaked through the glassy complexion where micro-organisms had migrated and air bubbles formed. Nearer the shore, in the shallows, algae and weeds were frozen into the ice, immovable and trapped until the spring thaw. Nothing here escapes the grip of winter. Yet, still life goes on. It survives.

The surface of the lake wasn't all smooth. In places it was pockmarked with dips and dents that were infilled with fresh snow giving a mottled effect. In another stretch, the surface consisted of a series of serrated edges like a saw. The jagged teeth broke off and rang like percussion as I cycled over them. Now that my fear had subsided, I found it all fascinating. Until, all of a sudden, I was back on solid ground.

4.

Was that to be the end of my cycle over Lake Baikal? I hoped not; it had ended so soon. I pedalled off with sadness through the undulating countryside, along dirt tracks. The climate in this region is very dry; there was little snow covering the yellow grass. By midday, the temperature had risen so much it hardly seemed like winter at all. I could sit out and drink tea, eat lunch and enjoy the gentle warmth of the sun on my face. Sheltered from the wind, there was no chill at all. My thermometer read minus ten degrees Celsius.

I found a hostel to stay at in Kuzhir on the island. The village is isolated. But alive. Smoke rises from the houses dotting the hillside. Dogs bark from behind a wall as you walk past. Cats crouch under the eaves of wooden homes. Little tits and other birds with feathers plumped line the fenceposts. People wander to the shops to buy food.

By the jetty in the bay, boats lie pitched askew like ancient headstones in an overgrown graveyard, fixed in place until the lake releases its icy grip in three months' time. Looking out at the lake, all is absolutely still, concealing the life below.

On the inside wall of a crumbling building by the jetty, a face had been painted. I find street art and graffiti fascinating the world over. This was the face of a large weathered man with a wild beard surrounded by fish. His eyes stared out from a hole where a window should have been, looking out over the boats in the bay like a protector.

I leant against the wall beside Neptune and watched with curiosity as two men dug into the ice in the distance along the shore. After they had finished, they returned with their cattle. The cows walked cautiously towards the hole and took turns to drink the fresh water. Every day the cattle would have to be watered and every day the ice would have to be broken.

I had thought the men were making a hole for ice-fishing, a popular pastime for locals. There were many makeshift signs around the village advertising fish for sale. Omul, a whitefish endemic to Lake Baikal, is the main catch. Considered a delicacy, it is often eaten salted or smoked.

Back at the hostel, three French ladies invited me to a barbecue. In the afternoon, we drove into the forest on the south side of the village with Sergei, a local man they knew. We parked beside a small stream, its surface covered with a thin film of ice that held a light sprinkling of snow. With a light tap, the ice cracked to reveal clear flowing water beneath. Sergei gathered wood and started a huge fire. With an iron tripod stand, the pan of water hung precariously over the flames. We cooked sausages on a metal grill whilst waiting for the water to boil.

It was cold in the shade of the trees, only shafts of sunlight reaching through. As we stood round the fire drinking tea, it was obvious who was used to the Siberian winter. Sergei stood with only a thick woollen jumper on. His bare hands were thick and slightly swollen. The rest of us were wrapped up in thick down jackets and hats and gloves, stomping our feet to keep the blood flowing.

I wandered across the stream using the makeshift bridge of fallen tree trunks. Where the forest thinned out, the white ground sparkled in the sunlight. Animal footprints criss-crossed the otherwise untouched snow and birds darted through the trees.

Around Khuzir, it was thick enough to walk and even drive on the ice, but the local drivers were not yet crossing directly to the mainland shore. They claimed that there were channels of open water around the northern part of the island. I was interested in going to see. It's not that I didn't believe them. I didn't want to. Cycling the short distance over the ice to the island was a taster; it had only made my desire to ride up the lake even stronger. In my naivety, I imagined that the channels might be narrow enough to throw my bags and bike over and step across.

Whilst cycling from Irkutsk, I had come down with a terrible cold and hacking, chesty cough. It was due to wearing my neoprene face mask, which would get soaked from the moisture of my breath and then freeze. For days, I had been cycling with this frozen mask wrapped around my lower jaw and sitting on my chest. The sensible thing to be done now was to keep warm and rest. So the next day, rather than cycle, I joined a Chinese tourist group and went to the north of the island in an army green Russian UAZ truck, a type of minibus that can go almost anywhere you dare drive.

There is no real road beyond Kuzhir, only forest tracks accessible by 4x4 or the Russian UAZ. It was easier to travel over the ice near Khuzhir, where it was thick enough and safe to do so.

Close to shore near Khuzir, there are several smaller islands, pinnacles of rock that protrude from the ice. By one rocky island, we left the truck to explore the needle-like icicles, several feet long, hanging precariously from the roofs of small caves. I walked over the morass of broken ice surrounding the island, a crater-field of slippery obstacles to negotiate. Where the ice remained flat, I took large steps over the darker bands where the ice had been pulled apart and fresh water had recently frozen in its place. I was sure I could feel it flexing under my weight. It creaked and groaned with my heavy-footed intrusion. It made me uneasy. It was as though the rock did not want me there, its low moaning voice a final warning to stay away.

I walked further out where the ice felt more solid underfoot. The silence returned.

When the ice became too thin, we drove back onto Olkhon Island using a track alongside a farm and continued north overland through the forest. Deep in the woods, where little sunlight reached through the canopy, leafless pine trees struggled to survive, bleeding orange sap and covered in a yellowy moss. They struck out of the ground with spindly fingers, as though clawing to escape the deadly grip of the frozen earth.

Towards the northern tip of Olkhon Island, this forest gave way to an open snow-covered plateau where a cluster of hardy horses sheltered in the lee of some trees. High up and exposed, the wind whipped across. It was no wonder few people live here. There were only a couple of farms poorly sheltered in the valleys and a weather station down by a sandy inlet on the east coast.

Whenever the UAZ stopped, we all donned hats and gloves before opening the door, when a rush of cold air filled the inside. Then we climbed out and clambered up onto the rocks. The wind soon froze our exposed cheeks. Out on this promontory, I kept a tight grip as the wind gusted and howled. It was beautiful and bleak and damning.

Looking north, cutting through the white ice all the way to the horizon was a dark blue open channel. Another wide crack towards the northeast formed a scathing 'V'. With only ice and the horizon, it was impossible to tell the true size of the gaps – perhaps the width of a football pitch, possibly more. The only thing I could be sure of was that the ice could not be crossed. Those dark cracks breaking the ice into giant shards shattered my hopes of cycling up Lake Baikal.

The disappointing truth was unavoidable. It was time to move on. I could always come back another year. The lake will remain; the winter will surely return.

I decided to return to Irkutsk and take the first train to Neryungri, a large mining town directly east of Lake Baikal. I could cycle from there to Yakutsk and continue my journey.

Rather than cycling the return route, I took a *marshrutka*, a minibus used as shared public transport, back to Irkutsk, which was much faster. My bike and bags were crammed into the back seats, piled up with other people's rucksacks. Unable to stare through the window for long – soon after we started moving, the windows began to steam up and frost over – I made smalltalk with three young Russians while eating cabbage cakes they had given me that tasted as awful as they sound. Sometimes, I stared blankly at the window frosting, watching my breath spread slowly like a tree of tiny veins across the glass. The branches spread and divided and smaller threads grew from those and very soon what had started in the corner now covered half the window. I put my finger up to the glass and the warmth melted the frost, but soon my fingertip was cold too. No matter how hard I rubbed, nothing else melted. Warming anything up here requires a lot of effort.

Irkutsk had undergone a transformation. All the trees were sugar-coated in fine snow. In the crisp, clear air, it sparkled as in a fairytale winter wonderland. But this wasn't the time for me to explore this dream world further. I had a new plan, in the real world.

The train journey to Neryungri reminded me of when I'd travelled from Moscow to Irkutsk in the summer: bundles of Russians and one English *turistka* trundling across industrial city sprawls that churned smoke to the skies and spewed cars along straight roads that cut through the vast swathes of taiga. We went silently through the night except for the clickety-clack of steel wheels on the rail tracks or whistle of wind as two trains passed side-by-side. Then we slowed into a town and ground to a stop. And we waited. I gazed through the window at the people climbing down off the train to stand on the platform and smoke. Then the whistle would blow and they'd clamber

31

aboard for more hours of sitting and talking and listening. When we were hungry, we'd buy noodles from the *provodnik* and add water from the samovar that was always at the wagon end. I watched young people connive and imbibe a vodka or cognac, tear at a chocolate bar to take away the foul flavour, and then down another shot.

When the sun set over the broad sky and darkness fell upon all, the lights were dimmed, and I crawled onto my narrow bed that rocked hypnotically to and fro, shuddering and jolting as wagons collided. Sleep came easily until daylight arrived once more. It always came fast, travelling east as I was.

Train travel is timeless. The difference was that then, in the summer, the forest had been fat and full and green. Now, in the midst of winter, looking out of the window, the world outside was bleached white and the taiga looked lean with the trees in their bare-branched state. The contrast between the seasons was as stark as life and death.

5.

As the train approached Neryungri, passengers about to disembark began to pack up their bags. This is an exercise in teamwork. First, everyone has to clear up their belongings and place them together with their rolled up mattresses onto the upper bunk beds. Then everyone squeezes onto one of the lower beds, so that the bags that have been neatly packed underneath can be accessed. One person lifts the lid of the empty seat, removes the bags and passes them over to the other passengers. They either launch the bags onto the upper bed if there is space or they simply remain squashed under the pile. Once the baggage space under the seat is empty, the struggle to lower the lid begins. The locking mechanism that holds it up regularly gets stuck. So the person who has removed the bags is now bent over with their backside undoubtedly in some poor person's face, fighting with this inanimate object and working up a sweat. The other passengers, squashed under the pile of luggage, sit silently as the battle continues.

There are two types of people who travel by train in Russia: those who can close the seat lid and those who can't. I am not talking about the toilet, just to be clear. I sincerely hope that no one ever touches those on a Russian train.

I sat through all this, partly in mild amusement and partly with desperate restraint, the urge to take over and close the seat lid myself growing ever stronger. I sat on my hands and focussed on not revealing the smirk on my face. I had one of the beds along the aisle, out of the way of the mayhem in the compartment.

I looked at Sonya, an Uzbek lady, sitting next to me. Our eyes locked and the smiles we'd been trying so hard to restrain suddenly spread across our faces. I instantly returned my stare to the continuing seat struggle to avoid an audible snigger. Sonya gave her husband, Radyk, a nudge and a nod of the head that meant, *go on, put them out of their misery*. With that, Radyk got up, took over and quick as a flash the seat was down. Then he turned his attention to the bags, which he arranged on the empty seat, much to the relief of everyone.

Finally, the only luggage still to be retrieved was that on the uppermost shelf – mine. I looked up at the bike; in that moment, it disgusted me. I stepped up onto the lower seats, inelegantly straddling the aisle and hoped no one would choose this moment to pass through to reach the toilet or have a smoke. Taking a moment to balance myself, I gingerly let go of the upper bed with one hand, then the other. As the train rocked along, I reached up for the tyres. This is good training for anyone considering equine acrobatics. You'll have no problem standing atop the saddle of a cantering horse once you've mastered this balancing act on Russian trains.

Fortunately Radyk, who happened to be a foot taller than me, came to my aid and took over. I stepped off my precarious perch and waited as he passed the wheels first, followed by the rest of the bike. I looked around helplessly, wondering where on this crammed train I was supposed to put my gear now. Everyone else in the carriage was quietly clutching bags, waiting and watching.

Seeing my bewildered look, a big lady stood up, smiled at me, took charge of the wheels and handed them to her friend. She then returned for the bike, disappeared down the aisle and left it at the end of the carriage. As Radyk continued to hand down my roll mat and dry bag and panniers, these too were passed down the aisle with everyone getting involved.

I reluctantly put on my polar-rated boots and stuffed my hat and gloves into the pockets of my fleece, which I now noticed was smeared in oil from the bike chain. This wouldn't have been bad if only it hadn't been brand new and white, and all the other women hadn't looked so smart wrapped up in their fur coats.

With peace returned, I focussed all my energy on calming down. Sitting in a room where the temperature is close to plus thirty degrees in clothing suitable for minus forty degrees is a most unpleasant experience. The heaters below the seat were blowing hot air straight onto my minus one hundred degrees temperature rated boots. My feet were soon drenched in pools of sweat. The more I tried to ignore it because there was nowhere else to put my feet, the more I thought about my rapidly reddening face, the beads of sweat on my forehead and moisture trickling down my back. I couldn't have felt more out of place if I'd been sitting there in a bikini. At least then it wouldn't have felt so damned hot.

As the train slowed, people made their way to the end of the carriage. Realising that my bike and luggage were probably blocking the exit, I apologised and pushed and squeezed my way through as far as possible, trying not to rub the black grease on my fleece onto anyone's pristine fur coats. Halted before the exit, I watched as various passengers stumbled past my gear when the doors opened. As the chaos continued, some people started picking up my bags and taking them off the train. There are some countries in Asia where I would never have seen my luggage again, but when I reached the door all my stuff was heaped on the platform.

The rush of cool air through the doorway was instantly refreshing. I stepped off the train. Winter had arrived. Cycling in northern Scandinavia and by Lake Baikal had been mere hints of cold, like standing on the far side of the kitchen while the freezer door is open. Now I was standing in the freezer. Actually, standing in a freezer would have been a lot warmer. It was minus forty degrees here.

There are no words in the English language to fully describe that kind of temperature. England, after all – where I grew up – is a temperate isle. We complain when the thermometer drops near zero. Unless you have experienced snow in England, you would not believe the utter chaos an inch of the stuff can cause. Trains don't run, roads become impassable, schools close, businesses shut early. It's great to be a kid on those days: build snowmen, throw snowballs, make snow fairies and yellow snow. Grown-ups prefer to head indoors and wrap up next to the log burner with a glass of wine and comment, 'Gosh, it's rather nippy out there now.' Or they head to the pub and over a pint of beer comment, 'Hell, it's freezing out, colder than a witch's tit.' Not exactly Shakespeare or Wordsworth, but I'm pretty sure they didn't have any words for the Siberian cold either.

So there I was, surrounded by my bike, four panniers, a dry bag and handlebar bag, fumbling with my gloves and trying to zip up my jacket and put on my hat all at the same time. It had been so hot on the train and I'd been stuck in it for two days sweating away that the idea it could be anything else but tropical outside was almost unthinkable. Now I was outside, and it was anything but palm trees and bikinis.

The advantage of it being so cold outside was that the crowd of onlookers was confined to a hardy few. It didn't take long to reassemble the bike. It's surprising how efficient you can be when faced with freezing temperatures. Only mosquitoes make me pack up faster.

Muttering to myself, I pedalled out of the station. *God, I hope it doesn't get any colder than this.*

It did.

Oh yes, be very careful what you wish for …

The first thing I did the next morning was pull the curtains back in the hotel room and peer out at the thermometer I'd stuck on the snow-covered window ledge. It read minus forty-three degrees Celsius. My courage disappeared with the daunting prospect of beginning the cycle ride in these temperatures, with the unknown of the road ahead and no safety net of a place inside to warm up that night. Suddenly, any enthusiasm for the winter bike ride vanished. All that remained were doubts and questions. One question summed up this whole ridiculous scenario I'd voluntarily put myself in:

What the fuck am I doing here now?

The only thing forcing me to start riding that day was that I couldn't bring myself to pay for another night in an expensive hotel. Besides, I checked the forecast online and the cold looked set to continue. I was in the middle of Siberia in February – what else was I to expect? I'd only be in exactly the same predicament the next day, and the day after. I hadn't started yet and I was already wondering when it would end.

As a compromise, I decided to stay until checkout time. Hopefully by then, with the sun out, it would have warmed a few degrees. My second compromise, to ease my churning stomach, was to give up on breakfast and get my calories in liquid form from highly sweetened instant coffee. Let the sugar flow and teeth rot, I say.

Before leaving town, I needed to buy some good mittens. I stopped outside to ask directions to an outdoor shop. There is a skill in finding the right person to ask. I knew when I saw the fishermen standing behind a table with their catch piled in boxes that one of them could help. Wearing thick camouflage jackets and fur-lined trappers' hats, they stood around joking amongst themselves without a care or concern, as if it were a clear spring day in England.

The one I approached stood well over six feet tall and clearly lived on a fat-heavy diet like most people here. He looked an unsavoury character; there's no way I would have approached him alone in the wilderness. But appearances can be deceptive; I considered that perhaps his rough, unkempt appearance was down to the fact that he'd been out hunting and fishing for weeks and only just returned. Who was I to judge? I might be in a similar unwashed state by the time I reached Yakutsk.

You should have seen the look of wide-eyed horror on his face when I said where I was going to cycle. 'You're going on this bicycle?' he asked, clearly disturbed. 'Like this?'

'Yes.'

'You have nothing with you.'

'Oh, no. My luggage is back in the hotel.' I laughed, realising he thought that I was going with only the clothes on my back.

A look of relief washed over his stubbled, red-cheeked face, and the wrinkled-brow concern transformed into a wide, rotting-tooth grin. I guess he'd been drinking sugar-heavy coffee for decades. 'So you have a tent and sleeping bag?'

'Of course,' I smiled.

He looked over the bike. 'Good tyres,' he commented as he inspected the metal studs on the treads. 'Do you have tools to repair your bike?'

'I've got everything I need: camping gear, good clothes, spares for the bike, a stove and lots of food,' I said. 'Everything except some good mittens.'

Perhaps I was asking the wrong person after all. This tough fisherman, I now noticed, wasn't wearing gloves at all. His rough, thick hands were cracked with dirt engrained under the nails and two fingertips short.

He suggested I buy mittens at the market as they'd be cheaper there.

'They'll be good enough to stop me getting cold hands?' I asked.

'Oh no, there's not much you can do to stop your hands getting cold. But the mittens are the best option.' And he grinned again. I was

38

beginning to like this guy. He had a warm heart and a wicked smile. He was one of the few people who didn't question why I wanted to cycle here in winter. For him, it was perfectly natural to spend a life outdoors whatever the weather.

6.

No more delaying. It was time to leave. Bike ready, panniers packed, fully clothed. First, though, I needed a quick stop to buy the last vital item I'd forgotten, namely loo roll. Outside the shop, I leant my bike against the railing next to a parked car and debated whether I should lock the bike. I weighed up the situation, which ultimately came down to the time required to lock my bike, resulting in cold fingers, against the risk of theft considering the people about and time I'd be in the shop. I looked around to assess the type of people on this mining city street.

I laughed. Who in their right mind is going to steal a fully-laden bicycle in the middle of winter when there's a car with the key in the ignition and engine running right next to it? If you turn the engine off when it's this cold, you won't get the car started again until spring. You must even keep the engine running overnight, unless you can park the car in a heated garage.

I also needed fuel for my stove. The petrol station was on the outskirts of the town. There was a pretty blonde girl sitting in the kiosk with a steaming mug of tea. I looked helplessly towards her when I couldn't figure out how to start the old rusting pump. She shouted something back to me and pointed. I looked around, none-the-wiser. She explained again. It was no use; I couldn't hear anything through my hat layers.

Come off it, shouting isn't going to help, I thought. *Can't you see I'm an idiot foreigner who doesn't have a clue how things work here? Why don't you save us both some pain and come help me?*

Shit, I'm gonna have to go out and help this guy, she was thinking. *Why the hell does he need petrol for a bicycle anyway? Why should I have to suffer the cold just because he's idiot enough to be cycling in this weather?*

I was about to leave, figuring I'd find fuel at the next village, when she emerged from the kiosk, turned on the pump and waited for me. I inserted the nozzle into the fuel bottle and gently squeezed the trigger. Nothing happened. I squeezed a little harder; petrol sprayed everywhere as the nozzle took on a life if its own. It shot out of the bottle, which toppled over and spilled fuel all over the icy concrete. My mittens stank of petrol. The girl swore at me and picked up the bottle.

'Don't touch anything,' she commanded as she walked away. I stood motionless like a naughty schoolgirl wondering what punishment was in store. She came back carrying a small bucket.

'How many litres do you still need?' she asked.

'Two, I think.' With that, she emptied two litres into the bucket, magically produced a plastic funnel from nowhere – Russians are very resourceful – and poured the fuel into my bottle.

'Thank you and sorry for the mess.'

'It's OK,' she replied and, for the first time, looked at me. 'Oh, sorry, I thought you were a man.' I saw the hint of a smile crack through her frosty exterior. 'Where are you going?'

The ice was broken. Now she didn't want me to leave. 'Would you like some tea? You can come and warm up inside. I'd love to hear more. It's boring here all day with no one to talk to.' It was a tempting offer and clearly would have meant a lot to her, but I wanted to get going and make the most of the short day. It had taken long enough to reach the edge of town.

She waved goodbye and wished me luck. I pulled up the air-filter mask over my face, flipped up the hood and zipped the jacket fully up over my chin. Then I wheeled my bike to face the road. In a stable position, I paused a moment for composure. With considerable effort, I swung my foot up and over the cross bar. Still unused to wearing these cumbersome, thick-soled winter boots, I'd misjudged the clearance one time, inadvertently kicked the bike out of my hands and had fallen over backwards to land with a thud on the ice.

Finally, I was on the road cycling towards Yakutsk. The sun was out and the gentle incline had me warm soon enough. The going was slow, despite the clear tarmac road. I was crawling along, getting more and more out of breath. *Am I really this unfit? Perhaps I should have trained more. Too late now.* If this was as fast as I could go, so be it. Get on with it. I tried to settle in to a slow steady rhythm, but it just got harder and harder to breathe. *Shit, I don't feel so good.* I struggled to force the air into my lungs. Then I began to feel pressure on my ears as if my skull was being squeezed. *What the hell is wrong? Too hot … Can't breathe. Need air!*

I stopped pedalling, dropped the bike, forced my jacket hood down, fumbled with the zip and ripped the filter mask from my face. This time as I gasped for breath, the icy air rushed into my lungs and the blood rushed to my head. I crumpled into a heap on the ground taking long, deep breaths. I couldn't understand what had happened. Once my heart rate returned to normal, I felt OK.

It wasn't long after I resumed cycling that the same laboured breathing returned. *Something's not right.* I lowered my mask and breathing became easier. That's when I realised that the moisture from my breath had condensed in the air filter and frozen solid when I'd stopped to get petrol. It had been suffocating me. I tried to knock the ice out, with no effect. Instead, I pulled up my scarf over my mouth and nose.

The road now took a straight line up a steep hill – too steep to pedal up with sixty kilograms of bike and baggage. It was a slow slog pushing. At the top, I stopped for tea from my thermos, picked at the trail mix and looked back at Neryungri below. *I hope that's all the uphill today.* But, like I said before, be careful what you wish for. It wasn't long before I would cherish the uphills. It's the downhills that are the winter cyclist's bane and torture.

The next problem, I soon realised, was that my softshell trousers were not windproof enough when cycling at a reasonable speed on the flat. My thighs soon froze. My butt, too. It was cruel that I could be so hot and sweaty, yet the fattest parts of me – those well-insulated hips and thighs – were so icy cold, painful and itchy. I struggled to fit my ski trousers over the top. Resembling the Michelin man and significantly less agile, it took several attempts and much hitching of trousers until I had a wedgie to get sufficient flexibility to be able to swing my leg over the cross bar again.

It had taken a long time to cycle the ten kilometres to reach the main highway going north to Yakutsk. Once there, I set my sights on Chulman, the next village. With no more reasons to stop, I intended to pedal all the way with only a couple of short breaks to drink tea. Then I'd keep going another twenty kilometres, maybe, before setting up camp for the night. That would be reasonable for the first day, I thought. Reasonable, if it wasn't so cold. But it wasn't the cold in itself that was the main problem.

Sure, my goggles steamed up and quickly iced over, so I couldn't see, and no matter how hard I tried, I couldn't de-ice them – because it was cold. Sure, ice formed on my eyelashes, so it looked like I'd mistaken the Tipp-ex bottle for mascara, and the ice stuck my eyelids together – because it was cold. Sure, the windchill when freewheeling downhill soon numbed my toes – because it was cold. And my fingers hurt when I stopped and had to fight to open the stiffened panniers, or hold my thermos mug, or touch the metal camera to take a photo – because it was cold. Sure, my camera battery died and the replacement was useless because the lens had frozen shut anyway – because it was cold.

I could deal with all of this – make allowances, adjust, adapt, re-assess or simply put up with it. But the main problem was one thing I hadn't counted on and could do nothing about. Every time I stopped, which was frequently, no matter how briefly, a driver would slow down and pull over beside me to make sure I was OK. Now, how could I begrudge that? It was comforting to know that the locals would stop to help if I needed it. But the conversation never stopped there.

'Are you sure you're OK?' the driver would ask.

'Yes, I'm fine,' I'd reply and clarify the reason I'd stopped was to drink tea, or eat something, or take off a pair of gloves because my hands were hot, or put a pair on because they were cold, or take off a hat, or adjust a zip, or take a photo if my camera would work. Oh, there were many reasons I was stopping so often.

There were always so many questions. And with every question, while the interrogator sat inside with warm hands and feet without the need for hat or gloves, I stood outside getting colder by the second. No, I wasn't cold when the conversation started. By the fourth question I was.

'Can I take a photo?'

'Of course you can take a photo.' *Of course I'd love to stand out here all freezing day. I'll be a real ice sculpture soon.* There was hatred behind my eyes in those moments.

'OK, smile!' And I smiled away those cold-hearted thoughts because you can't begrudge a person whose heart is in the right place; even when that place is a fucking warm car and you're freezing your tits off outside.

Click.

When every time you stop for a moment (and sometimes when you don't), a concerned or curious Russian delays you for five or maybe ten minutes, you don't do much cycling. It's a double-edged sword; the longer you stop, the colder you get, until you have to put on more clothes, which is a laborious affair. But then, when you finally get pedalling again, you soon warm up. You warm up so much you have to strip off a layer, which inevitably means stopping again. And it is during that briefest halt that another vehicle pulls over and the questions and photos begin afresh.

Progress. Was. Slow.

When I reached Chulman, I stopped at the little shop at the top end of town. Inside, the lady behind the counter smiled when I entered. I asked for a couple of chicken *kurniks*, which she heated in the microwave. I devoured the pasties, shovelling them in so fast the chicken burned my mouth and pastry flaked over me while I stomped my feet to get some feeling back in my toes.

During my pastry-flake dance, a local man walked in and walked straight out. I furrowed my brow in confusion. Then he walked in again carrying a gilet and put it around my shoulders. I smiled and said thanks. He commented that it was cold out. Yes, I had noticed. We talked while I got my thermos refilled and began the re-dressing palaver.

I was determined to cover more kilometres before darkness. Although I didn't want the day to end as that would mean the start of a long, cold night. It's funny how things turn out sometimes – the day was far from over. That's the thing with first days – they're always the longest. So many new things, first times, every moment a fresh experience. Shock and awe, over and over: everything so shockingly awesome (or awesomely shocking).

The local man turned to leave, hand on door, and gave it a yank. You needed strength to open outer doors in Siberia; they're all so heavy and well insulated and padded, especially when there's only one door. That said, most buildings have two doors – the space between

45

a freezer box and insulator.

'Your jacket!' I called out.

'It's a gift,' he replied, popping his head back round the door. 'You need it.' Then he was gone.

Do you know what was my first thought? It wasn't: *oh that's so kind* or *such a generous man to be giving gifts to a stranger* or *won't he be cold without it?* Those were second, third and fourth thoughts. No, my first thought was: *great, another thing to carry. As if I don't have enough baggage already.* How ungrateful can you get?

I wore the gilet all the way to the bottom of the hill at the end of the village. Then I passed the wooden church, crossed the bridge over the frozen river, began pedalling uphill, and before I had rounded the first bend on the hillside, I was hot and had to let the bike wear it instead.

It was while I was strapping the gilet to the top of my bike rack that a truck slowed beside me.

'Are you OK?' the driver enquired.

I laughed, knowing how this scenario was going to play out – with me getting cold and having to put the gilet back on. 'Yeah, I'm fine. No problem.'

'It's hard going up with that,' the driver commented, nodding towards my bike.

'Yeah I know, but it keeps me warm.'

'*Molodets*!' the worker in the passenger seat called out as he leaned over the driver to give me a thumbs up through the window. *Molodets* – I heard that word everywhere. There is no direct translation for it. It means good work, or nice job, or amazing, awesome, fabulous, congratulations! It always made me smile.

'Sure you're OK?'

'Yeah, thanks.'

'OK, then. Good luck!' the driver called out as he pulled away. *Now that's more like it.*

I set off on foot, pushing the bike. Less than a hundred metres further, a blue pickup slowed to a crawl beside me.

'Are you OK?'

'Yeah, I'm OK.'

'Want a lift?'

'No thanks.'

'It's a long walk up this hill. I'll give you a lift to the top where the road flattens out. You'll be able to cycle then. Much easier. Come on, let's put the bike in the back.'

I hesitated; a lift always felt like cheating. Then I agreed; this was my trip, and I got to make up the rules. There was something about the way he said it, as though it was the natural thing to do and I didn't really have a choice. Who knows if we really control our own destiny anyway? As long as we don't know what that destiny is, we can fool ourselves into thinking we are in control.

Cycle-touring tends to foster a fatalistic attitude. Out there alone on the road, unable to move faster than your own strength allows while exposed to the forces of nature and reliant upon the goodwill of humanity, you quickly realise just how vulnerable and insignificant we all are. Sometimes, rather than resist, it is better to accept the forces acting upon us, like a message in a bottle released out to sea with the hope that one day it will wash up on a distant shore.

The driver jumped out of his truck and started to move my bike. 'Go sit inside. Warm up. We can do this.' He called to the other two men.

It was always hard handing over responsibility of my bike to anyone else. While it was in my care and under my protection, I knew it was safe. Cutting the umbilical cord and releasing it from my icy white-knuckle grasp was a leap of faith every time. It got easier with each sever and reconnection. I came to realise that the bike would be fine without me. It always came back in one piece, unharmed. More or less. Sometimes, it was a little battered and bruised, but it was always the same bike I knew, and sometimes loved and other times loathed. This time it came back, I would loathe it.

In the meantime, Andrei drove me to the hilltop, acting as a tour guide on the way, though the sights were limited. Even the airport was hidden from view somewhere beyond the wall of trees that the road cut through. There could have been a thriving Disneyland hidden away for all I knew, except there's more chance of the thermometer rising above zero at this time of year than a Disney theme park coming to Russia.

On the dashboard of Andrei's truck was a statue of the Eiffel Tower. He'd not been to Paris, or France, even Europe and had no desire to. It was a gift from a tourist. *Perhaps I should have brought some souvenirs to give as gifts.* Although I would have needed a trailer to carry enough for everyone who helped me during the three months.

The other sights were the river I'd crossed earlier and the cafe at the top where we stopped. We lifted down the bike, shook hands and parted ways. If only I had come to that cafe when I actually needed a rest. They would be few and far between on the road ahead. It seemed such a waste to cycle past without going in, but I was still determined to cover more ground that day. I was naively optimistic that I could reach the next town, Aldan, 270 kilometres away in three days and two nights camping. *If only I can rack up seventy kilometres today, I can surely do a hundred on each of the others. Oh hell, who am I kidding? OK, rethink. If I can just make fifty kilometres for today before dark, then I only need to do seventy kilometres each of the next three days and I'll be there. Yes, that's much more realistic.*

I needed to cover fifteen kilometres more before camping. It didn't sound like much. In any other temperature, I could cover that in less than an hour. At my current rate, more like two. Still, it was flat now; I'd already covered the last kilometre faster than any other that day.

Yeah, I'm getting the hang of this. Easy riding. Oh yeah, I'm cycling through Siberia and it's freezing cold and it's amazing! Look at the sky – so many colours. Er, hang on, something doesn't feel quite right. Ugh, no. I know that feeling. Surely not …

I ground to a halt simply by stopping pedalling and leant the bike against the wall of snow banking the road. I squeezed the rear tyre. Flat. I looked around helplessly. If I expected to see anything other than snow and trees, I was severely disappointed. I was going to have to sort this out myself. It's not that I can't fix a puncture. I've had more than enough practice at that. It was the thought of fixing it in that goddamn hellish temperature.

In the hope that it was a slow puncture, I tried pumping up the flat tyre. The pump wouldn't work. I pumped furiously, but the tyre remained deflated. *No problem, I'll get the spare pump out – thank God I brought a spare.* I wrestled to get into the rear pannier, which was frozen stiff. I reached in for the bag of bike spares and tools. Fortunately, the second pump worked. The pumping action kept my body warm, but with every minute the metal from the pump, even though I'd wrapped it over and over in electrical tape, sapped the warmth from the hands. As I was screwing on the dust cap, a truck came up the road and stopped.

'Are you OK?'

'Yeah, I'm fine.'

'What are you doing here?'

'I'm cycling to Yakutsk.'

'You're not fine.'

'No, really, I am. No problems.' He looked a dubious character.

'You are definitely not fine. You're crazy!' By now the driver was out of the truck and walking towards me. 'You're crazy!' he repeated, screwing his forefinger against his temple. 'You're wrong in the head!' We laughed.

'Do you want some tea?' Tea would have been nice. Tea is always nice. But what I really wanted was to get cycling again.

'No, thank you. I want to go further before dark.'

'OK. You really are crazy. Tomorrow, when I see you ... then we'll drink tea.' That sounded like a good idea. Behind the stubbled face and scruffy clothes more fitting of a homeless drunk was a guy working a shit job at the local mines, on his way home to wash, have dinner and sleep until the next shift. We could each brighten the other's day.

Less than five minutes down the road, I felt the back end of the bike wobble. I stopped. For some moments, I stood staring at the bike, then up at the sky, and back at the bike. *Is it worth pumping up again and repeating every five minutes until I camp? If I fix the puncture now, is there time to cover much distance before dark? Should I just camp now?*

During this deliberation another truck came along and stopped. 'You OK?' the driver asked.

'Yeah, fine.'

'Want some tea?' I was feeling the cold. The temperature had dropped now that the sun was well below the tree-line. I hadn't warmed up at all in the five minutes of cycling I'd just done.

'Yes please.' I could decide what to do whilst in the truck. As soon as I clambered up into the cabin and closed the door, I felt safe inside this cosy womb. My predicament in the freezing world outside evaporated away.

I removed hats, gloves, mask, neck scarf, gilet and jacket, and laid them out on the dashboard over the heaters. Bogdan, the driver, watched in silence. Where most people would raise their eyebrows and shake their head in disbelief, Bogdan wobbled his head from side-to-side; his blue eyes and salt-and-pepper hair floating in the air above his shoulders. It was his signature move. He felt my jacket, which was damp with sweat, and laid it against the big blower that he used to heat the cabin at night.

'Let's bring your bike inside,' he said.

'It's fine out there,' I replied.

'Look, your clothes are wet; it's not good. Bring your bike and bags in and warm up the rest of your stuff.' It was easier to do as he said than protest further. It didn't take long.

Soon I was watching Bogdan transform his cabin into a kitchen and dining room.

'Where are you cycling to?'

'Yakutsk.' Bogdan wobbled his head.

'Where are you staying tonight? It's a long way to the next cafe.'

'I'm camping.' Bogdan wobbled his head.

'But at night it gets really cold.'

'I know. I've got good gear. I've been camping out in winter before.'

'Where?'

'Near Lake Baikal and also northern Scandinavia.'

'But there it does not get cold …'. He checked the temperature reading from the truck. 'Here, it's thirty-eight now. Tonight it will be forty-five. Further on …' he nodded out of the front windscreen, down the road in the direction of Yakutsk, 'it can be fifty, sixty.' He meant minus numbers, of course. That's how everyone here talks about the temperature. They exclude the minus. It's obviously minus; there's no need to say it.

'I know,' I said. Bogdan wobbled his head.

'You don't know.'

'No, I do. I'll be fine.' Bogdan kept wobbling his head with a smile I couldn't decipher until the boiling water grabbed his attention and he turned his blue-eyed stare away from me.

We drank tea and picked at the salami and *salo* (a slab of cured pork fat) and bread. He handed me a hard-boiled egg and opened up a plastic container of potato salad. Occasionally he looked at me and wobbled his head as though wondering what to do with the stray animal he'd picked up.

'Let me give you a lift to Aldan,' Bogdan offered. Getting a lift up a hill was one thing. Getting a lift 250 kilometres to the next town was something entirely different. If I had wanted to hitch my way across Siberia, I wouldn't have brought the bike. I refused.

'Then let me give you a lift to the next cafe. It's not very far.' This made more sense. With the bike inside the cabin, I could no longer ignore it. The rear wheel, visible over my shoulder, was a nagging reminder about the flat tyre. I could stop in the cafe while I repaired the puncture, get a hot meal and then go camp. The thought of being ejected back into the cold and first having to repair the flat tyre was not appealing. Unappealing doesn't actually describe the feeling of dread rising up from my stomach at the thought of it. And I didn't want to take up Bogdan's time fixing it now in his truck.

'How far?' I asked.

'Fifty kilometres.' Not very far in a truck and not very far on a bike are very different measures. Even so, I agreed. I'm glad I did. Now I didn't have to contend with the cold, I could sit and stare out of the window and marvel at the scenery; I didn't have to squint through fogged up, frozen goggles.

We drove along the plateau, where the road ran like a narrow vein through the deep forest, until the view opened up to reveal dark, tree-covered, undulating land with white scars of snow where electricity pylons ran. The road continued endlessly, switchbacking down into one valley and rising slowly up into the next range and winding round the hills in large sweeping arcs where every turn was a different view, although every view was much like the last. More forest. More snow.

In the twilight, the snow covering the trees took on a ghostly hue like thick cobwebs and dust blanketing an old abandoned house. The haunting beauty of it sent shivers through me even though I wasn't cold any more.

It was dark by the time we reached the cafe. Bogdan turned to ask, 'What are you going to do now?'

'I'm going in the cafe and will fix the flat tyre.'

'But it's not open all night.'

'That's OK. I am going to camp.'

Bogdan was seriously concerned about this. 'You can't camp,' he exclaimed. 'It's too cold. Let me drive you to Aldan.'

'No, you don't understand. I want to cycle. That's why I'm here.' My insistence was met with a head wobble. It made me smile. Bogdan put on his coat. He opened the door and climbed out. 'Don't go anywhere.'

Moments later he was back with a work colleague. We drank more tea and discussed the weather and why I should not camp. In the end, we came to an agreement. I would ride with them for another seventy kilometres to where a truck that they were going to repair was stranded. They would be sleeping there that night; I could stay in Bogdan's cabin. We'd eat dinner, I'd repair my puncture, and they'd work until the truck was fixed. I could go to sleep anytime I wanted, then set off early the next day. Bogdan saw me look suspiciously around the cabin.

The year before, getting a lift to Dushanbe in Tajikistan, I'd accepted a lift from an unshaven, portly Russian Tajik who was driving goods back from China. He hadn't slept in three days. It looked like it. His eyes were so bloodshot there was no white left in them. It was late afternoon, and I did wonder at the time exactly what he planned to do that night. The truck cabin was on the small side. My bike and bags were strewn across the bed space. I presumed he'd be stopping with friends or at a guesthouse to have a proper sleep. But if you haven't slept for three nights, one more isn't much worse, I imagine. Neither of us slept that night. He wanted sex. I didn't. I avoided it by leaping round the cabin like a mountain goat, always out of his reach. Eventually he gave up and we drove on. I didn't want a repeat of this scenario played out in Siberia.

The ride from the cafe was made in darkness. I looked out of the window longingly. *I could be cycling this*, I thought. But I knew if I was, I wouldn't be enjoying it the same.

The broken-down truck was parked by the side of a long straight stretch of road. While the men worked, I fixed my tyre. Bogdan came in from outside, and we ate dinner together before he went back out to finish the job. We slung my bike and bags out into the snow bank. They'd be safe there. No one in their right mind would be out here at night looking to steal bikes. It was almost midnight when I crawled into bed.

Bogdan's cabin had a bunk bed. That avoided any confusion in the sleep-not-sex stakes. Well, it did until the middle of the night when I went out to pee. I came back and Bogdan was awake, sat up on his bed, feet on the floor, waiting for me. He held his arm out, beckoning me to join him. *I don't think so. Oh bugger, what have I gotten myself into?*

'But it's cold,' he reasoned. 'Let's snuggle together. Much warmer.' My sleeping bag was even warmer and less likely to grope me. I said I wasn't interested and clambered back onto my bunk.

'OK, good night then.' Bogdan was one of the good guys. A guy who likes to try his luck, but a good one still the same.

And that was the end of my first day on the road through Yakutia.

7.

When I looked out of the truck the next morning, the sun was beginning to rise. All around, it was white. The thick forest was gone; snowfields spread out to the horizon. The few trees were covered in snow and blended chameleon-like into the land.

Waving goodbye to Bogdan, I set off down the road. Although the temperature was minus forty-five degrees Celsius, I was soon sweltering. It was as if I were pedalling up a steep hill, except I was on the flat. With the bike outside overnight, the grease in the bearings and oil in the hub had thickened drastically. Together with the added friction from the spiked tyres, it was incredibly hard work to get the bike moving at all.

There was no way I was going to stop before I was out of sight of the truck though. I didn't want Bogdan thinking I'd had a problem and coming to offer me a lift to Aldan again. *Dammit, I'm gonna cycle this road.* The truck remained in view a very long time.

The one advantage of it being very early in the day in the middle of nowhere was that no one else was around. Even though pedalling was hard work, progress was more successful than the day before because no one was stopping me. I only had myself to blame now. I should have used cold weather grease on the bearings, but I was too tight to buy a whole expensive tube. Maybe it wouldn't have made a difference anyway.

Although it was less than twenty kilometres to the next village, it took all morning. Time was fluid here. It sped up and slowed down against my will. It warped and shifted, so I couldn't tell how much time had passed. I didn't think it mattered. I would just cycle until it was nearly dark and then pitch my tent for the night. It sounded so simple. It had served me well everywhere else.

Cycle-touring was like writing a book. The trick was not to look at the big picture, but instead just write or cycle for a good portion of the day. If you put the time in, then words would become sentences and paragraphs, then pages and chapters. Rotations of the pedals would turn into kilometres and eventually, after enough hours and days, you would have a manuscript or have cycled across a continent.

Here, though, every pedal rotation was exhausting. The bike inched along the road and the view rarely changed. Even the sun rose slowly and set slowly, and it never reached its zenith but lingered near the horizon, lethargic and powerless like a teenager who stays out late and must be dragged out of bed.

Villages were always next to a river at the bottom of a valley. My feet were numb blocks of ice by the time I freewheeled down to Bolshoi Nimnyr. It looked an uninviting place. Soviet-era concrete block buildings lined the hillside. There was no sign of a cafe, but two workmen pointed me towards a wooden door. I didn't need to say anything. When you're outside in the freezing cold, there are only two things you could possibly want: a warm place to sit and a hot drink to sip. And once you're in that warm place, there is only one thing you really don't want: to go back out into the freezing cold. Procrastination reached an all-time high. Never before had my journal been such a concerted focus of all my attention.

Back on the road later that day, two trucks passed and pulled over.

'Want chai?' the driver asked.

'Sure.' *Must work on that willpower thing.*

'Get in from the other side,' he directed. I ditched the bike against the snow bank and ran round to the passenger door and clambered up, followed closely by the guy from the second truck. We squeezed in amongst the oily spare parts, rags and other random stuff that resourceful Russians find uses for, but many would consider junk.

Sergei cleared the dashboard by sweeping everything into his arms and slinging it behind the seats. Out came the gas hob, pan and water. Then a wooden block appeared on the dash and a smorgasbord of meats and cheese and bread was cut and laid out.

Sergei and his friend Alexei were both thirty-two, hadn't slept in two days, had driven almost two thousand kilometres and were determined to reach Aldan that evening. It was only fifty kilometres further. There, they were going to get raging drunk, party, and then pass out in the back of their trucks before continuing the journey to Yakutsk.

'Join us!'

'Oh …'. *Willpower. Stay strong.* 'I can't.' Thankfully they didn't push it because I probably would have caved in. I'm a sucker for the suggestion of alcohol and a good laugh and not having to camp in the snow-covered Siberian taiga.

They wanted to know if I was married. They smiled and shook my hand when I said I wasn't. They were single too. Why would they want to get tied into marriage too young, when there's so much to do in life without a woman to look after as well?

'You're travelling alone. What do you do when the bike breaks?'

'I fix it.'

'You can do that? Fix tyres and the chain and …'.

'Of course.'

'Why would you ever get married? You don't need a man; you can look after yourself,' Alexei laughed.

'Men must feel useless in England,' Sergei contemplated. He was the quieter of the two; Alexei was the joker and centre of attention. We all have our roles to play in life; these two were a double act, one where the whole is greater than the sum of the two halves. 'I'm glad I live here in Russia. The women here need us. What would we do in England?'

'We'd drink even more,' Alexei announced. We all laughed at that.

Looking out of the frosted window, the sky was still clear but the bright blue was fading to pink. The shadows were lengthening across the white road that wound down deeper into the forest. It was time to go.

Sergei drove off and I began to pedal. I looked back to wave at Alexei before he departed too. *What the hell's he doing?* Alexei was shouting and waving frantically from in front of his truck. I turned around and pedalled back up the hill towards him. 'You OK?' I asked.

'I'm locked out!' The keys were in the ignition, engine running; only, the door was locked. Now, my Russian is not great, but I am certain that the next words to leave Alexei's mouth were not for innocent ears.

'Fuck. Sergei!' Too late; Sergei's truck had disappeared round the bend. 'Fuck. Russian truck!' Alexei, I now realised, knew three words of the English language.

'What will you do?' I asked, a little bewildered at this unexpected predicament.

'No problem. Do you have a knife?' Alexei asked. I handed over my pocket Leatherman. Alexei laughed. I handed over my hunting knife. He laughed again. Size mattered out here. Instead, he rummaged around in the toolbox and grabbed a huge, solid steel wrench with his bare hands. I offered him my mittens. 'No, you wear them. Russian hands.' He waved his fingers at me and laughed again.

With the wrench, a screwdriver and the aid of my diminutive hunting

58

knife, he wedged down the window enough for the contortionist he turned out to be to climb onto the cabin and reach an arm inside to pull the latch. As he yanked open the door, he turned to me and said, 'Normal. This is Russia!' And he laughed again.

The tools were chucked hastily into the truck. He rubbed his hands together vigorously, blew deep breaths into them, and then shook my own mittened hand. As he put the truck into gear, he called out, 'Good luck!' Then he was gone – another character to leave my life as abruptly as it had entered; my life a little sweeter for it in the long run, but in that moment a little sadder and emptier.

I stood, silent and alone, in the middle of the road long after Alexei's truck had disappeared from view. Something snapped me out of the trance. I looked over to my bike – reality in steel frame form. My mind switched back on, and my body automatically went about the tasks it needed to do: cycle and find a place to camp.

Across a river, the trees parted to reveal a wide tract of hummocks covered in pristine snow that glowed faintly golden from the sun that was kissing the horizon. The road then wound uphill through more trees. I pushed the bike instead of straining to cycle up the incline, yet I could still feel myself overheating and sweating. I took off my outer jacket, but the sweat, rather than freezing on the outside of my fleece top where I could brush it off, froze within the fibres of the fabric. Soon the sleeves were frozen stiff, and the skin of my arms was getting painful and numb. I put the jacket back on.

A 4x4 pulled up. The driver asked the usual questions and then drove off, leaving me to my fate. I was looking forward to camping and was determined that no one would stop me this evening. I began cycling when I reached the top of the hill. I was torn between freewheeling down and getting cold from the inactivity or pedalling fast to raise my heart-rate and stay warm, which would inevitably increase the wind flow and cool me at a similar rate.

The 4x4 passed again going in the other direction, slammed to a halt, made a U-turn and drove back towards me.

'Are you sure I can't give you a lift to Aldan?'

'No, I want to cycle.'

'But aren't you cold?' *Sigh*.

'No.' That was rapidly becoming a lie as the conversation continued.

'But it's forty.' He meant minus forty. 'And it will get colder tonight. You should come with me to Aldan.' I refused again. The driver shrugged his shoulders, gave me a bottle of ice-cold juice and drove off. I pedalled like a Duracell bunny on steroids to warm up and tried to marvel at the beauty of the land unfolding in front of me. The reality was that I had to focus on scanning the snow and trees for a place to camp and think about what to do to warm up.

At the bottom of the hill, I saw the brake lights of the 4x4 go on. A wave of dread passed over me as I anticipated another conversation with the temperature rapidly plummeting now that the sun had fully set. The driver was out of his 4x4 by the time I reached him. 'Please, let me take you to Aldan. It is too cold for camping.'

'OK.' I was too cold for camping to be anything but survival now.

'I'm Andrei,' he said as he shook my hand. *Another one*.

The bags were squeezed onto the back seats. I wondered where the bike would fit.

'Go sit inside and warm up.'

I watched through the wing mirror wondering what Andrei was doing in the middle of the road waving at the oncoming orange truck. The truck stopped, fortunately. Andrei had words with the driver. My bike was put in the truck and the truck departed. *Er … my bike?*

Andrei got back in the 4x4. Without a word, he leant over me, reached into the glove compartment and took out a bottle. He twisted the cap and broke the seal, then poured the clear liquid into a glass he had pulled out from under the handbrake and necked the contents in one swig as he threw his head back. Once he'd fumbled with the plastic wrapper, he took a nibble of flapjack because a Russian never drinks vodka without *zakuski*, a little tapas style snack or bite of some food. Then he put the bottle down by my feet, released the handbrake and put his foot to the floor.

'Don't worry. We will get your bike in Aldan,' Andrei declared as I sat transfixed by the speedo that was indicating ever increasing speeds. *Oh shit.* 'You see? There's the truck. Your bike is safe.' Yes, but right then I was more concerned for my own safety.

We closed in on the truck until I wondered if Andrei were going to ram into the back of it. Then he slammed on the brakes and we slid to a halt.

'OK, calm. Everything is fine now. Let's drink.' Out came the vodka. I accepted my fate and joined in; I took my glass, downed it and coughed.

'You need medicine,' Andrei exclaimed. *Oh God, no. More vodka is not going to help.* 'Your cough is because of the cold. Here ...'. He handed me a tablet. Locals in Siberia handed out medicine like sweets. Now I know we were taught at school not to take sweets from strangers, but they never mentioned anything about pharmaceuticals.

We set off again at top speed until we caught up with the truck. Again, the brakes went on and the vodka came out.

'*Tvoye Zdarovye.*' Andrei toasted to my health as we raised our glasses.

Race. Stop. Drink. Repeat.

'Why Yakutia in winter?' Andrei asked.

'To see ...'.

'See what?' he exclaimed. 'There's nothing! Come in summer. It's beautiful then: the lakes, the rivers, the wildlife. But winter? It's cold. Forty ... fifty ... sixty. Look!' Andrei took out his mobile and started searching on it for photos. The 4x4 weaved across the road and swerved back when Andrei glanced up.

As I looked through the photos on his mobile and then outside, I began to think he had a point. 'I'll have to come back in summer. Though, at least in winter there are no mosquitoes.'

'Well, come in spring – April or May – before the mosquitoes. You can go fishing. The fishing's great. You see this river ...?' He pointed to the snowy white line winding through the valley. 'It's frozen now, but in the spring, when it thaws, you can catch fish like this.' Both Andrei's hands came off the wheel and spanned to fill the inside of the 4x4. He looked over to me, smiled and turned his focus back to driving. I couldn't tell if the smile was at the thought of an impressive past catch or at the anxious look washing over my face because of his lax driving style. Still, we made it to Aldan – Andrei, bike and I – all in one piece.

Once we'd retrieved the bike from the truck, we went to Andrei's workshop. He drove one-handed with the window wound down, wheeling the bike beside the driver's door with the other hand. I was convinced the bike would end up under the wheels. You'd think he had done it countless times before by his unconcerned attitude. That's the vodka-effect for you.

The rest of the evening flew past in a tiredness-and-alcohol-induced haze: the depositing of my bike in the workshop, the impromptu visit to Andrei's friends for dinner, the drive through town involving a close encounter with a black cat and a one-eighty wheelspin, the quick stop at a late-night shop, and then to a hotel and the moment I'd been dreading.

Ever since Andrei had mentioned a hotel, I had envisaged two scenarios. The least appealing option was that he would assume we would be sharing a room. It was a relief when he asked for a room for one. The next scenario was that the price of a room would be extortionate. A wave of dread washed over me when he said to the receptionist that I'd take the deluxe suite. When given a choice, I always take the cheapest room, especially in Russia where they don't come cheap. Despite my objecting, Andrei insisted. It would be worth it, he said. Frankly, I was too tired to argue. Then he paid for two nights out of his own wallet.

The selfless generosity that is dished out to the passing cyclist is always humbling. At first, it was hard to understand what I had done to deserve such kindness. Later, I learnt to graciously accept what I was offered without worrying how I might repay it. The only way to do that is to hand out help in turn to someone else when they need it. The karma-cycle, it should be called.

Wide-eyed with wonder when I entered the massive room, I soon collapsed on the bed, overwhelmed with exhaustion from the previous two non-stop days. Andrei had put the bag of groceries on the side table and left. A minute later there was a knock on the door. *Oh no, what does he want?* I still couldn't believe he had no hidden agenda. But all Andrei did was place some ruble notes on the table. 'For breakfast and dinner tomorrow,' he said.

'No …'.

'Quiet,' Andrei interrupted. 'For breakfast and dinner,' he repeated. And with that he left and closed the door behind him.

Seconds later there was another knock and Andrei's head appeared round the door. 'And lock this door after me.' Then he was gone.

I locked the door.

I slept a deep, dreamless sleep until another knock in the morning. It was the receptionist.

'There is a man here asking for you.' *Oh no, not Andrei already.* I had hoped for a restful day and dreaded that Andrei would come along and insist on taking me sightseeing or drinking, assuming I needed entertaining.

It wasn't Andrei. And that made me feel bad because, if it had been him, he would have come with only my interests at heart.

It was Sergei (another one). Sergei was a friend of Bolot. I knew Bolot, one of the few English-speaking Russians in Yakutia, through Facebook. They were both in the tourism industry. Bolot had hoped I might be able to help his friend, Sergei.

'Would you like to do an interview with the local TV?' Sergei asked. *About as much as sticking a sharp hot poker in my eye or lying in the road and being run over by a bus.* I had successfully avoided both in life. I intended to keep it that way. A TV interview in a language I understand as well as a brain-damaged chihuahua was something I also wished to avoid. Fame is not something I crave. I wouldn't be cycling through obscure, sparsely-populated parts of the world if that were the case. Unfortunately, however, I find it hard to shake off that inherent British politeness at times like these.

'Yes, I suppose I could, but my Russian is very bad.' I said, hoping this would be a sufficient deterrent without appearing rude.

'No problem. It can be in English.'

'Great,' I said. Sergei smiled, acknowledging the word, but not understanding the sarcasm. *Crap.*

8.

That was how I spent the morning I left Aldan. Then I cycled to the edge of town and tied a ribbon to the small tree next to the town sign for the TV crew to film. Finally, I was free to begin the ride north.

Since it was a late start, when I reached the next settlement I stopped at the shop to buy a *kurnik* for lunch. I didn't need to stop, but I couldn't pass up the opportunity. 'Do you want it hot?' the young man serving asked.

'Yes, please.' He put the *kurnik* in the microwave while I fetched my thermos from the bike. When I came back in, the young man was talking with a couple. There wasn't much room to move, not with us all wrapped up in several layers.

As the couple asked me about my bike and I explained my passing presence, the young man passed me the piping hot *kurnik* wrapped in a napkin. The greasy smell was so tantalising that I took a massive bite and instantly regretted it. *H-h-hot.*

'That's not enough,' the lady in the fur coat commented. 'You need real food.'

'No, this is fine. I have lots more with me.'

'No, why don't you come back to my house. You can have a proper meal and warm up. Then you can get on your way.' I must admit, I didn't protest too hard.

We wheeled the bike into the shop storeroom. Then we drove up a snow-covered side road past a number of housing blocks. Like all large buildings and apartments in this region, they were raised off the ground, so they wouldn't sink in the spring thaw.

Within moments of entering the flat, the plastic cloth on the small kitchen table was covered with soup and stew, *pelmeni*, cheese and meats and *salo* and bread, with a pot of tea brewing. Anna spread my wet clothes on the hot water pipes to dry, leaving a musty, sweaty aroma in the entrance hall, but she didn't care at all: she was enjoying giving me all her motherly attention. Sometimes it feels good to be needed and even better to be appreciated. As I tucked into the hot, hearty food, Anna shuffled around the flat in her slip-on slippers filling a bag with what she considered essentials for a winter cyclist.

'Really, I don't need anything,' I commented while thinking about the extra weight.

'No, no, it's OK, don't worry. I am only giving you a few important things. Things you need. Because I know you have to carry it.' She emptied the contents of the bag to show me what she'd packed: noodles and packet soups, a brick-sized slab of *salo*, cheese, one fat salami, sugar and teabags, a bag of sweets and chocolates, a jar of honey, a pot of jam and a loaf of bread.

'Thank you, but it's too much,' I exclaimed, not only worried about the weight but how I would actually fit it in my bags.

'OK, maybe you are right.' A wave of relief washed over me, until she put aside a couple of bags of noodles and repacked the rest. *Oh no. Quick, say something.*

'Not the bread; it is too big and will freeze.' She nodded and took it out. 'And the jars; they are heavy.' She shook her head.

'No, you must take those. Honey is good for energy. It's lovely in tea. And the jam is home-made with local fruit. You have to take it. It is my gift to you.' *Oh well, that does it.* I couldn't refuse a gift.

Fully satiated and thawed out, I set about getting ready to go.

'Ivan, look at her socks. We have some thermal socks don't we? Go fetch them for her. They're in the drawer in the bedroom …'. Ivan wandered off. 'Have you seen her gloves?' Anna called out. 'These are not good,' she commented to me.

'They're fine. I have mittens too.'

'These? No,' she replied adamantly to me, then called out to the bedroom, 'Ivan, where did we put those mittens? You know the ones …'. There was no point protesting.

Back at the shop, once we'd retrieved my bike from the store room and I'd shoved the food and gifts into my least full pannier, I waved goodbye to the wonderful couple.

'Wait!' the young shopkeeper came running out. 'To keep you warm,' he said as he thrust a bottle of cognac into my mittened hand.

With less traffic and fewer people to ask me questions, I covered a good distance that afternoon. I didn't stop to take a single photograph – it was too damn cold. When it came time to look for a place to camp, I kept seeing little tunnels under the road. They would be good to sleep in if only I could get down to them and shovel out some snow. At dusk, I stopped at a side track, wondering whether to venture up the hill in search of a good spot or to try one of the tunnels. I knew I had to make a decision quickly – darkness was imminent. The village I'd hoped to reach was nowhere in sight.

The tunnel. Decision made.

All I had to do was wait until there was no traffic to see me make my escape from the road. Traffic may have been a rarity, but right when you want an empty road because you want to camp, it turns up on cue. You can guarantee it. It's the sod's law of cycle-touring.

A small car passed. *Go on … keep going, don't stop now.*

It stopped.

I waited, hoping it would move on quickly.

It didn't.

The driver, short and slim, got out and stood behind the car, rubbing his hands together and blowing on them to keep them warm. He was underdressed to be standing idly for long outside. He was overshadowed by a tall lady in a thick fur coat and hat. It was easy to tell who gave the orders.

With no alternative, I cycled over.

'Hello, the lady would like a photo. Is that OK?' the young man asked as he shook my hand, then shoved them back into the warmth of his armpits.

'Sure,' I smiled. *Let's get this done quickly.*

'Oh gosh, you're a girl. That's great!' the lady exclaimed. 'Where are you staying tonight?'

'I'm camping.'

'No. Come to my school.'

'But …'.

'No buts. It's not far. It's in Yakokit.' *Ah, the village I'd hoped to reach …*

'How far?'

'Very close.' *Be precise, dammit. I need numbers.*

'How many kilometres?'

'Three.' *That is close.* 'It's downhill to the river. The village is on the other side. We will wait for you at the shop.'

It was dark now. I freewheeled downhill, and the wind chilled the skin around my eyes and tore through my jacket like it was tissue. Rather than stop and put more clothes on, I pedalled furiously. The wind bit deeper. In the darkness, those three kilometres seemed to take forever. The ice road was faintly illuminated by starlight. The forest was black, the trees lined up like a heartless, impenetrable army.

I began to doubt. *What if I don't find the village? What if I misheard and it's thirty, not three kilometres away. What if I have to camp?* I started

68

scanning the forest for a way in. I couldn't risk getting any colder.

And then I saw the lights: civilisation. The little car, barely visible through the misty fumes it was churning out, pulled away slowly. An arm thrust out of the side window signalled me to follow.

The village looked ramshackle and decrepit and beautiful at the same time. The wooden homes were haphazardly built, each coated in a thick white blanket that sparkled. I couldn't tell if they were abandoned or inhabited. There were no lights on or smoke coming from the chimneys.

The school, though, was different. Inside, it was bright and clean and light and warm. Once we'd squeezed my bike through the doors, I attached myself like a limpet to the hot water pipes lining the corridor. Nothing would tempt me to move. Or so I thought. When Tatiana, the head teacher, asked if I would like tea and something to eat, I quickly released my grip. School dinner never tasted so good.

After that, I was left to my own devices. I moved a couple of the wooden desks – old-school ones with the integrated chair and flip-up desktop – to make space on the floor for my sleeping bag. I was ready to sleep. The late evening coffee and sickly sweet chocolates and candy I devoured had boosted my energy levels, but it was a temporary revival. I was exhausted.

Tatiana took me under her wing like a pupil. She came back and informed me that she had found a better place for me to sleep. I somehow doubted it. All my needs were met with this warm, dry classroom.

We walked back through the village, listening to the crackle of the compacted snow underfoot. We huddled arm-in-arm to keep warm and to catch each other when we slipped on the ice.

At the end of the street, we stepped into the doorway of a three-storey traditional wooden building and walked up the rickety stairwell. Tatiana didn't knock on the door at the top, but walked straight on into the apartment.

'I'm back,' she called out.

'Come on in,' I heard a voice reply.

'Helen, this is Baba Liliya. She is a good woman. She has said you are welcome to stay with her tonight.'

'Yes, yes. You are welcome. Sit down. Sit, sit. Would you like something to eat?'

'OK, you will be fine here,' Tatiana said to me, her comforting hand on my shoulder. 'I must go now. I will see you in the morning. Good night.'

Once Tatiana had left, Baba Liliya took over my care with grandmotherly attention. 'Let's get you some borscht and tea.'

'But …'.

'No buts.'

'OK.' A second dinner wasn't exactly a hardship.

'Would you like a bath?'

'Oh, no. Really, I'm fine.'

'You should have a bath.' *Do I smell that bad already?* 'It will warm you up. Besides, you don't know when you'll have the next one. Tatiana told me you're cycling to Yakutsk. It's a long way. *Molodets*! You will have to wait, though. The water is too hot.' *Too hot? That doesn't make sense. She must mean to wait for the water to heat up.*

How little I knew. Huge hot water pipes ran through the houses providing warmth and scorching hot water from the tap. Getting cold water was the hard part. You had to collect snow from outside and melt it. Baba Liliya wasn't interested in braving the outdoors. Instead, we sat at the kitchen table and talked while the hot water cooled.

Mostly, Baba Liliya did the talking. I think she was lonely in her apartment. She talked and talked as if she hadn't had a conversation with another person in a long time. Any solo cycle-tourer knows what that verbal diarrhoea is like. You talk about anything and everything and don't care if the first unfortunate person to meet you is listening or not. It is an uncontrollable flood of anecdotes and personal confessions and revelations. Very soon, you are no longer strangers. Either you will quickly become good friends or they will be assured that you should be locked away in a lunatic asylum. Baba Liliya babbled to me as I polished off a second bowl of borscht.

'Call me Baba. Now, let's have another drink.' She had poured a shot of vodka even before Tatiana had left, and as soon as the front door had shut, she had come back into the kitchen and necked it. I never saw a Russian flinch and wince at the alcoholic aftertaste. Baba was no different.

We lifted our glasses and drank. Baba never bothered with trivialities like actually toasting to someone or something – none of that malarkey such as to your health, your family, your journey or to world peace. Baba drank for drinking's sake.

'Do you smoke?' Baba asked.

'No.'

'That's good. It's bad for you,' she said as she lit up a cigarette and took a deep drag. 'Look at your hair. It's beautiful,' Baba said when I finally took off my hat. I'd been resisting removing it because I knew my hair would be one sweaty, knotted matt underneath, but the overwhelming heat of the house was too much to bear. 'Mine was beautiful once too.' She brushed her fingers through her fine, wispy black hair that had thinned badly on top. I imagined she was quite a catch before age and the Siberian climate and the effects of cigarettes and alcohol had caught up with her.

'Do you have a husband or any children?' she finally asked after a long exhale, her elbow on the table and the cigarette held loosely between her fingers, the smoke rising and swirling, dispersing and disappearing.

'No,' I replied.

'Me neither,' she said. 'I never met the right man. That didn't matter. There are too many bad men in Siberia. It's the alcohol makes them bad. I would have liked children though, but I couldn't have them. Too much smoking and drinking.'

'Who's the girl in the photo in the hall? The one with the horse,' I asked.

'Oh, that's my niece. I don't see her much.' She leant away from the table and stared distantly in the direction of the hall.

Baba was only a little crazy, I thought. That lonely, harmless kind of crazy. It seemed the only thing keeping her sane was her cat.

'Chapa!' she cried out suddenly. 'Chapa,' she scolded, 'stop that. Come here.' And she leapt up from the table and chased the playful furball into another room. Chapa, the six-month old kitten, had found a new toy with my fleece gloves. I heard the sound of claws racing across the carpet as Chapa darted into the kitchen and took refuge under my feet. 'Oh Chapa, you naughty little kitty. What will I do with you?' Baba muttered as she sat back down at the table, poured another drink, then picked up the kitten and stroked him affectionately as he pawed at her lap.

'Where was I? Oh yes …' she remembered. 'But your bath. Now come with me. Let's see if it is still too hot.'

'It's fine,' I commented as I dipped my fingers in the shallow bath. It was scolding hot, but I didn't want to wait any longer. Besides, I was still under the illusion that I could simply run cold water from the tap.

Baba found me a dressing gown to wear and left me to it. I turned on the tap. *Ouch*! It was scolding hot. I searched around the bathroom for anything that might provide cold water. Only then did it dawn on me that I had understood Baba correctly. With no alternative, I gingerly dipped my toes of one foot into the water. *Hot*! And yanked them back out. I tried again, but the same reflex sent water splashing. After a few more minutes of staring at the bath, I decided to grit my teeth. What a waste of water if I didn't have a bath.

I swung my legs in. My toes burned with pain and went red. Steam filled the room. I sat down and quickly leapt back up. Too damn hot. Why could nothing in Siberia be a normal, pleasant temperature? I'm just a girl from England and not used to such extremes. Everything had to be hellishly cold or scorching, scalding, burning hot. There was no chance of washing my hair, so once I'd splashed the water over me, I got out, put my feet on the cool bathroom mat and breathed out.

Baba was lying on the sofa watching TV when I emerged, half-roasted. She then sat upright with her feet on the floor, in a formal way that didn't suit her or the room. I took a seat in the armchair and listened as Baba started to gabble on about I've no idea what. Whatever it was, she found it highly amusing. As she giggled childishly, her feet rose off the floor and she kicked them around excitedly. She was still a young girl at heart.

That night I slept in her room, which she had given up for me. The fish tank in the corner glowed iridescent through the night and lit up the posters on the wall of teenage heart-throb Robert Patterson.

The next morning, after we'd had tea and more borscht for breakfast, two young lads came in. They sat and talked with Baba while I collected my gear. Then they escorted me back to the school. They were in no rush to return to lessons. If I'd have known what Tatiana had planned for me, I wouldn't have been as eager either.

Thrusting me to the front of the classroom, Tatiana introduced me to the class as a girl from England who was riding her bicycle across Yakutia. That essentially summed it up, and my limited Russian didn't allow for much elaboration.

9.

'You must stay with my good friend Svetlana in Tommot. The town is only twenty-five kilometres from here,' Tatiana explained after I escaped the classroom. 'This is her number. I have called her already. She said to phone her when you get to Driver's Cafe on the edge of town.'

So that is what I did. It was a short and easy ride to the cafe. I drank three sugary coffees while I waited for Svetlana. She didn't say a word when she arrived. She said later that she had known who I was because I had smiled at her, as if no Russian stranger would smile.

We loaded my bike into the taxi and went to her home, a modern apartment, where she lived with her husband, son, a lion-sized cat and a cat-sized dog. Once again, the table was laid with an array of food. It was the typical Russian affair.

Once I'd showered and changed, we went to see Svetlana's school. Like Tatiana, Svetlana took me under her wing as if I were a new pupil. She showed me round the school and introduced me to her colleagues. Then we bought some supplies for dinner and collected German from his home on the other side of town. German was, ironically considering his name, the English teacher, and had been invited to dinner for my benefit.

German was a big fellow with a broad smile and kind eyes that slanted slightly and beamed brightly. His English was excellent. In a selfish way, I wished I could spend all evening talking with him, learning about the town and way of life here. It was clear, however, that he and Svetlana were old colleagues and good friends; the kind of good friends where it doesn't matter how long you go without speaking to one another, it's always like it was only yesterday. And as is the case when you live so close to someone, you often see them less frequently than those further afield. Svetlana and German had much to catch up on.

Oh, how I wished for a rest day to do nothing. But I knew a day off in Tommot would be anything but restful. I envisaged talks to be given at the school and outings around town. I had no desire to be a burden on Svetlana and her family, who had already been so kind.

When they realised that it was my birthday in a couple of days, they suggested I stay and celebrate with them. I found it hard to refuse, but the idea of vodka-induced hangovers was enough to steel my resolve to keep moving.

It would be two days' cycling to the next settlement. My intention was to splash out there on a guesthouse and indulge in a few beers and a good book. Not exactly living it up for my thirty-third birthday, but it sounded like the perfect present to myself out there in the Siberian winter.

Beyond Tommot, there was even less traffic, mainly orange trucks going back and forth from their bases to various locations for road construction, maintenance and repair. In places, the road was badly rutted and the ice broken up. The cycling was a slow, hard slog. I had to stop regularly to rest, each time taking a cup of tea from the thermos and moving on quickly before cooling down too much. Eventually the road conditions improved. Then, I had to stop regularly, not to rest but to race and stomp up the road in an attempt to bring back life to my toes. Even though the sun came out and by mid-afternoon the temperature had noticeably risen, I was suffering with cold feet.

Whereas the forest had been tall and dense, today the trees had withered to nothing more than stumps. Thin, tilting trunks appeared like an army of drunks wearing hats of snow. Where thin twigs branched off, snow clung to their sides like warts and white boils. This forest was dying, the trees slowly sinking into the swamp.

Towards the end of the long day, as the sun dropped below the horizon and the temperature plummeted again, my breath froze over my jacket. My goggles frosted over until I couldn't see, so I had to cycle without them. I was worried that my exposed face would freeze with the windchill. When I saw a truck parked by the roadside and two men outside, I stopped to ask if they could defrost my goggles. I had no desire for frostbitten cheeks and no qualms asking for help.

Misha, the younger of the two men, suggested I put the goggles inside the truck and put myself in there at the same time to thaw out. I leapt in with the speed and agility of a snow leopard; well, that's how I prefer to think I looked.

Once Misha had finished working, he joined me and asked where I was going. There was a cafe ahead at the Amga River. I had hoped to reach there before nightfall; if I didn't, it was highly unlikely I'd make it to Uluu, the next settlement, in time for my birthday.

'Amga is twenty kilometres from here. Do you want a lift?' I did the maths. It added up to the desired solution.

'Yes, please.' And with that, we shoved my bike on the back of the lorry with its cargo of huge sections of pipe. It was a bumpy ride to Amga. 'Are you sure my bike is OK? It won't fall off, will it?' I asked Misha.

'It's fine,' he replied complacently. I stared hard at the wing mirror hoping to see if my bike did fall off. I squinted, but couldn't see through the white cloud of fine snow that was billowing out behind the truck. Part of me hoped the bike would fall off and be irreparably damaged. I could give up on this cycle ride then. I pondered what I would do.

I knew what I would do: I would chastise myself for being careless, then I'd hitch a ride to Yakutsk, buy whatever bicycle I could find there and continue the journey. If I really wanted to give up, I could stop any time. The reality was: I wasn't ready to quit.

As we drove over a series of massive bumps, it felt as though the entire truck had taken off the ground. It landed heavily and the suspension bounced the cabin around. Misha carefully put on the brakes and we ground slowly to a halt. We looked at each other. Misha grinned. 'Do you want me to tie down your bike?'

'Yes, please.'

When we arrived at the Amga River, Misha asked, 'Why don't I drive you to the next village?' He looked out of the window towards the tiny cafe down in the dip beside the road. 'There's nowhere to sleep here.'

It didn't take much to convince him that I would prefer to stop here. I don't think he understood why I wanted to, but he realised I was old enough to make my own decisions. I respected him for that.

A week later, I met Misha again. He was not the only truck driver I met more than once. He was in a little car, parked at the roadside in town. 'Helen! You're here,' he called out. Without the truck, it took a few moments to realise where I had seen that grinning face before. 'I was worried about leaving you at the cafe. Looks like I didn't need to.' He put his arm through the window and shook my mitten fiercely. His hand dwarfed mine.

The cafe at Amga was a small wooden room with a couple of rickety tables and a bench lining the wall where the hot water pipes ran. I stripped off my wet clothes and hung them to dry, put on my down jacket and wool hat, fought with my boots and took out the liners to air. My sweaty socks went on the pipes too. How I pitied the other customers. That was not the aroma they expected with their tea and *pelmeni*. At any other time, I would have been so embarrassed that I'd have hidden away the dirty, stinking clothes. But when they're your only clothes and you've got to go back out into the winter's night, quite frankly, you don't give a damn.

I don't know how long I sat in that cafe. I watched workmen stopping in for dinner at the end of their day. Invariably, they had a bowl of steaming *pelmeni* in a thin stock-like soup flavoured with dill and a dollop of sour cream. Of all the herbs you could add, why on earth anyone would choose dill is beyond me. It is vile. The Russians put it in everything. Even those mini pizzas you can buy at train stations across the country, which are glorified rounds of dough smeared with mayonnaise and ketchup, with a token piece of ham and slice of tomato shoved on top and heated in the microwave, are sprinkled with dill. That's how you make the worst fast food taste even more terrible. I don't think I'd ever had dill before I went to Russia, but once you've tried it, you never forget the flavour.

There are changes a traveller observes as they cross countries and regions. Dialects and customs and tastes and fashions gradually morph from one thing to another or fade from view entirely. Dill heaven must be centred somewhere in western Russia. Fortunately, as I made my way east through Siberia, the propensity for the vile stuff diminished. Pickled gherkins, on the other hand – don't get me started on the Siberian love of pickled food. No, it is safe to say, Russian cuisine is not my favourite in the world. Give me Thai, Indian, Chinese, Italian, Turkish, Lebanese or Greek instead. Even give me McDonalds or a mayonnaise sandwich, so long as it doesn't have dill in it.

Rather than a second bowl of dill-flavoured *pelmeni*, I opted for three Mars bars and a coke. That was when Sasha and Len came in and joined me at the table I had commandeered. They reminded me of George and Lennie in Steinbeck's *Of Mice and Men*. Len was the simple one, childish and innocent in his behaviour. Sasha was quiet and accompanied Len everywhere, making sure Len stayed out of trouble. I wondered if Len was his real name, he was so similar to Steinbeck's Lennie. It was probably a coincidence; the world is full of Lens and Lennies and coincidences.

Len was no trouble. Instead, he tried his damnedest to recollect English words he'd learnt at school and engage me in conversation. That evening, his English was better than my Russian. 'It's too cold to camp. You should stay in my truck,' Len said as he nuzzled his head like a dog against my arm. *Hmm. What do you have in mind tonight, young man?* I looked to Sasha for help clarifying. Sasha didn't give anything away, probably because Len didn't have an ulterior motive. Len, I realised later, didn't know what an ulterior motive was.

Len saw my look towards Sasha. 'You stay in my truck. It's warm. And I will sleep in my house.' My experience with truckers was that their truck was their home while on the road. What I didn't realise was that behind the cafe was a work camp. All the trucks returned there each evening and the drivers slept indoors.

'Let's drink vodka,' Len suggested. *Not a good idea.* 'Or beer.' *Better idea.* Still, all I really wanted to do was sleep. Climbing into my sleeping bag outside was becoming more appealing with every yawn I struggled to hide.

'One beer. Then I have to sleep.'

After one beer, Len said, 'Another? Yes, another.'

'No! I'm going to go. I have to sleep.'

'Where are you going?'

'To camp.'

'No, we'll take you to the truck now.'

We walked along a path up behind the back of the cafe and came to a floodlit yard that had been hidden from view. Len's truck was in the middle of the yard with about twenty other trucks, all with engines running, churning out fumes that lingered low in the cold, heavy atmosphere.

We climbed into Len's truck and closed the doors. 'You see, it's warm in here,' Len commented. He wasn't lying. 'Very warm. Outside it's too cold. Here you will be warm,' he repeated as he pointed to the temperature controls and the vents that could be opened and the buttons I shouldn't touch. 'And here is the music.' He turned up the CD player to an unbearable volume and started nodding his head to the techno beat. 'Do you like rock music?'

'Sure,' I said, downbeat with tiredness. *I just want to sleep.* Len switched over to eighties rock and grinned at me.

'Will you spend the day with us tomorrow? Join us in our truck. We have to work, but in between we can talk. Go on. Pleeease!'

'Thanks, but not this time. I want to reach Uluu tomorrow. It will be my birthday, and I'm looking forward to a rest.'

'Your birthday. When? Tomorrow?'

'No, not tomorrow,' I butted in. 'On the fourteenth.'

'No!' Len exclaimed. 'You and Sasha are twins!'

'What?'

'Twins,' Len repeated. 'It is Sasha's birthday on the fourteenth too. How old will you be?'

'Thirty-three.' Len looked disappointed with this answer.

'Ah, Sasha will be thirty-four. He is old.' Sasha looked down and smiled bashfully. 'Yes, he is old, but you do not look thirty-three. You are not real twins; you are almost-twins. So you *must* come with us tomorrow. We will celebrate.'

'Really, thanks, but I can't,' I replied.

Temporarily, Len looked even more disappointed, but then a smile washed over his face. I don't think Len could stay angry at anyone for very long, no matter what they did. 'OK then. It makes me sad, but we are still friends, yes, and you and Sasha will always be almost-twins. If you must leave tomorrow, then we must let you get some sleep.'

'OK. Thank you.'

'OK, good night. I start work at eight. See you then. You must be ready to leave then. You are not really supposed to be here, but me and Sasha can keep a secret.' With that, he clambered out of the truck, shut the door and wandered off with Sasha.

I turned off the music and lay down where I was, spread out over the seats, not caring about the ridges digging into my back. The smell of fumes inside the cabin was overpowering and left a sharp acrid taste in the back of my throat. My last fleeting thought was concern that I would die right there from carbon monoxide poisoning. I couldn't work out if it would be better with the vents open or shut. The whole truck park was engulfed in smoke. There was no fresh air, inside or out.

The cafe, whose sign said it opened at eight, was shut when I wandered over to it the next morning at eight-thirty. There was no sign of it opening soon. I shovelled down some frozen cheese and salami, drank a cup of precious tea from the thermos that had cooled overnight and hit the road. It was too cold to wait. The sun hadn't risen.

10.

Warming up was no issue. The road was so rough and rutted and rocky from all the work trucks; for most of the morning I had to push my bike. Bumping along. Frustrated. Exhausted. Fortunately, later in the day, the road improved. Then, when my water had run out and I needed to get my stove out to melt more snow, a lorry stopped up ahead.

The driver wound down the window. 'Where are you going? Are you OK?' This was my opportunity. You learned to recognise them pretty quick out there.

'Do you have some water?'

'Yes. Come on in.' That's how I met Slava from Aldan, who told me about another woman who had travelled this road alone about five years before. That woman was walking, pulling a sled. I'd heard about her. Women travelling alone in winter, and camping (although I was yet to camp) along the way, were a rarity – a memorable one. I was beginning to realise why no one cycles in the extreme cold. It's too damn hard. Walking and skiing are easier.

Dimitri Kieffer had tried to tell me. I had met Dimitri in Ulaanbataar while cycling through Mongolia earlier in the summer. He had a zest for life and curiosity about the world I could identify with. Whereas travelling eventually takes its toll on me, and what should be memorable and exciting eventually becomes mundane, Dimitri never tired of new experiences and meeting new people. He had walked across the Russian Far East in winter. He had walked across the Bering Strait from Alaska and had kept on walking. Now, that was a challenge. But when I told Dimitri that, which no doubt he had heard many times before, all he said was that walking in winter was much easier than cycling, even if it did take longer. He was right. Siberian winter is not the season for cycling.

With any other location or season, I thought, the hardships endured while cycle-touring are far outweighed by the highlights. Siberian winters seemed in a league of their own. It was a close call whether the outstanding highlights – few and far between – outweighed the extensive periods of hardship and monotony. That was my view of the two weeks it took to reach Yakutsk. Of course, this was the coldest two-week period in February in the heart of Yakutia. It would get easier, I kept telling myself. But out there, at the time, it was difficult to comprehend that the region could ever warm up.

By late afternoon, the sun was ringed with a halo. *It's a good omen*, I mused. I began dreaming of the guesthouse in Uluu and all the luxuries – chocolate and beer – I would buy in the shop. I'm not superstitious. I don't really think that an optical display occurring due to all the ice particles in the air, natural considering the location and time of year, is anything other than a scientifically explainable effect. But I had recently been pondering all the apparent good luck I'd been having – not just on this trip, but in life generally – and wondering when it was all going to run out.

Over the last few days, I'd also been thinking about getting old. When I was young, I never imagined I would ever grow up to be an adult. Not in a Peter Pan, child forever, kind of way. Only that I could not see me concerning myself with those issues that grown-ups have to deal with: exams, jobs, owning a house, having children, getting old and frail. It seemed far more likely that I'd meet an early end in life. I've had a few close encounters where I could easily have lucked out – those moments when it could all have gone so horribly wrong – but it wasn't my time then.

Mind you, in the way I imagined as a kid, I still haven't grown up. I dabble in a job and career as a means to an end; I don't have a house and don't intend to get a mortgage; I've no kids either. I did have to take exams, though I didn't concern myself with them too greatly; they were a minor inconvenience and distraction whilst having the time of my life as a student.

This got me thinking that with all this good luck I'd had in my life until now, perhaps it was about to run out. I had been wondering, would I live to be thirty-three? That was my lucky number. I don't really believe in luck – I think we each make our own luck – but sometimes things just happen that are beyond our control.

When I was younger and first started to play hockey, I had to choose a shirt number. Choose your lucky number, I was told. Well, I didn't have a lucky number, so I chose the number thirty-three for no good reason at all. It's just a number.

It's just a number until you are cycling through Siberia in the winter wondering about the possibility of dying out there (you have so much time to think while cycle-touring, there are few topics you won't have considered or debated from all angles) and it's just days until your thirty-third birthday, which is your number. Now, is it just a number? Or is it a lucky one? And if it's a lucky one, is it the good luck or bad luck sort?

Of course, this all sounds quite ridiculous writing it down surrounded by comforts in England, having returned from Siberia alive and kicking. Most people living in a stable country, such as England, in the developed world of the twenty-first century, have no need to entertain the possibility of dying by any means other than old age or ill health. Paying into a pension is their most pressing concern. This is unprecedented in the history of humanity. Danger to life has been all but eliminated. It makes for comfort and easy living. That is not what we, as a species, have evolved to deal with. If I were going to die before getting old, it seemed possible that I could die out there in the depths of the Siberian winter. There were so many things that could go wrong: I could get hit by a truck or another vehicle with a drunk driver; I could stumble and fall in the snow and not be found before the cold had overcome me. So far, I had not had to camp except near Lake Baikal, which was much milder than here. But I was well aware how quickly everything could go tits up in this extreme environment. Was thirty-three to be a number with meaning after all – signalling the final whistle of the game to end all games?

That day with the haloed sun on my back was only one day away from my birthday. As the hours and kilometres passed, the chances of my successfully reaching Uluu before nightfall and checking into a guesthouse increased. That would guarantee me the birthday rest day my body was so urgently craving. It seemed increasingly unlikely that anything could go wrong. I would live to be thirty-three. *Yeah, I'm one lucky girl.*

Long after the sun had set, I rolled down the hill into Uluu, another village beside a frozen river. There were not one but three cafes to choose from. You would think that a village big enough for three cafes would also have at least one guesthouse. But that's where you'd be wrong. *Shit, my luck has just run out. Guess I'll live to be thirty-three; only it'll be spent on the road in the freezing cold. I only wanted a beer and a bed. Was that really too much to ask?*

With a second plateful of pancakes smothered in sweetened condensed milk, I drowned my sorrows at the thought of camping cold and waking up with only the road ahead to pedal on my birthday. I love condensed milk, which conjures memories of drinking instant coffee at street cafes in West Africa. Oh, what I'd have given right then to be transported into the searing heat of the Sahara.

The truck driver sitting at the other table paid for my dinner. Whether the gesture was out of admiration or pity, I don't know. At that moment, I didn't care. My thoughts were focussed on whether my clothes would dry before the cafe closed when I would be evicted into the bleak winter's night. *Maybe I should go and crawl into my sleeping bag*, I wondered. My body was so tired.

Reluctantly, I began pulling on my boots. Then, while I was gathering up my gloves and scarf and hats, the lady owner of the cafe, an intimidating woman if ever there was one, came and stood over me. *Oh no, what's the problem?*

'Are you going to camp?' she spoke sternly, as if it were forbidden.

'Er ... yes?' I replied hesitantly, as if asking her permission.

'You know, there's no guesthouse here.' I was about to reply, but she interrupted. 'If you want a place to stay tonight, you could sleep in the house of the woman who works here. How much would you pay?'

'OK.' Now I paused, unsure what the going rate for a room was before realising that the only thing that mattered was how much I was willing to pay. 'Five hundred rubles?'

'She said five hundred rubles,' the lady called out. I heard a mumbled reply from the kitchen.

'OK. Five hundred rubles for one night with dinner and breakfast included. Get what you need now. The rest we will put with your bike in the shed next door.'

And that is how I got to spend yet another night warm indoors, insulated and cut off from the white world outside.

I walked slowly with Veronika to her home. She wheezed through the streets and had to stop, puffing and panting, halfway up the stairs to catch her breath. She had a steely look in her eye and spoke without affection, although she also had a kind heart.

She served me borscht and tea, turned the TV on to the Sochi Olympics. It was the main news coverage besides the current protests in Kiev. Watching the news only added to the sense of isolation. It reminded me that beyond the white wilderness there was another world. But the effects of that other world did not reach here. It was like watching a soap opera, more fiction than reality.

Veronika returned to finish her shift at the cafe. 'Make yourself at home,' she told me before she left. That I found easy to do. No doubt, it was helped by having spent so many nights under different roofs over the years of travelling. It was the same with every Russian household: people made me feel at ease.

Veronika's home was in one of the concrete apartment blocks scarring the hillside. Externally, they looked decrepit and abandoned. Soviet by design, their slow, gradual collapse continues long after the end of communism. I sometimes think that the people still living here are all that holds these places up. They don't want to let go of the old times, which they remember as the good times. It is as though this part of Siberia has been forgotten by the Russia that is run from Moscow, some five thousand kilometres to the west. And where people are forgotten and left to fend for themselves, they remember the days when they were a part of something. Even if that something only used those people for its own advantage. It reminded me of the older people I spoke with in the Congo. They reminisced about the bygone days of colonialism under King Leopold of Belgium. It was hard for me to imagine how life was better there either.

Inside these decaying buildings, once you've negotiated the crumbling stairs and rotten bannisters, stepped warily over the creaking wooden floorboards covered in dirt and dust, ignoring the stench of urine, and entered through one of the heavy set doors, you find yourself in a homely, warm, well-kept, clean apartment.

The entrance hall of Veronika's apartment was furnished with a full-length mirror and dresser with hairbrush and makeup on it. At the base, the pile of the deep red carpet was worn down from daily use. On the wall were the antlers of a reindeer, a trophy and emblem to the close interaction people have with nature here. The large poster of a gushing fantasy waterfall in bright, gaudy colours was typical of the pictures used to decorate homes and restaurants alike throughout Russia, Mongolia and Central Asia; just as posters of food and Mecca adorn cafe walls throughout West Africa.

I was in bed before Veronika returned from work. The next morning, I woke to the sweet smell of cooking. In the kitchen was a plateful of pancakes stacked higher than it was wide.

'Come. Eat,' Veronika beckoned when she saw me. I did as I was told. I was still tired and not looking forward to facing the cold and cycling that day.

'What time do you need to leave today?' Veronika asked.

I don't need to leave at all. Hmm … no harm in asking.

'It doesn't matter. The thing is … I don't actually need to leave. Er …' *Just ask, dammit.* 'Erm … if you don't mind, would it be OK to stay another night?' I mumbled in my jumbled Russian. 'It's no problem if not, of course,' I added quickly because, more than anything, I didn't want to impose.

'Of course. Of course,' she smiled. 'I don't have to work today. You can rest here, have a bath and wash your clothes. These pancakes I made for you to take. They will do for lunch. Help yourself whenever you want. If you need anything, ask.'

Oh yes. Happy thirty-third birthday! My luck had not run out yet. A beer would've been asking too much. It could wait.

Veronika busied herself for most of the day, washing and cooking and cleaning. She sat down to watch TV in the afternoon when she changed the channel from the Olympic curling competition to watch an old drama, like a Russian *Little House on the Prairie*. I could understand enough to know it was terrible. I wrote my journal instead.

Ilya, her husband, returned from work later in the day. He was thin and grey and unshaven. His clothes hung off him, and he had a smoker's cough. He didn't look well, although he had a youthful glint in his eye and was enthusiastic to talk with me. I got the impression that the couple didn't often talk; either Veronika would be watching her period dramas on TV on her day off whilst Ilya was out at work, or when Ilya was in, he would be watching the sport on TV and she would busy herself with the housework. That's what I liked about the Russians I met. Once they'd welcomed me in and made sure I was OK, they left me to get on with my things and they got on with their lives. I felt less of an imposition or intrusion.

Ilya had been finding things around the house with English writing on. He didn't speak any English, and I think this was his way of showing he was trying. He'd shown me the packaging on some food and a couple of glasses with writing on the underside. Then he took out a condom from a little wooden box in the cabinet and showed it to me, pointing at the writing on it, which was also in English. Was this innocent enthusiasm for the English language or an unsubtle tactic to show his interest and desire? I gave him the benefit of the doubt and laughed.

When he heard Veronika come in, he whipped the condom into his pocket quickly so she wouldn't see. Then he winked at me. That wink whispered, 'This is between us.' *Sigh*. It was no surprise then, when shortly after Veronika left for work the next morning, I heard a gentle knock and the creaking of the door as he pushed it ajar.

'Helen. Are you awake?' I ignored him. 'Helen. Helen?'

'Yes.' I sighed and sat up. The door opened fully. Ilya walked in and sat down next to me. I stood up.

'Helen,' he was holding the condom up to me, 'She has gone to work.' The youthful glint in his eye had returned.

'Yes, and I have to cycle to Yakutsk.' It was clear that I would be getting no lie-in that morning. I started to pack.

'No, no. No rush,' he stammered. 'Time for sex.' *Oh God, did he really have to say that out loud.* As if the condom left any doubt what he wanted.

'No. That is why I'm leaving now.' I went into the bathroom to get dressed. When I came out, he had gone back to his bed in the living room.

As I finished packing my bag, he knocked on the door again. 'Helen. I'm sorry. Don't leave. You must have breakfast first. Please. I will go back to bed. I won't disturb you. There's no need to leave yet.' He was genuinely apologetic. I could tell from the tone of his voice. I opened the door. 'I'm sorry. I will make you some tea for breakfast. You must eat something before your long journey.'

With all that, the early wake-up call still meant I was on the road before sunrise.

11.

It was hellishly cold out. Fortunately there was a big hill to get up first thing. That, at least, got the heart pumping, chest heaving and feet stomping as I pushed the bike up.

A few minutes in, an old yellow school bus, empty except for the driver and his mate, came chugging along and stopped beside me. 'Do you want a lift?'

'Only to the top of the hill,' I replied.

'OK. Get in.' I pushed the bike as the guy behind the driver took the handlebars and heaved. The panniers wouldn't squeeze through the door. I heard snapping of plastic.

'Hang on,' I said and removed the bags on one side. Now the bike fit through.

We talked on the way up the hill, but I was distracted. A plastic hook on my pannier for fixing it to the bike rack had broken. Without it, the pannier wouldn't attach. I took out a cable tie to fix it. The cable tie broke. That's what happens when it's below minus forty outside.

The driver's mate saw the problem and took the pannier from me. 'No problem. I'll fix it,' he said. He put the pannier down, walked the length of the bus looking at the floor under the seats, leant down to pick something up and came back. It was a piece of wire. He then said something to the driver, who rummaged around under his seat without taking his eyes off the road and handed over some pliers. He threaded the wire through the broken clip and attached it to the pannier, then used the pliers to tie it together tightly.

'There. Is that OK?' It was more than OK. 'Plastic. Those,' he pointed at the cable ties, 'are no good. This wire is good. It's strong, even in the cold.'

And at that moment we rounded the crest of the hill and came to a lay-by. There were several other trucks there. The sun was beginning to rise; the yellow ball peeking above the horizon. Rays of glorious light flooded through the trees lining the road. *This is going to be a good day.* I knew it. I thanked the two men, lifted my bike out, attached the panniers and found the metal wire holding well, and set off before I cooled down too much.

It was a good day with steady progress, albeit slow at times when the road became overly rutted and potholed. The sky was clear and blue. When I stopped, I could even feel some warmth from the sun. By mid-afternoon my thermometer read a high of minus twenty-five degrees Celsius – the warmest day since Lake Baikal. Even another puncture failed to dampen my spirits. There had been virtually no traffic and hence no unwanted distractions from cycling. I stopped briefly and often to have a little tea and snack, and to stomp up and down to keep my toes from going numb. I had plenty of time to think ahead about where I might camp, what I needed to do and in what order to make sure I didn't have any problems.

Late in the afternoon, a truck came over the ridge of a hill and stopped. As I neared, the driver wound down the window and waved. I squinted, trying to make out the face through the half-light. *That truck looks familiar. It's not Bogdan is it? It is. Unbelievable.*

I cycled over. 'Helen. Come and have some tea. Hello!' I pushed the bike to the roadside, leant it against the wall of snow, picked up my thermos and climbed into the truck. Bogdan was already transforming it into a kitchen.

'I did not think you would get anywhere after I last saw you. So, it is possible to cycle in this cold. I certainly did not expect to see you again,' he said, and he wobbled his head from side to side in the way only Bogdan did. That made me smile. It's always nice to see a familiar face.

'How long has it been? A week?' I counted up the days in my head. It was easy to remember each place I'd slept as they'd all been so memorable, unlike the days that all merged into one cold hard slog of cycling.

'Nine days.'

Bogdan's head wobbled.

'Nine days and you've still not reached Yakutsk.' His head wobbled again. 'And I have been there, rested and am now going home. Why do you do this?' It was a rhetorical question. We'd already had that discussion.

'Where are you sleeping tonight?'

'I'm going to camp.'

'No. Why don't you sleep in the truck?' It was easy to argue my way out of it this time. We were heading in opposite directions, and I was sure that Bogdan had planned on driving many more kilometres before stopping for the night. Instead, he put the heater on full blast to dry out my damp clothes. We ate *salo*, bread and salami, and drank lots of tea. Then he filled up my thermos with hot water. The sun was setting by the time I left. It gave me time to cover a few more kilometres while still warm before finding a place to camp.

The temperature plunged, as usual, as darkness fell. Rather than waste time erecting the tent, I dug out a shelf in the snow and laid out my bivvy bag. Just doing that, my fingers were painfully cold. The stove wouldn't stay lit. My fingers hurt badly as I tried to relight it. The fuel bottle wouldn't stay pressurised, so I had to pump it every minute to keep it burning. As I waited for the weak flame to heat the water, I ran and jumped to keep warm between pumping the fuel bottle. Eventually the water boiled. I scoffed the noodles and got quickly into my sleeping bag.

It was silent out there in the Siberian wilderness. I lay in the darkness, peering through the slit between my hats and the scarf I'd pulled up over my nose, looking up at the blanket of stars overhead. The moon rising above the trees glowed huge through the haze and shone a yellowish heavenly light across the horizon, as though something great and godly was rising up.

I listened for any sound, but when all around is silent except your heartbeat and slow breathing, any muffled sounds emanating from your sleeping bag are confusing and the mind transforms them into real things – images of fear and fantasy. *Is that a truck pulling up and men talking?* No, it was my hat rustling on the sleeping bag. Even if it were men, they'd be unlikely to see me, hidden in my snow coffin next to a huge pile of wood. *That pile of wood, though, would be a good place for a bear to hibernate. Oh God, I hope I'm not camping next to a bear.*

I'd seen bears the previous summer while biking a trail in Buryatia, south of Lake Baikal. I'd been happily pedalling, mindlessly gazing at the stream rushing over rocks beside the track and the bright orange and yellow flowers amid the lush undergrowth. When I looked up, only twenty metres ahead of me was a little black bear. *So cute.* Then I saw the mother turn her head and stand on her back legs. Long leaves were hanging out from the sides of her mouth, which would have been comical at any other time. The cub ran off into the bush. The mother followed once she realised I wasn't a threat. That brief bear encounter was wonderful. I had no desire to see one now.

Someone had told me not to worry about bears because, as we all know, they hibernate in winter. But if I did see a bear, then I should be prepared to run very fast. Because a bear that's not hibernating in winter has just been woken up, and it'll be angry and hungry in equal measure. Yeah, very funny.

What's that sniffing sound? Not wolves, surely. I was an easy, defenceless target cocooned in my sleeping bag. I'd have had more chance of making an escape from a straight-jacket. I half sat and peered out. There was nothing. It was just the sound of my feet moving over the Thermarest. *Stop thinking about bears and wolves and dangerous men; you'll never get to sleep.*

I did sleep, because I was tired, but it was a restless night as my feet were so cold. I woke up periodically and shook my body as though I were having a fit, and I did sit-ups in my sleeping bag – anything to warm up my feet. Whenever I drifted off, I wondered if I would wake up with frostbitten toes.

When I woke up and it was daylight, I noticed how unnaturally quiet it was. There cannot be many places on earth that are silent at dawn. Nothing disturbed me; there were no cockerels crowing, no donkeys braying, no songbirds sweetly chirping, no dogs barking or traffic roaring.

I rolled over to look at the thermometer. It was max'd out at minus fifty degrees Celsius. God knows how cold it really was. All I wanted to do was roll over and go back to sleep, but I had to warm up my feet.

Moving around fixed that. My fingers, though, were another matter. I had more struggles with the stove, which didn't help. But the worst of it was trying to unfreeze the Thermarest valve to let the air out; and fighting with my sleeping bag, which seemed to have bloated in size overnight, to squeeze into the pannier; and struggling to unscrew the lid of the thermos, which had frozen shut. My fingers were swollen numb by then. The effort required to drag the bike through the snow back to the road had me puffing and steaming. As the blood returned to my hands, the tears streamed down my face, and I held back the urge to shout in agony at the pain burning in my fingertips. I dropped the bike on the road and whimpered as the feeling returned.

It was forty kilometres to the first cafe. After that, I was determined to reach Katsikattsi, the next village, another thirty kilometres on before finishing for the day. Bogdan had said there was a cafe there also. A hot dinner indoors before camping appealed.

The endlessly undulating road was tiring. As I picked up speed going downhill, the road became rutted; I had to put on the brakes. Without much forward momentum, I was soon pushing the bike. My thighs were too sore, my load too great, and the hills too steep to cycle.

Whilst pushing, I often stopped to look behind me at the sun edging closer to the horizon. The sky was a changing kaleidoscope of colour throughout the daylight hours. In fact, it seemed as though there were no day. The sun was always either rising or setting, the temperature rising or falling. It was neither light nor warm enough to call it 'day'. The nights, however, were both long and dark; unless you were indoors, where you slept deeply, unaware of the passing night and woke at sunrise as though it were only moments since you shut your eyes. But I couldn't admire the red, swollen, setting sun and horizon bruised purple behind me; my cold feet pervaded every thought.

I knew I would reach Yakutsk. I only had to persevere, to keep moving forward. But was all this hardship worth it? What exactly was I getting out of this? For me, to say 'I did it' is not a good reason. The cycling was not enjoyable. I had not camped as much as I had wanted. When I was outdoors, the focus was not on the scenery or the sunsets, but on survival. Survival is not fun. Surviving is not living. Surviving is having your life in the balance, suspended delicately on a thread that is wavering in the flow of life going on around you. Survival is being on a knife edge. No, I did not come to Siberia only to survive; I came here to live. These were the thoughts plaguing my mind as a distraction from my cold feet. What was the point, and why was I doing this? If it was not enjoyable or the rewards commensurate with the hard work put in, why would I continue beyond Yakutsk? *No, stop with these negative thoughts. They are not helpful. Decisions are for later. Take one step at a time. First, reach Katsikattsi this evening.*

12.

It was pitch black by the time I reached the junction at Katsikattsi and was drawn to the wooden cabin with smoke rising from the chimney. Never did such a little word – cafe – on a sign above the door mean so much. It meant food and drink and warmth. That was everything I desired.

I never left that cafe until morning. I was given the bed in the back room, which the women working there slept in when taking a break on the night shifts. With nothing to offer in return for this kindness, I quietly left a big tip for my breakfast pancakes.

I had only to cross the Lena River and cycle north a total of ninety kilometres to Yakutsk. So many long, slow days had passed where I'd finished the day seemingly no closer to my destination. Yet now, Yakutsk was finally within sight. *I might even make it today.*

Oh, I should have known better by now than to get my hopes up. I should have known that things rarely go according to plan when cycle-touring and almost never when winter cycle-touring in Siberia. That hope was crushed before I'd even crossed the river.

The day started like any other morning. After breakfast, I packed my panniers, loaded the bike and wheeled it outside ready to cycle off while I was still warm. Other people always had other intentions. First, photos were taken. I stood awkwardly by my bike feeling the warmth in my fingers and toes fade and watching my breath freeze into a fog around me. I had learnt by now that these photo shoots would go on forever unless I drew an end to them. Only after that was I free to cycle away.

I freewheeled down the steep hill winding through the forest until the trees opened out into a wide, flat expanse. I reached a crossroads. There were no signs and no one around to ask the way to the river crossing. I turned towards the village. The single-storey wooden houses peeked out of the snow blanket that thickly covered everything. Smoke rising from chimneys and spreading horizontally in the air above was the only sign of life. It was picturesque. Picture perfect. It's what the postcards would have you believe Siberian life is like. It was beautiful. But the softness of the pure white snow belies the harshness of the reality when you step inside that picture. Where there was no smoke, the half-buried houses were like skeletons, the snow a shroud covering the dead, not a blanket protecting the living.

The road through the village veered away from the river, so I turned around and returned to the crossroads. The second exit took me closer to the river. I could see one poor track going down to the bank. *Surely that isn't what the vehicles use.* Instead, I continued on the wider, maintained road. It ran parallel, separated by a long thicket of bushes and shrubs, so that I could not see the frozen river. On and on it went. *Is this really going to take me across the river? Perhaps it was the other track.* With heavy legs, I turned around. The track petered out at the river, where a sign warned car drivers against accidentally driving over the bank into the river, presumably a summer warning. Here, in winter, the river looked much like the riverbank: snow-covered. I ventured out onto the river and looked up and down it. There was no obvious ice road across. The only visible tracks were from horses and people.

When I had enquired in the evening as to the best route to Yakutsk from Katsikattsi, one truck driver had said to stay on the east side of the river and cross further on at Nizhny Bestyakh. Everyone else had said that, being on a bicycle, it would be better to cross at Katsikattsi and take the road up the west side straight to Yakutsk. I was beginning to think I should've listened to the truck driver. If this so-called track really was the best route over the river, the four kilometres across would be a tough slog. I was determined not to go back up the hill to the main road now. I sighed and set off.

Within metres, I was struggling to heave the bike through the deep snow and over the horse tracks. This was harder than dragging the bike through sand in the Congo. Then, at least, I had about half the weight of luggage. It took less than twenty metres for me to know this was not going to work. Even if I had to cycle back up the steep hill to the cafe and go on the main road, it would be easier and quicker than crossing the river here. Reluctantly, I retraced my steps. At the junction, a van drove past. I flagged it down and asked the way. The driver said I needed to keep following the road running parallel to the river. If only I had just kept going a little further. But that is the difficulty when unsure of the way. Just how far do you go before turning around? How far is too far?

Eventually the road turned to the river and there it was – the ice road – smooth and wide and clear, cutting through the thick snow. It had taken two hours and much wasted energy to find. Although temporary while the ice remained thick enough through the winter, the road was like any other, complete with speed limits, road signs and route markers.

Out there on the exposed ice, the wind cut through my clothes. I put on another top, another hat and my mittens over my gloves. There was nothing to be done about my feet. Walking on the flat no longer warmed me enough to thaw my toes. It was too slippery to run. The thick ice was a milky blue, not like the transparent ice of Lake Baikal, which showed the black deepness of the lake. Here, in the middle of winter, the ice was many feet thicker. There was little risk of falling in.

By the time I reached the opposite side, the idea of reaching Yakutsk that day had sunk into the river. Instead, I could only think about reaching the next town where there was a guesthouse. Even those twenty-five kilometres took an inordinately long time.

Pokrovsk was a big town. The hotel took a while to locate. I went into a shop to ask directions. It wasn't far away, the lady assured me. Lazy with tiredness, I didn't bother to put my mittens back on when I went outside again. In less than five minutes, my hands were painfully cold. I quickly put on my mittens, but in that time, without my body heat near them, they had frozen. My hands went numb. *Quick, do something.* The thought of running up and down the streets waving my arms like a madwoman for all the town to see was too embarrassing, so I rushed to the first shop I came to. I couldn't open the door; my hands wouldn't do what I wanted them to. When a man walked out, I stepped in.

Inside, in the warm, my hands immediately began to warm, and my eyes welled up with the pain. The women at the counter looked on at me silently. I pulled off my face mask, so as to look more human, and then turned to them and smiled and said hello, by way of introduction and excusing my intrusion.

One lady replied, 'It's the cold, yes? Are you OK? Do you need a cup of tea?' They spoke as if it was an everyday occurrence for a crazy foreigner overcome by the cold to rush in, clearly with no intention of buying anything. This was a hardware store, after all, not a cafe. I said that I would soon be fine, which was true. They said I was crazy and brave to be cycling here in the winter. I don't think you can be both crazy and brave, not at the same time. I said they were probably right about the crazy part. Bravery – courage – is the uncomplaining way people who live here go about their lives under the most extreme conditions. The same can be said of many people throughout Africa. I, on the other hand, like to complain. That's something we Brits excel at, especially when it involves the weather.

Once checked into the hotel and showered, my first priority was that birthday beer I'd never had in Uluu. Yakutsk seemed even further from reach than at the start of the day – still a full day's ride away and now with legs that were even more tired. I knew the beer wasn't going to help with that, but it sure would taste good. Further along the street I found a shop selling beer. I walked with my gloved hand in front of my nose and mouth, the way the locals did, to prevent the skin from freezing.

Back in the warm hotel, drinking that bottle of Sibirskaya Corona, I was content. I didn't once think about the cold or worry about frostbitten toes or where I was going to sleep that night or what direction I should go from Yakutsk when I finally got there. No, I didn't have to think at all; I only savoured the taste, and that was a good thing.

13.

Everybody thinks I'm crazy. 'Why?', they ask. Why, oh, why would you want to cycle through Siberia in the winter? Why! It's a rhetorical question, an exclamation. Any answer I give leads only to incomprehension. The questions I am asked rarely deviate from a select few.

Where are you coming from?

- Irkutsk.

Where are you going to?

- Chersky.

Aren't you afraid?

- No.

But what about the bears?

- They're sleeping.

Do you have a gun?

- No, I have a knife. (They laugh)

But what about the wolves?

- They don't come near the roads.

Aren't you cold?

- Now, no. Soon, yes. Of course, this is winter in Siberia.

Where do you sleep?

- Anywhere; I have a tent.

What do you eat?

- Anything; the same as you.

Would you like some vodka?

- No.

Would you like some tea?

- Yes.

But why come to Siberia in winter?

Silence.

And there it is. My entire trip can be summed up in a song of questions and staccato answers. All of it except 'why?' It's not that I don't know the answer or lack the Russian; it's because it cannot be nicely summed up in one sentence. There are many reasons why, but I would be really cold by the time I managed to explain it all. So they think I'm just crazy.

I've been called crazy before. Crazy for quitting my job and crazy for cycling through Africa. Crazy because I get a wild look in my eye and a grin as the corner of my lips crease when someone mentions tough tracks and mountain passes (oh, and beer). I'm OK with crazy. None of it seems so crazy to me. Crazy to me would be sitting at a desk my entire life staring at a computer screen and daydreaming of all the things I would rather be doing or places I'd rather be. Better to just go do them. Get up. Get out. Live.

Why, oh, why would you want to spend your entire life working a mundane nine-to-five job you don't enjoy? That's what I would ask in return. I don't *want* to, is what they say. As if there is no other choice. There is always a choice. Usually it involves a compromise. Life involves lots of compromises.

Now who is the crazy one? I'm spending my life doing what I want and what makes me happy. That's my dream. It doesn't have to be yours.

We are all going to die some day; some sooner than others. We can't do a thing about that. But we can make sure we die with no regrets. That's not crazy. So I go out and do the things I love. I love a challenge. I love to learn. I love to travel and see and hear and listen, and try to understand – make sense of – this world. That is why I went to Siberia in the winter.

I am not travelling because I am running from anything. I am not travelling because I am searching for something. Perhaps, if anything, I am trying to figure out what part I am playing in this world. I suspect that nobody truly knows what their part is in life. That is for other people to decide, after the final curtain call when our time is up.

I tell you what, though, for anyone who didn't think I was crazy before I went to Siberia, they should've seen me in the midst of a tyre change. Damn, I hated the tyre change.

You see, when it gets cold, the rubber tyres get really stiff, the inner tube too. Sometimes the tube just splits. It's as though, when the temperature drops below forty – that's minus forty – all your gear has a mischievous, impish mind of its own whose sole aim is to cause you grief and misery and revel in letting the world see you shout and swear.

Fuck. That's my word of choice when I've frozen my fingers fiddling with the quick release that is anything but quick or releasing. Fuck this, I mutter under my breath as I rummage through my panniers to get the repair kit and spare tube and pumps. And I say it louder when I realise the pump won't work and throw it across the road because I'm getting pissed off now. Fuck that's cold, I exclaim as I shove the spare pump deep inside my jacket to warm it with my body heat and feel the cold metal close to my skin. Fuck this for a laugh, I say to no one as I run and stomp up and down the side of the road trying to bring back feeling into my toes and thaw out my bike pump. So I'm running and jumping and stomping and swearing and waving my arms about, flapping and flailing like I'm trying to take off but am too fat and heavy to fly. And there are tears in my eyes, because all this exertion is bringing the feeling back into my fingers, and the pain is excruciating. Then, when a vehicle drives past and keeps going – the one damn time nobody stops to ask if I'm OK, or would I like a cup of tea, is when I'm clearly not OK, and yes, tea would be nice if I could sit in a warm vehicle at the same time – you know what I shout out with bitterness on my breath to the disappearing taillights? Bastards!

Then I laugh. Because you've got to laugh, really. I must've looked like a raving nutcase. A madwoman. A lunatic. No, if you didn't think I was crazy for going to Siberia in winter, you'd sure have thought it to see me trying to change a tyre there.

And it was right then, during the fourth tyre change in two weeks, less than two kilometres from the hotel I'd stayed at in Pokrovsk, that a car did stop. I'd made an early start, and because the sun was yet to rise, it was the coldest time of the day. And at the coldest time of the day, in the depth of Yakutia, on a clear February morning, the temperature is below forty. I mean minus forty, of course. And when the temperature plummets below forty, well, that's when everything stops working as it should. It is precisely at these times that you wish everything would work as it ought, which is kind of why it doesn't. Sod's Law and all that.

Yakutsk was only seventy-five kilometres – one day's ride – from Pokrovsk. Two hours later, I was still no closer.

I had thought that a day off in Pokrovsk would have helped to rest my tired legs. What I really needed was several days off. Usually, with twenty-four hours rest, the muscles in my legs are so tight, they burn just to walk upstairs, not to mention when cycling. So those first two kilometres were a slow, painful affair as the lactic acid coursed through my quads. I was barely through town and back on the main road when I felt the ominous loss of control with the rim on the road and thump … thump … thump … as the valve ran underneath.

By the time a car stopped, my feet were numb. The driver, a local from the next village, instantly realised why my bike pumps weren't working.

'Come on, let's take you back to my garage. We will warm everything up and fix it there.' With his brother, he had a garage next to the family home where they repaired anything and everything. While the bike pumps were laid on the stove to warm, I was invited in for tea and breakfast. We repaired the puncture, then loaded up the bike again, and I set off once more.

The road was flat following the Lena River. Keeping up a decent speed wasn't too laborious. The problem was that with the prolonged days outside, I was feeling the cold much more quickly. Soon my feet were numb. The only way to bring back the feeling was to get off and run with the bike. There were no hills to work up a sweat. Running was slow and exhausting and made me look ridiculous to all the passing cars on their way to the regional capital.

I had set my sights on the next cafe to defrost my digits when another car pulled over. 'Can we take a photo of you? You are cycling to Yakutsk, yes?' That seemed obvious. 'You are from England, yes?' Not so obvious. Not, unless you'd watched the local news that morning on the station that had interviewed me back in Aldan, which aired that day. During my five minutes of reluctant fame, I posed for photos and got colder and colder. The smoke rising from the cafe teased me; it was so tantalisingly close.

Unfortunately, the cafe was nothing more than a small wood cabin with a stove in the centre. There were no hot pipes to dry my clothes on. I ordered coffee and a *kurnik*, then another, and another. My feet remained numb. It was midday now and I'd barely cycled twenty-five kilometres. With a fourth *kurnik*, I reconciled myself with the concept of camping out one last night. Then I made a concerted effort to thaw out my feet. I took off my boots; the lady serving food placed them beside the stove and pulled up a chair for me. I leant back with my feet up against the walls of the stove and felt the warmth drawing through. I placed my fleece gloves on the edge of the stove and breathed in deeply, savouring the mouth-watering aroma of freshly grilled meat that was being cooked outside and had been carried in on a large plate. A strange plasticky stench wafted my way.

Then the lady shouted out so loudly, I nearly rocked off the back of my chair. 'Your gloves!' Her hand shot over the stove, knocking off a paper plate of pancakes. It was too late. One glove had melted to the stove; the other was singed beyond repair. And that is why you carry spare sets of anything essential like gloves. I'd never have anticipated that scenario. What an idiot. Unfortunately, my other gloves were not as effective at keeping my hands warm; I quickly got cold hands as well as cold feet. The coffee and *kurniks* had done nothing to revive my energy levels.

Yakutsk seemed as far away as ever.

It was then that I again began to wonder why exactly I was cycling here. With so much traffic on the road now, it seemed pointless. I wasn't going anywhere a car couldn't. It wasn't fun or interesting or challenging to cycle, only tiring and boring and … *I could just get a lift*. But I couldn't bring myself to ask for a lift, to admit defeat. I wondered whether, if someone stopped and offered me a ride, I would or should take it? I figured I probably would. Over the years I have been cycle-touring, I have reconciled myself with the idea of occasionally taking a lift. With every vehicle that passed, I silently hoped they would stop. Sometimes they did, because they too had watched the news that morning and wished for a photograph. Each time I got a bit colder. The colder I got, the more I wondered, why?

My feet were completely numb again. I was going to have to stop cycling and run for a while. This was the other war raging in my mind: to keep pedalling and risk frostbite to reach the destination sooner, or to stop and run to warm my feet up, which would extend the time outside in the cold where the risk of frostbite increased as day turned to night.

It was similar to cycling through the desert with a limited amount of water and a long distance before a chance of a resupply. Your throat is dry and all you can think about is quenching your thirst by taking long refreshing gulps of water. As there is only a little water remaining in your water bottle, you must satisfy yourself with a few sips instead. The sensation as the water touches your tongue and slides down is tantalising and tortuous. You don't dare to drink more, although your body is screaming for it. Instead, you save some because you don't know how much thirstier you're going to get. And what if there's no water where you're expecting it and you have to go further? No, it is safer to save some water, if you can. All this time you are cycling along with your mind focussed entirely on the dwindling water supply, you fail to notice the beautiful scenery around you. The wildlife and nature you have come to see is now irrelevant. There is only one thing of importance: water. You want to drink again, but think it best to go further before stopping. Each kilometre appears to go by more slowly. The distance to the next water supply seems to get further away. *Drink all the water now or save it until later ... What to do, what to do?* The risk of running out could be disastrous. The mind games rage on.

Don't want frostbite ... Want to get to Yakutsk ... A van stopped up ahead on the hard shoulder. Even though I knew it was probably someone wanting a photo, I couldn't help thinking my bike would fit easily into the van.

The driver, wearing a leather jacket and fur trapper's hat, was standing at the back of his van by the time I reached him. 'I saw you at the cafe earlier. Now when I saw you cycling, I had to stop and ask ... Can I give you a lift?'

I didn't hesitate for a moment. *Hell, yeah*! In my mind, I did a little happy dance. If only my body had really done the same dance, my feet might have warmed up without the need for a ride.

The last twenty kilometres to Yakutsk were over in a flash.

14.

The last two weeks felt like they had been merely a practice, a shakedown, a chilling warm-up. Now I was at the start line. But where was the finish line? The difficulties of the previous two weeks had made me seriously question whether I could reach Chersky up on the north coast. It had been my dream to go all the way there; the idea of giving up on it left me with an empty feeling in my stomach.

Failure is not easy to swallow. Would I be failing to achieve my own goals if I stopped or didn't get to Chersky, or would I only be failing in some other people's eyes? It was not the destination, Chersky, that mattered to me; it was the journey there.

Physically, I was exhausted from prolonged exertion, too little sleep and continuous exposure to the cold. I was also exhausted from always having to think ahead and having no one to share these difficulties with, and coming to terms with the fact that I was extraordinarily close to reaching my limit.

This was not an absolute limit where I would collapse, unable to continue. It was the limit of what I was willing to endure for the pleasures of new experiences. Would I enjoy the journey enough to make it worth the considerable effort?

I had come here, in part, to experience the cold and see how you can live in such an extreme environment. My cycle ride in northern

Scandinavia had shown me that winter camping could be enjoyable and fun. Out here, though, only on a couple of afternoons did the temperature reach a high of minus twenty-eight, which was the lowest I had experienced in Scandinavia. This was a whole new realm of cold. When it is colder than minus forty, living becomes surviving. Every day since Neryungri the temperature had dropped well below that. It felt like I had bitten off more than I could chew. I was cycling through the very coldest inhabited region on earth at the very coldest time of year.

I knew that soon the temperature would start to rise as spring drew near. And with a rise in temperature, everything would get easier. I knew that. People kept telling me that. But something in my brain prevented me from believing it. The only cold I had known in Yakutia was this February cold. A ten degree increase in temperature was all that was needed to transform this extreme cold into something manageable, even pleasurable. But a ten degree rise was as incomprehensible at that moment as the plus forty degree temperatures it soars to in midsummer.

I had also come for the challenge of facing the unknown alone. I wanted to leave the familiar road behind and travel through the remote, barely populated region in the north. The risk would be greatly reduced by going with another person or close support; it wouldn't be half so scary. By myself, though, I would have to deal with whatever came up; I alone would be responsible for the outcome of my decisions. I wanted to know how I would cope without someone to turn to for help. Would I be able to push past the fear, yet recognise the point that is a step too far and turn back if necessary? This was how I expected to be tested on the remote journey to Chersky.

Then I realised, I was being faced with this question now, much sooner than I had expected. It was disheartening to realise that I'm not half as fearless as I thought.

At some point, I was going to have to make a decision about my destination – to push for Chersky or make an alternative plan – because I would need to book a flight back to England.

Another option was to continue on the Kolyma Highway to Magadan instead. The distance was less; I would have time to rest. With a real road, it would be easier and carried less risk.

But a significant reason for cycling here in winter was because an overland journey to Chersky is only possible then, when the ground freezes and ice roads are created. Taking the real road to Magadan made being here in winter a bit pointless. I could have cycled it in summer (and put up with the mosquitoes and bears instead).

I was also concerned that it would be too easy. Sure, the last two weeks had been a challenge, and whichever route I took, there would be adventures. There are always adventures on the road; around every bend a new experience lies in wait. That's the appeal. But I sensed I had a good idea of what lay ahead on the road to Magadan.

This journey wasn't meant to be all about pushing my boundaries; I wanted also to learn about different places and people. On the road to Magadan, there would be more to learn about the history and development of the Kolyma region and, I suspected, more people to meet.

What I had read about the history and people of Siberia, Yakutia and Chukotka fascinated me. Based on my journey to Yakutsk, I was beginning to suspect I would meet an entirely different group of people to those whom I had expected – fewer Even, Evenk, Kopik and Chukchi; more Russian, Tajik, Uzbek and Ukrainian immigrants to the region.

The longer, complete journey across Asia was a chance to explore the lands inhabited by nomadic cultures. Nomadic lifestyles intrigue me. I am, as a cycle-tourer, a kind of twenty-first-century nomad. What is it about this transient way of life that is so compelling to those restless among us who are unable to remain content when settled?

Few of the traditionally nomadic cultures have survived intact. Those people who have managed to retain at least some of their nomadic customs and identity are still spread, albeit thinly, from the Central Asian Steppe through to Chukotka in the Russian Far East. Kyrgyz shepherds, Mongolian horsemen, Chukchi reindeer herders and cycle-tourers – what is it that we have in common? But my time in Siberia was not being spent amongst the traditionally nomadic people; it was spent with the nomads of the modern world – the truck drivers and migrant workers – and with settled people.

My fighting spirit hadn't given up on Chersky and the challenge yet. I debated the options endlessly, over and over and over. I would wake from my dreams in the morning and be certain I would take the road to Magadan. Then over breakfast, I had changed my mind and was sure that I would try to reach Chersky. I would start making plans for that eventuality when something – anything, nothing in particular – would cause me to reverse my decision again. It was exhausting.

The pros and cons, the advantages and disadvantages, the risk versus benefit analysis all came from me. Counter-arguments are one of my specialities. Give me an opinion or point of view and I can disagree with it, whether I believe it or not. Devil's advocate, that's me. There was no one to ask for advice. The decision was mine alone. Decisions, however, are not my speciality.

Finally, I made a decision: to not make a decision yet. I would wait until I reached Ust-Nera. It would probably be the last chance I'd have to get online to book my return flight. Situated on the bend in the road, it would be the last town before having to choose between the Artik Road north to Chersky or continuing along the Kolyma Highway to Magadan.

15.

Egor had offered me the spare room in his apartment to stay in whilst visiting Yakutsk, having originally contacted him through the Couchsurfing website. I met up with him in Lenin Square. I was easy to spot – the only person with a bicycle. He walked towards me – the only person with a knitted beard tucked under his hat and covering his chin.

Yakutsk was modern and lively. Although the main industry was mining of gold and diamonds, it had the feel of a city thriving on the service sector. Businesses were booming and there were more office workers in suits walking through the main square than workers in heavy industry.

Whereas Yakutsk is geographically isolated, technology and the internet age have served to connect it globally and transform it into an international city. In the evening, I went with Egor to meet his friends at The Wild Duck, an English pub, in the city centre. We listened to American music while discussing Japanese movies, inter-railing around Europe, holidays to southeast Asia and the delights of Thai food.

Egor had told me early on that everyone knew everyone here, despite Yakutsk being a sizeable city with a population of some 300,000. It was his way of explaining how the first person I met in town knew him.

I'd been standing outside, trying to work out which entrance to which apartment block was Egor's, when a lady wrapped up in furs had asked me what the problem was. There was no problem. I was finally in Yakutsk and that made me very happy. All I had to do was figure out from the address which door to use, which would be an entry into the warm. It would be like returning from Narnia, back through the wardrobe into a world I understood.

I showed her the address. She couldn't work it out either.

'Who are you staying with?' she demanded to know. I told her. She spoke in English, which took me aback. I'd hardly heard a word of English for weeks.

'Ah, Egor. I know Egor. Do you have a phone and his number?' I nodded. 'Then give it to me. I will call him. You cannot stand out here; you will die.' That was an exaggeration, but she believed it.

Some locals embraced the winter; others lived in fear of it. The comforts of modern living had not liberated them from the harsh environment. Sucked unwittingly into the vortex of modernity, some were spiralling further and further from the freedom it offered, where fear of hardship became an insurmountable barrier.

We have been taught to fear death – health and safety and a compensation culture. We have been taught to revere immortality – the dream of eternal youth sold to us by airbrushed models through anti-ageing creams, super-foods and diet pills, making us feel guilty about any small pleasure in life that is only a risk to longevity when taken in excess. But those who fear death become scared to live.

'Egor? Egor. There is a girl here from England with a bicycle. She is here to see you. You must come quickly; she is dying. She is outside your flat; she's cold and dying.' I asked to speak to him.

'Hi Egor! It's Helen. I'm not dying.' I was not dying. I was very happy and just a little cold.

'Are you OK?' Egor asked, understandably sounding concerned.

'Yes, yes. I'm fine. I just arrived and was trying to work out which

116

is your flat when this lady stopped.' He laughed.

'OK. I'm still at work. Can you come to the town centre? We can meet up for lunch and I'll give you the key.' We arranged a time and place. Then I hung up.

The lady asked, 'Are you sure you're not going to die?' *Some day I will. But not today. Not here.*

When she was satisfied I wouldn't die immediately, the lady was curious to know what I was doing here. 'My nephew, Slava, he rides a bicycle. I'm sure he would love to meet you. Do you mind if he contacts you?' I said I didn't mind. I couldn't really say anything else.

It was a couple of days later that I met up with Slava. He was slim with a fine wispy beard and blackened ear tips from recent frostbite. He was quiet by nature and softly spoken. He knew enough English that we could converse in halting sentences as he showed me the city sights.

Slava took me to the Archeology and Ethnography Museum where his uncle worked, located within the university buildings that look out onto the Lena River. The surrounding streets were full of students walking in groups, the girls all wearing fashionable *unty*, reindeer fur boots embroidered with traditional designs, smart coats and fur hats and scarves. I felt distinctly scruffy. Russian women never go out looking anything other than their best. The men walked with hands in pockets and shoulders hunched, so there was no gap between their hats and jacket collars for the cold air to reach. Everyone walked the same way, in a fast shuffle so that their feet were never far from the ground. That way, if you slip, you don't fall. Not once did I see a Russian fall on the ice. I crashed inelegantly with a thud twice before I learned the technique.

I also went with Slava to see the ice sculpture display that is created every winter down near the port. I expected something similar to the sculptures I'd seen in Irkutsk's Kirova Square, where there was also a massive ice slide for kids to slide down again and again as the parents watched. The display in Yakutsk was far grander. Replicas of famous landmarks like the Eiffel Tower and Statue of Liberty stood alongside ice carvings of the Sochi Olympic mascots. One of the sculptures was still being finished. Two men were working on it armed with a chainsaw and chisels. It was slow work creating such detailed, intricate patterns. It must take a certain kind of person to put so much time and effort into work that is only temporary because at the end of the winter the sculptures melt away.

Whilst in Yakutsk, I also met up with Bolot. I knew him through Facebook and his incredibly informative website, AskYakutia, where he answers queries about the region for anyone who cares to ask.

'Do you know Bolot?' I had asked Egor one evening.

He laughed. 'I told you, Yakutsk is a small town. Everyone knows everyone. And especially anyone who speaks English and is involved with tourists knows Bolot. Of course, I know Bolot.'

I met Bolot at the bar and restaurant Be Happy. Its name, bizarrely, was in English. It's my suspicion that there is no direct Russian equivalent for the phrase. Happiness is not so common on this continent; not in the way that Africans are happy. That was the main difference I could see between the Siberians and Africans I had met on my travels. While both may live under harsh environments, the Africans go through life with smiles on their faces, whereas the Siberians tended to be glum about it. OK, I know I'm stereotyping, and that's not something I like to do. And I know that it is not fair to paint everyone with the same brush. But really, it was so startlingly clear to me, I can't help but mention it. Yes, the Africans are a glass half full lot, going about life with a kind of childish innocence. The Siberians, though, are not so much glass half empty as glumly propping up the bar with only the dregs remaining and not enough spare change for a refill. I'm not saying they don't know how to laugh

– that's a different matter – but there is a darkness to their humour; sarcasm and irony seeps out of them like a weeping wound. In that way, as a Brit, I feel their pain. I am sure it has something to do with the weather. The sun can put a smile on anyone's face. And the freezing cold of Siberia is enough to shatter any smile into shards.

The five days in Yakutsk flew by. I could easily have stayed longer, but if I was going to try to reach Chersky, I needed as much time as possible for the journey. My body felt rested, which was the main thing.

Bolot had drawn me a crude map of my route on a scrap of paper. There was not much to put on it: one squiggly line dotted with the names of a few towns, distances between cafes, a couple of rivers and where the mountains were. Yakutsk was at one end of the line, Magadan at the other. The line represented 2,000 kilometres. Halfway along the road was the town of Ust-Nera, and 100 kilometres beyond that, Bolot had drawn an arrow north. That was where the Artik Road to Chersky began. He had nothing more to add about that route. He'd never been. It remained blank. That's why it intrigued me.

Egor had gone to work and said to leave anytime I wanted, just close the door behind me. I made coffee and sat at the kitchen table, staring out of the top floor window at the flaming red sun rising above the apartment blocks and smoke stacks that gave Yakutsk its skyline. It was the same fiery sunrise every morning I'd been in Yakutsk. I loved to sit and watch the city stir from the comforts of indoors.

As with every other morning, Kate and Oskar, Egor's tiny black cats, vied for my attention. Kate, named after Kate Moss because of her beauty and sleek silky body, sat on my lap. It was her favourite place because it was out of reach from the claws of her tormentor Oskar, named after Oskar Schindler because he was a womaniser and not very nice in the beginning but he turned out all right in the end. Egor was clearly an optimist and still had hopes for Oskar the cat, despite the overwhelming evidence to the contrary.

When I got out the bread and cheese and salami from the fridge, both cats began meowing loudly. I put Kate on the floor and got ready to fend off the attack on my food by Oskar, who always tried the stealthy approach from the chair on the other side of the table. I threw down a couple of pieces of salami and watched as Oskar waited for Kate to grab the first piece before launching an attack on her, stealing her salami and running off with it. Kate hunted around until she found the second piece. I ate some myself and put the rest back in the fridge, then poured another coffee. I was in no rush to leave; outside it was cold.

When I finally left, the thermometer wavered above minus twenty. During my stay in Yakutsk, the temperature had turned; Egor had called it, without a hint of sarcasm, 'the first week of spring'. I almost believed him. As I cycled out of town, tiny flecks of ice crystals floated in the air, sparkling like glitter. It was magical and mesmerising like walking through a fairy tale. No one else took any notice.

I had no trouble finding the ice road across the Lena River. There was no wind this time. *This is what it's meant to be like.* Even after the river crossing, the main road winding its way through the forest was easier to cycle than the journey to Yakutsk had been; the road smoother, less hilly. My feet didn't feel the cold for twenty kilometres at a time. Finally, I was making good progress. I had a routine now; I'd cycle twenty kilometres, then stop to have a cup of tea and some snacks. Meanwhile, I would walk up and down the road and stomp my feet to get the circulation flowing again. Then I'd cycle another twenty kilometres before repeating the refuelling and reheating process.

By putting continuous pressure on the pedals, it was not surprising the blood flow to my toes was reduced. I was hardly wearing the most appropriate boots for cycling in. They were, however, the most appropriate boots for cycling through Siberia in winter. They were the best I could find. Where my hands and feet were concerned, I was only going to use the best gear. I valued my extremities highly.

There was nothing I could do with the fact that I had poor circulation, a condition not uncommon for women. Even sitting at home in England in autumn, I get cold feet unless I am wearing socks and slippers. That said, home in England is a very large, very old Tudor building with no insulation and drafts through the windows and doors. By home, I mean my parents' home, the place I spent half my life growing up and the place I always go back to.

Over the New Year, before I left for Siberia, I had put my newly purchased thermometer in my old bedroom. It never wavered above plus ten degrees Celsius, and that was middle of the day with the radiator on. That is not warm for a home in England. However, to have cold feet in plus ten temperatures gives you cold feet about the prospect of going anywhere it is expected to be minus fifty. So I bought some really warm boots and thick socks. I also took a supply of chemical hand warmers. I could place these in my boots in an emergency, I figured. I had no intention of using them up before I started the Artik Road to Chersky where, unlike on the Kolyma Highway, the prospect of help was slim.

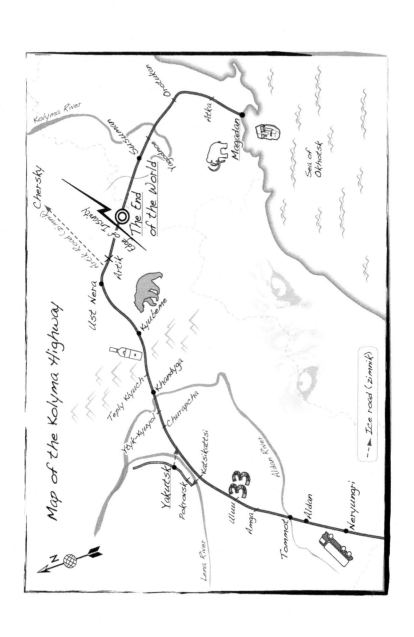

Map of the Kolyma Highway

N

Kolyma River

Chersky

Ust Road (zimnik)

The End
of the World

Edge of Insanity

Chersky

Ust Nera

Artik

Kyubeme

Teply Klyuch

Khandyga

Churapcha

Ytyk-Kyuyol

Katsikatsi

Yakutsk

Pokrovsk

Ulu

Amga

Tommot

Aldan

Neryungri

Lena River

Aldan River

Kolyma River

Susuman

Orotukan

Yagodnoye

Atka

Magadan

Sea of
Okhotsk

- - ▶ Ice road (zimnik)

16.

I always have to go that little bit further, always try to squeeze a little bit more into the time available. Sometimes, it would be better if I stopped, sat back and relaxed. But now I had this idea, I couldn't let it go: if I cycled another twenty kilometres and then camped, I could reach the next town, Churapcha, the following day.

My leg was shaking and my foot tapping on the floor unconsciously. I was pinned to the radiator with a mug of coffee between my hands, staring out of the cafe window, longing to be on the move. The sun was low and casting a pale yellow light across the wide, snow-covered flood plains of the frozen river. It looked so inviting. The sun called to me from across the snowfields. 'Come out to play,' it whispered. And like a puppet on a string I did as commanded. I put on my hats and gloves and boots and walked outside to my bike. 'Sucker!' the sun hissed with a sadistic smile. *Damn, it's cold.* Every time I stepped outside, I got the same bite of shock. It always surprised me how cold it felt. Like some kind of short term memory loss, I would forget the feeling that the cold induced as soon as I stepped foot indoors. Our brains are very good at forgetting pain and suffering.

It became clear very quickly that I had left it too late to cover twenty kilometres before dark. But I was enjoying the cycling and didn't care when the sun set. I kept cycling as the first stars appeared in the sky.

123

I pedalled steadily and stared out across the wide valley with the trees silhouetted in the foreground. It was a pleasant evening. I wanted to continue, but then the trucks came thundering past. My concern was that a truck coming from behind would not notice me in time and might knock me over. With my headband and hat on and jacket hood pulled up, I couldn't hear them approaching. With diminished sight and dulled hearing, my sense of smell was heightened. The pungent odour of fuel lingered in the air long after the trucks had passed. As much as I would have liked to continue, it wasn't safe.

It was at this point, when I began looking for a place to camp, that buildings appeared on the raised bank. Ahead, I could see a factory. In the heavy night air, the chimney smoke spread out and cloaked the buildings in an eerie, diffused orange glow from the fluorescent lights illuminating the area. Trails of smoke snaked and curled around the outline of the buildings and wavered over the roofs. It reminded me of the ethereal shifting of the aurora borealis I had seen in Norway.

I hoped to see the Northern Lights again, although I doubted I would on this trip. For most of the journey, I wouldn't be far enough north. In any case, cycle-camping is not ideal for watching them. When looking for a place to wild camp, good views of the night sky are not usually a top priority, and after a tiring day on the road, you go to sleep early. If by chance you are awake when the lights appear, you need a strong will to go out into the frigid air to get a better view. I enjoy photography and would have loved some decent pictures of the aurora whilst in Norway, but I loved my sleeping bag more.

Beyond the ghostly orange glow, where the darkness returned, I knew I would find a place to camp among the trees. Then I saw a log cabin. It looked like the Russian equivalent of an American diner with an 'Open 24-hours' sign. Cafe 99 was, presumably, named after its distance from Yakutsk. Irrationally, it annoyed me that I was stopping short of one hundred kilometres. I like round numbers.

But I like hot meals on cold nights even more. *I can always cycle the last kilometre before camping.*

I ordered food from the canteen and took a place at one of the tables by the window. Once the crowd of people left and it was quieter, the ladies in blue aprons who worked at the cafe sat down at the table in front of me. They talked over cups of tea and sometimes asked me questions. They enquired about my accommodation plans.

'You know there is a *mini-gostinitsa* here?' I didn't know there was a mini-guesthouse. 'It's very simple, just beds in a room at the back of the cafe. It is warm. There's no one there now. Why don't you stay? You won't have to pay. You'll need a sleeping bag as there are no blankets, but I think you must have one if you were going to camp.' *If I stay, I'll have only cycled ninety-nine, not one hundred, kilometres.* It was still irritating me. As I said, I like round numbers. But I like warm beds on cold nights even more.

Despite stopping one kilometre short of one hundred, I made it to Churapcha the next day. There was nothing in Churapcha that grabbed my attention. But beyond Churapcha, there is a large statue. As I ascended the road to the brow of a hill, a mighty, powerful-looking warrior upon a great horse grew to dominate the skyline.

Horses have always been important in Yakutian culture. As I cycled through the region, I saw several horses roaming the snow-covered fields near villages. They are small hardy animals like the native ponies of Britain. Their shaggy winter coats of long, thick hair insulate so well that when it snows their backs become covered with a white layer of flakes that their body heat fails to reach and melt. They have a heightened sense of smell, so they can detect grass below the surface snow. I watched them with their heads down, pawing at patches of ground with their tough hooves to clear the snow, nibbling the exposed grass and pawing again. Grazing the low-nutrient winter grass is slow, laborious work. In the summer, they store massive fat reserves and then shed up to twenty percent of

125

their weight in the winter. The Yakut horse has evolved to cope with the extreme conditions and is the only breed of horse that survives above the Arctic Circle. They reminded me of the desert horses in Namibia, which cope equally well with extreme heat and lack of water.

The statue I passed was of Njurgun Bootur the Rapid, legendary hero of one of the most well-known *Olonkhos* or epic folk tales from Yakutia that are performed by singers and storytellers. On the statue was written that Njurgan 'possesses a mettlesome fast raven horse born at the horizon of a clear white sky'.

The four days of cycling from Yakutsk were a joy, especially the fourth day. It had been a short ride north from Ytyk-Kyuyol, where I'd spent my third night, to a sharp bend in the road. There, a brand new, two-storey wooden building rose up from the snow in a forest clearing. To my amazement, there was a sign with that wonderful four-letter word 'cafe' beckoning me in.

This cafe was not on Bolot's map or my GPS. I didn't even need a coffee to warm up then, so soon was it after I had set off that morning. But I knew it was a long way to the next one, and I wasn't going to pass up this opportunity. The cafe was new. It was bright and clean and warm; the food on offer was fantastic. I sampled extensively. To hell with the bill.

Imagine my surprise when the young lady there spoke to me in excellent English. Although she hesitated often, unconfident with her choice of words, it was only an innate shyness overwhelming her.

'Where did you learn such good English?' I had to ask.

'Born Mouth,' she replied. I looked at her quizzically and racked my brain wondering where in Russia this distinctly non-Russian-sounding place was.

'Born Mouth? Where's that?' I finally asked.

'Born Mouth. In England. It is not very big; perhaps you do not know it.' *England?*

'Oh, Bournemouth!' I blurted out. 'Yes, I know it. It's on the south coast.' When you have spent so long in a foreign place, it is surprising how the smallest connection with home and what is familiar takes on a huge importance.

'Yes. I lived there for a while. But now I have returned to open this cafe with my husband.' She smiled at Ruslan who was sitting beside her. He smiled back. He seemed proud of his wife, especially then, speaking with me in English. It was clear he hadn't got a clue what we were talking about, so his wife, who introduced herself as Kate, summarised our conversation for him. He smiled. Then he spoke, and Kate translated:

'Can you tell her that I think what she is doing is great? More people should get out and see the world as she is. It's the only way for us to begin to understand one another.'

They invited me to spend the day at the cafe, sleep there and continue the next morning. I looked out of the window at the bright blue sky and midday sun glare off the snow. It was too nice to be indoors. As I gathered up my clothes, Kate handed me a bag of *kurniks* and pancakes. 'These are good to eat, even when they are cold.' *Too right. Beats frozen cheese and salami, my staple trail mix.*

I spent the afternoon cycling up a very gradual incline from the valley floor. It was enough to keep me warm all the way. When I reached the top of the hill where the forest closed in on the road, the sun flickered through the trees. The treetops were all drooping under the weight of snow clinging to them, bent over this way and that as if standing erect were too much effort. Every now and then, a slight breeze dislodged the snow and a fine powder sprinkled to the ground in a light shower. As it did, the treetop rose to stand tall, freed of the burden. I watched the powder fall, sparkling in the sunlight, leaving a fine mist that lingered long after I had cycled past. Then another noise distracted me. Looking ahead to where the strange sound came from, I saw another tree shaking off its load. The sound was a hiss and a whoosh and then the crackle of Rice Krispies as the snow fell on the ground. So accustomed was I to the Siberian silence, the sound startled me like a gun shot. But this dramatic orchestral crescendo only made the snowfall appear more graceful and beautiful.

I was in a buoyant mood; the kilometres were flying by in this beautiful white wilderness. I'd be in Khandyga early the next day at this rate. Everything was going so well ...

And then it wasn't.

Just like that.

17.

According to the map and GPS, there was a village at the bottom of the hill. Although it was late in the day, I thought it wise to continue rather than have the downhill first thing the next day. *Who knows, I may even find a place to sleep indoors.* Going downhill, I started to get colder. The sun set. Where I thought the village should be, I saw only a couple of unused wooden hunter's huts, beyond reach from the road. *Is this all of the village?* If it was, I needed to find a place to camp soon. The roadsides were too steep. When I saw another hut, barely twenty metres from the road, I decided to check it out. *Perhaps I could bivvy inside.*

I leant my bike against the snow and looked for a pathway. There was a faint indentation in the snow indicating a trail. Many fresh snowfalls had fallen since the last feet trod that path, but at least I knew there was solid ground underneath. I took a couple of tentative steps and sank up to my knees before the snow compacted enough to give a sure foothold. It wouldn't be possible to push the bike through, but I could carry the bags first and then the bike. I took another step and …

'Oh shit!' I exclaimed as I plunged down, now buried in snow up to my waist. I instantly turned around and scrabbled for solid ground. It took considerable effort to climb up the embankment, invisible under the snow. I was puffing profusely by the time I landed back on the road. Snow had forced its way up my jacket and was ice cold against the bare exposed skin around my waist. I brushed it off and tucked my top back into my trousers. *Maybe I won't stay in a hut tonight.*

Around a few more bends was a sign to the elusive village – seven kilometres away down a side road. *Sigh.* By now, it was dark except for the stars. It was not safe to be on this road; it was too narrow, and I didn't have lights. I tried to find a path near the river, but everywhere was covered with a thick layer of untouched snow. Instead, I found a wide track into the forest, compacted by turning lorries. That would do for the night.

As I started to change out of my softshell jacket to put on my down one, I realised it would not come off over the gloves I was now using, my good fleece ones having been burned on the stove. There was no alternative than to quickly take off the gloves to make the swap. It only took moments but my hands froze, numb with pain and useless.

I had to warm them up. I knew that. I fumbled to put on my mittens. But having put these down for a minute, they were frozen and only served to suck the remaining life from my hands. I ran as fast as possible in my heavy boots. Up the track. Down the track. Up and down. And I waved my arms like windmills on overdrive to get the blood flowing. I ran until I could run no more. It was no use. My hands would not warm up. Only the searing pain intensified. *Run more. Must run more.* My head knew what I must do, but my legs had nothing more to give. They were weak and wobbly and wouldn't move. I had to do something else, fast. *If I can just get in my sleeping bag, then I know I will be fine.* It was my cocoon that fought the cold on my behalf without me having to do anything.

The sleeping bag was in the rear pannier. I focussed all my attention onto it. The pannier was frozen and stiff. I fumbled to prise it open.

Nothing was simple. I had packed the sleeping bag in so tightly; my fingers couldn't grip it. I tried to grasp it again. And again. My fingers failed me. I had lost all feeling in them now. Even the pain had gone. *This is no joke.* I tried pulling the bag again, but it remained lodged in the pannier. I looked around, hoping help would appear from somewhere. It didn't. I was alone. I thought about going to the roadside and waiting for a vehicle to pass and get help. *No, you don't know how long you might have to wait.* Surely, I had not exhausted all my options. *Think! You're an engineer – a problem solver. This is just a problem to be solved. Use your strengths; use your head … Yes, my head!*

I shoved my head, face first, into the pannier and took a bite with my teeth. And yanked. A bit of the sleeping bag loosened. I pulled again, like a rabid wolf tearing its prey apart. Eventually, enough bag was sticking out that I could grab it between the palms of my hands. Hands in prayer, I pulled, and the sleeping bag spilled out like guts from a torn stomach. I threw down my roll mat where I was, struggled out of my boots, shook the sleeping bag and climbed into it. I pulled the bag up around my head, assumed the foetal position, thrust my hands down my trousers and rubbed them vigorously between my inner thighs. In another context, this may sound exciting. However, I am convinced that this is the warmest part of the body, more so than the armpits, and allows you to be comfortably curled up within your sleeping bag. *That was a close call.* I lay there in silence with my heart pounding. Only a few minutes earlier everything had been great. It had only taken one mistake, one oversight.

The feeling in my hands returned, as I knew it would. By then, the idea of starting the stove and getting cold hands again held no appeal. It didn't take long to fall asleep. When I woke up in the middle of the night, I sat up to eat some cold pastries and biscuits, then rolled over and went to sleep again as best as I could with cold feet. It is not easy to reach your feet to rub them while zipped up in a sleeping bag. You have to bend and twist unnaturally. After a day's cycling and no dinner, this contortionist's act causes your muscles to cramp intensely. Unable to bend beyond the cramping pain, your feet remain out of reach. Instead, I went about exercises to warm up in my bag; sit-ups and leg raises were about all the motions I could manage. But these only tired me out. My feet stayed cold. I tried wriggling and shaking my legs violently like an epileptic, hoping to nudge the warmth from my body to my feet. I can't say that helped much either.

The motivation required to get out of a relatively warm sleeping bag when camping out in the winter is significant. Just a few more minutes, you say. And when those minutes have passed, you say it over again. There are only three feelings that can be overwhelming enough to make you rise: extreme thirst, excessive hunger and a bladder so full to bursting it hurts. Thirst can be quenched and hunger sated simply by sitting up and reaching for your drinks bottle or food, assuming you have been sensible enough to leave them close at hand. There is no such solution for the full bladder, unless you don't mind a pee-soaked sleeping bag. I did mind that and preferred by a margin to put on my gloves and socks, crawl out of my sleeping bag, put on boots and a jacket, take a few steps and then drop my thermal bottoms to expose myself to the freezing air.

I sat up to eat some more biscuits. Eventually I got up to pee. The sun had risen above the trees and was now shining on my bivvy bag. That made it easier. *Well, I survived another night outside.*

The events of the night before ran through my mind. I wouldn't make the same mistake with my gloves again. I couldn't afford to. From now on, I would also roll up my sleeping bag and bivvy bag loosely and simply strap them to the top of the bike rack. That way, it would be very quick to unstrap and roll out. No more fights with panniers.

That night was a harsh lesson in how things would be when all alone. If I was on the Artik Road to Chersky, there'd be no one to help. Did I really want to go to Chersky alone and battle this cold every day?

It was the question that kept going round and round in my head, spinning like a roulette wheel. Sometimes the pointer landed on Chersky: that was where I wanted to go. Other times, on Magadan: I'd had enough and was happy to take the easy road. This was the thought as I packed up and wheeled my bike to the road and began pedalling; the roulette wheel spinning round and round and bump … bump … bump …

You're kidding! Not another puncture? Give me a break. Not even five kilometres this morning. And with that, I grabbed the roulette wheel, picked up the spinning ball and slammed it down on Magadan.

If there is ever a choice of two options and you can't decide, leave it to chance and toss a coin. That is the only way to be sure what you really want to do. If you say heads and the tossed coin lands heads up and you are happy with this, it means that is what you want to do. If you are unhappy with the result, then you know you must ignore it and choose the other option. It's only when the bare metal is staring you in the face that you can know for sure what you really want to do. It is a feeling from deep within.

The puncture was my coin. It landed on Magadan, but I wasn't really happy with the choice. I knew then what I wanted to do: go to Chersky. Logic and sense warned me against it, but I wanted to ignore those feelings. Perhaps I was using them as an excuse. It was my gut instinct – an instinct that had got me through to my thirty-third birthday and beyond – and I couldn't ignore that. Gut instinct doesn't sound very logical or reasonable; it is far from a scientific justification. It is nothing more than a feeling. But feelings can be very powerful if you truly believe them.

OK, I don't have to make the final decision yet. Just remember this moment when you do: remember the cold hands, remember the flat tyres. You came to Siberia to live, not die or merely survive. And you intend to leave with all body parts intact. Remember this moment.

It was not far to Khandyga across the river – less than twenty kilometres, I presumed. I pumped up the tyre, hoping it would hold. It didn't. I began pushing. Up ahead, though, I could see a building. Perhaps there was a cafe by the river crossing.

It wasn't a cafe. The building was inaccessible. But by the ramp down to the river, a Russian UAZ truck was parked, engine running. I went over to find out exactly how far it was to the town. Perhaps I could just cross the river and walk there.

It was not twenty, but fifty kilometres away, the men said. I thought I had misheard so asked again, but I hadn't. My disappointment was audible with a sigh and was written all over my face. I would have to fix the puncture here. *Bring on the cold hands, again.*

The driver told me to get in the back. I climbed in and his mate hauled in my bike after me. I wondered what they were doing there. It seemed like they had driven here just to sit and stare at the river. That, or they had driven here to escape home. Perhaps their wives thought they were working. That seemed unlikely. People here didn't mind hard work.

They looked middle-aged, had dark hair (as had all the locals), and wore army green jacket and trousers (as many men wore here, since military surplus was cheap, readily available and well-suited for the cold). They never told me their names; I never offered mine. They will probably remember me as the crazy girl who was cycling in winter. Or they may not remember me at all. I will remember them as two more people who entered my life for a brief moment, helped me and made me smile.

'Are you OK?' one of them asked.

'Yeah, but my bike isn't.' I squeezed the back tyre by way of explanation. It didn't compress, although that was because the tyre was frozen stiff.

'Aaahh,' the other man breathed out, knowingly. He understood the problem exactly. 'Yes. Because it is very cold.' *Yes. Because it is cold.*

134

Every problem here is because of the cold. And every solution here is to get warm.

'Do you need help to fix it? We have time,' the first man said.

'I can do it,' I said. 'If you are staying here for a while, can I fix it in here?'

'Of course.' And so we set to work fixing the flat tyre. As I rummaged around in my panniers for the spare tube, the man in the back took off the wheel and removed the tyre. He had done that before.

'Sit down. Relax. He can do that,' the man in the front seat said, nodding over his shoulder towards his mate. Then he passed me a one-litre carton of fruit juice. I took a few sips and stretched to hand it back before the urge to gulp it down became too strong. I was very thirsty. 'No, you keep it for the road.' I drank the rest of it there and then. I had barely drunk anything since the night before.

'Do you want a lift to town?' the man in the front seat asked. *Yes, dammit, say yes.*

'No, I want to cycle. Thank you.' *Why do I always say that?*

'OK, but let me drive you to the cafe across the river. Then you can get warm before continuing.'

'OK,' I said. *That's more like it. Well done.* It was only across the river.

The cycle into Khandyga seemed endless. The road near town was well-used, so the ice had become chipped and rutted and potholed. I could only bump along barely faster than a walk. So I walked. It took less energy. When I saw smoke lingering like a cloud up ahead, I knew I was close to Khandyga even though I couldn't see a single building for all the trees. A smoke-cloud was the telltale sign of a town.

135

18.

I don't know what I was expecting. It wasn't the Khandyga I rolled into. My only other experience of a Siberian town besides Neryungri and Yakutsk, big cities by comparison, had been Aldan. Aldan was a pretty town. Khandyga, on the other hand, depressed me. It was as though all the colour had been sapped out of it. Its defining feature was the tall stack, churning out the smoke I had seen. The buildings were wooden or concrete; paint was used sparingly.

My GPS indicated there was a guesthouse on the main road in the town centre. The guesthouse was probably there, only without a sign to indicate its presence. Advertising was not something considered important or necessary. This was the case in every town. Every town was well-provided for and had all amenities one could possibly require. They were not bad places to live, and as a local you would know where everything was. For the stranger or newcomer, it was bewildering. The shops all looked the same and rarely had displays in the windows. I'd walk into one looking to buy a drink and chocolate and realise the only items on sale were car spares. The guesthouses and hotels were no different from private residences and apartment blocks. The owners saw little need to put up a sign saying 'Hotel' or 'Gostinitsa'; if they did, it was in tiny writing only visible once you'd actually found the place. Anonymity was preferable to business.

If you actually wanted something in town, rather than wandering aimlessly, it was better just to ask.

I walked into the first shop, which happened to be a grocery store, and asked where there was a guesthouse. I also bought a large chocolate bar and devoured it in front of the cashier while she took down a piece of paper off the wall with a phone number on.

'*Gostinitsa*,' she said to me as she pointed with one hand to the receiver, which was between her ear and shoulder. I could hear it ringing and ringing and ringing. She put the phone down. 'No answer. I am sorry.' Then she sat back down and resumed her vacant stare as if I were not standing right in front of her. She had done more than her job required and would clearly prefer me to exit her life as quickly as possible. I was an inconvenience in this convenience store.

Once, I would have been offended, but I had come to realise that this was the Russian way. I turned to leave. There were other options; I could wander aimlessly. Then I thought better of it. I stopped, turned to face the lady again, composed myself and mustered my energy reserves and my best Russian.

'Thank you for your help, but do you think there may be another place I could stay? I must rest.' She could tell by the way I stood that I wasn't going to give up easily.

Begrudgingly, she called out to someone. A voice replied from a back room. Then a man appeared. I had seen him walk through the shop earlier.

'Is that your bicycle outside?' he asked me. It was. Obviously. 'You need a place to stay, right? I will make a call. Follow me.' I followed. 'Would you like a cup of tea? It might take a few minutes. You look like you need to warm up.' I did.

And like that, I had a place to stay. I drank my tea. A young lad came by. The man told me to follow the young lad. He would take me to the guesthouse. It wasn't easy to find unless you knew it, he said. I knew that.

I followed the young lad up a side street. We walked under the large pipelines that arched overhead. Ice had built up around the bases. Along the top, a row of large icicles hung. It would be bad luck if one of them broke off while you were walking underneath. No doubt this was the cause of death for some poor individuals. We rounded a bend and walked up to one of the concrete buildings. It looked derelict except for the trodden snow up the wooden steps to the wooden front door. I left my bike outside and entered. Inside was a large empty room. The young lad knocked on the door at the far side. And he knocked. And knocked. No answer.

'Wait,' he said. I waited. He walked up the stairs. I heard knocking on another door. Then voices. And then footsteps on the stairs. The young lad returned with an older lady holding a key.

'You want a room,' she said sternly. She thought I was an inconvenience too.

'Yes,' I said quietly.

'OK?' the young lad asked me. I was. He left. Soon I would be in a room by myself, an inconvenience to no one.

As with every other room in Siberia, the heating was on full. I didn't need warm clothes whilst indoors. On the contrary, it was so damn hot I could walk around in shorts and T-shirt as if it were a midsummer's day. Too bad I didn't have any with me. I checked the door was locked, then stripped down to my underwear.

Ever since my hotel experiences in Mongolia, I always double-check that the door is locked. It was a regular occurrence there to have people knocking on my door. It was also a regular occurrence to have people walk right on into my room. Not all doors had locks, or sometimes someone had a spare key, and I couldn't always be sure it was the owner.

One hotel I'd stayed in, I was quietly reading a book on the bed when an old man walked in, stopped in the middle of the room, looked around, didn't even acknowledge that I was there, and walked out again. I closed the door and turned the lock behind him. The lock, I soon realised, didn't work; moments later a younger woman walked in. She said something to me in Mongolian, which I didn't understand, so I just nodded. Then she walked over to the television, unplugged it and walked out with it. I sat stunned on the bed. *What the …?* She then returned empty-handed, stuck her head round the door, apologised, and left again. Moments later I heard the television in the next room. Having the television removed was preferable to having another drunk Mongolian enter, sit on my bed, and try to kiss me.

The room in Khandyga was so lovely and warm that I didn't leave it for two days except to go and buy food and beer. In that time, there were only two knocks on the door. One was the scary lady owner who told me there was a washing machine I could use if I wanted. I did. I hoped my clothing didn't smell so badly that it was emanating from the room and wafting up to her apartment. She was, despite initial impressions, kind and thoughtful. The other knock was from a young guy who was staying in one of the other rooms. He and two friends were cooking dinner and wondered if I would like to have some too. I did.

Besides reading and writing, drinking beer, eating junk food and sleeping, I sorted through and arranged all my gear. I made sure that if and when I next had to camp, I would have absolutely everything easily accessible in the order I needed it. There would be no more mistakes. I thought I had already done this, but each day I learnt something new. Although winter camping in Scandinavia was a good experience, it had in no way fully prepared me for winter in Siberia. If anything, it lulled me into a false sense of security that I could deal with the cold without problems. Everything in Scandinavia had been great. End of. Everything in Siberia had also been great. Until, suddenly, it wasn't. One moment you'd be flying high, the next moment – BAM! – you'd come crashing down to earth.

Now I was ready to cycle to Kyubeme, the next town. Only 325 kilometres from Khandyga, I figured it would take four days of easy cycling at my current rate. I'd stocked up on enough food for those few days until I'd be able to rest again and resupply.

I should have learnt by now not to be overly optimistic about daily distances for cycling. And if only I had known that Kyubeme was not really a town …

19.

I cycled out of Khandyga in high spirits, blissfully unaware of what lay in store for me further on. After fifty kilometres, I came to a small bridge across a river. On the other side was a workers' camp. A number of containers, lined up side-by-side, had been converted into living quarters. Smoke was rising from one chimney. Outside, a couple of diggers stood idle. I waved to the men as I walked by. I was walking to warm my feet. One of the men called out and invited me over for tea.

The worker pulled back the thick blanket covering the doorway. I ducked my head as I squeezed through the entrance into the gloom of the unlit container. I stumbled forward and gradually my eyes became accustomed to the darkness after the blinding glare of sun on snow outside. Inside, there were two bunk beds at the back with a small porthole window that let in faint light through the smoke-smeared pane. Another bunk bed lay back-to-back with one on the right side, and to the left of the door was a blackened stove with wire tied between the pipe and one bed for drying socks and gloves on. In the remaining space was a small cupboard with an array of kitchen wares on it: mismatched cutlery stacked in an old recycled tin can, others now filled with tea and sugar and salt. Above that, two planks of scrap wood had been screwed to the wall for shelves.

I almost choked at the stagnant overpowering aroma of unwashed people living in close quarters. One of the men came in and put a pot on the stove. As it heated, steam rose and the smell of meat stew filled the room. My taste buds fired up on all cylinders. How could I be so hungry? It wasn't that I hadn't been eating enough; it was that instant noodles are not known for their full flavours or high nutritional content. It seemed an age since I had eaten a tasty, filling, homemade meal.

It wasn't long after I left the container that the sky became streaked with faint white clouds; the sun's feeble warmth blocked by the haze. Gradually, the clouds thickened and spread until the sky was a uniform grey and flakes of snow began falling to the ground. They were soft, fat flakes that soon covered the handlebar bag and panniers; only my jacket remained bright blue since my body heat melted the snow as it touched down. Whenever I unzipped my jacket and lowered my hood, a flurry of thick flakes of 'snow' that had formed from my sweat would fall to the ground like dandruff. When it had been colder, my sweat had frozen like ice, and when I brushed it off, it fell in tiny sprinkles. When it had been colder still, and I worked hard cycling uphill, I would watch my hot breath freeze into tiny crystals and float in the frigid air like billowing and swirling dragon's breath.

When the sky is cloud-covered so that not a single hint of sun shines through, there are no shadows to be seen in the timeless half-light. There is something disconcerting about travelling through a land without shadows. There are no shades of grey in this forested, snow-covered world. It is as though time itself has stopped and everything with it is frozen in the moment; only you continue to move, to change, to age; and the still world watches you pass through, an intruder breaking some hallowed, unwritten rule. Nothing else is moving. There is nothing else. You are alone with only the road and the trees.

It was strange, then, to see a neon-signed cafe as I entered Teply Klyuch. Bright orange trucks were parked outside with their engines humming and the choking smell of petrol fumes spreading. Inside the cafe, people mingled; their voices sounded loud and harsh even though they were talking barely above a whisper. The smells of freshly cooked food infused the air, and the warmth of the hot water pipes filled the room.

Walking into that cafe was an escape from the shadowless, timeless land, back into the world of the living. The clock on the wall went tick … tick … tick … as if counting down to the end of something. It was unnerving.

It didn't take long to adapt to this island of life. The clock ticked rhythmically like my heartbeat, on and on and on, until I was in sync. The thought of going back out into the cold was dreadful. I sat there until the grey half-light transformed into the black darkness of night. Outside remained a shadowless world.

Unfortunately, I'd been in the cafe too long and drunk too many cups of coffee. I had to go to the toilet. And the toilet was outside. Oh God, the Siberian toilet! I haven't told you about that winter wonder yet, have I?

Forgive me now, as I know that toilet humour is a low form of wit, down in the pit together with sarcasm. But no story of a journey through Siberia in winter is complete without some reference to shit. Everyone has their own toilet stories from travels beyond their en suite bathroom. Toilet humour is guaranteed to flush through conversation at some point upon meeting another traveller. No matter a person's background, nationality, ethnicity, wealth, opinion or style of travel, shitting is something we all have in common. No wonder this daily necessity indiscriminately breeds tales of woe, and I have my fair share of stories on this subject. They are best left unwritten, saved until a pint of beer acts as the laxative and unleashes the tirade of cheap laughs.

Roadside cafes along the Kolyma Highway vary in style, age, the food on offer and the type of person working there. When it comes to the outhouse toilet facilities, however, they are all, in essence, the same: long drops.

I imagine that in summer these are festering, stinking, fly-swarming obscenities best avoided in favour of the fresh open air of the tick-ridden, mosquito-filled forests. In winter, however, they are transformed into little wooden houses of modern art. Some of you may consider modern art to be a pile of shit, but here, in this surreal winter wonderland, shit is art.

Everything freezes when it's forty – that's minus forty. Shit too. And so, from the depths of the long drop, it piles up until out of the hole in the ground rises a brown stalagmite. I presume people peer down into the pit and consider the options as I did: do you aim directly over the column to make it grow taller or aim off to one side? Where people had aimed to one side or the other, branches had started to spread out. Branches or not, the shit stalagmite grows taller and taller until, eventually, it is not possible to squat over it at all. The toilet is then out of service until the spring thaw. That, however, does not always stop the desperate. Sometimes, in a corner, there's a frozen turd, like those unwanted 'gifts' of dead mice the cat leaves on the doorstep. But there are yet more hidden dangers with these Siberian toilets. Be careful not to slip. Some men, I suspect, with the benefit of being able to projectile pee, stand in the doorway and aim for the long drop hole. Sure enough, they miss and piss over the floor. This freezes and leaves a treacherous slippery route for anyone who dares to enter.

Having survived this hazardous trip to the loo, I returned to the cafe and ordered another coffee. The girls working in the cafe were having a break. At the table next to me, they were talking, texting and drinking tea. Occasionally one of them would ask me a question about my journey.

'If you don't have somewhere to stay tonight, will you come and stay at my house?' Masha asked.

'Oh, it's fine. I am going to camp,' I replied.

'Please. I'd love it if you came to stay with me. Of course, you'd have to wait here until I finish my shift. It would be lovely to have someone to chat with. It's just me and my two sons. Their grandmother is looking after them, but only until I get back. Go on. It's better than camping.' *True.* The way she said it made me feel that, by agreeing, I was the one doing her a favour. That was kind of her.

I pushed my bike, following Masha along the narrow, snow-covered footpath, and drew up alongside her on the wider road through the village. We talked all the way back to her house. I had no trouble understanding her. I think she was so used to speaking slowly and carefully choosing her words for her two young boys to understand that naturally she did the same with me. She didn't look old enough to have two sons.

After I'd had a bath, we sat down at the kitchen table and drank tea. She served it black with a slice of lemon. Masha was interested to know where else I had travelled. She was fascinated when I said I'd been to Africa.

'What's it like?' she asked.

I pondered the vague and open-ended question.

'It's like Siberia,' I said. I don't know what sort of answer she was expecting, but it certainly wasn't that.

'How?' Masha looked at me questioningly.

'They are both big regions, and people talk about them like they are countries. But Africa is many countries and Siberia is only part of one country.

'Africa has the hot, dry Sahara and forests of the Congo, just as Siberia has the taiga and the cold, open tundra, and both have many great rivers.'

'What about the people? Are there towns?'

'Of course there are towns. They are not like towns in Russia. They are busier and more crowded and dirty. But Africans are very much like people in Siberia. You think in a similar way.'

'I don't understand.'

'You know what's important in life. You value family and friends over money. You may not have a lot, but you make do with what you have and make things last. You don't need to buy new things all the time.'

I struggled to find the words in Russian, so I stopped talking. I wanted to say they all have a similar attitude to life – that what will be will be – as though they have accepted their fate and are content to go along with things the way they are.

Masha nodded, 'I understand.' Then she took a sip of lemon tea and continued. 'I would love to go to Africa. I'm scared that it is too dangerous because of what I see on the news.'

Whispered voices came from the bedroom. 'Quiet!' Masha called out sternly. 'Sleep.' The voices stopped. We sat quietly in the ensuing silence, waiting for another sound. The whispering resumed.

'Sleep!' Masha shouted. 'The boys are awake,' she said to me in a soft voice. 'It's late, isn't it? We should sleep too.'

The next morning I visited the Gulag museum at the school. Gulag was the government agency that administered the forced labour camps of the Stalin years. The museum contained a few rusted relics – a soldier's helmet, an adze, a mess tin and leather straps – found around the sites of some Gulag labour camps, but little mention of the history to explain them being there. One thing I noticed again and again throughout Russia was an unspoken accord to forget the country's murkier past.

Repeatedly, whilst cycling on the road, I saw parts of old wooden structures peeking out through the snow. I presumed they were parts of the original old road, the Kolyma Highway, that was constructed between Yakutsk and Magadan.

As part of Stalin's first five-year plan, a government agency, Dalstroi, was set up in 1931 to oversee road construction and mining. The work was carried out by forced labour: prisoners who arrived at Magadan by ship and were sent to the labour camps throughout Kolyma.

The Kolyma Highway is also known as the Road of Bones after the prisoners of the labour camps who died while building it. Overworked, malnourished and with insufficient clothing against the extreme cold conditions, the men and women died in the thousands. Their bodies were used as the foundations for the road; that was easier than digging into the permafrost to bury them in graves. The museum had little to say about this.

Instead, it documented the making of the modern road on which I now travelled. It celebrated modernity and improved accessibility. It did not dwell on the unsavoury past.

Further down the road, when I looked round another museum with the family I was staying with there, we spent hours looking at the cultural displays and carvings of wood and bone. When it came to the room on the history of the gulags, the family seemed uneasy and preferred not to look. They took a glimpse here or there and a few minutes later, someone said, 'This is too depressing. Let's go and look at something else.' So we went and looked at stuffed birds and pinned insects instead.

I'd felt a similar uneasiness when I looked around the old slave forts in West Africa. The difference there was that the locals strongly believed in educating people about this dark period of history. Only through remembrance and reconciliation would there be any hope of avoiding equally terrible crimes against humanity in the future. Perhaps the difference is that the slave trade was abolished 200 years ago, well beyond the memory of anyone alive today. For the survivors of the gulags and their families, the atrocities committed are still too painful with the wounds yet to heal.

That day, I only cycled thirty kilometres. Ahead, the mountains towered up as an impenetrable wall through the gap in the trees. The road ran straight towards them. It was a daunting sight. When I saw the sign for a cafe at the valley bottom, I stopped.

The simple cafe was open twenty-four hours a day. It was run by Lochijon and Sahim, two brothers from Uzbekistan. Sahim was the quiet one who spent most of the time preparing food. Lochijon was more confident and dealt with the customers, few as they were.

'Where in Uzbekistan are you from?' I asked Lochijon.

'Shakhrisabz. It's a little town not far south of Samarkand. You've probably heard of Samarkand.'

'Yes. I've heard of Shakhrisabz too. I travelled there last year.'

'You've been to Shakhrisabz!' he exclaimed. 'Then you know that it's the home town of Amir Timur.'

'Of course.'

'And now you know it's the home town of Lochijon and Sahim,' he joked.

'So what are you doing here?' I asked.

'Working,' he replied. 'It is hard work. There is not much time to rest, but the pay is much better. I send money home to my family. You are not working, are you?'

'In England I do, but not at the moment. I'm just travelling.'

'You are very lucky.'

'I know.' I knew that all too well.

'Why don't you rest and stay here tonight?' Lochijon suggested.

'Perhaps. I'll see.' I replied. The thought had already crossed my mind. The muscles in my legs were very tired and aching. I was thinking about the mountains ahead.

'If you want, you can stay in my bed. I have to work in here all night. I won't be there. It's in the old wagon outside. Did you see it? It's very warm.'

'Er …' I hesitated.

'Go on. We're the same, you and me …'.

'I don't understand,' I interrupted.

'We're both migrants in Russia. We should help one another. Besides, you have been to my home town. It makes me very happy that you know Shakhrisabz. Please, you should not sleep outside when there is an empty bed here.' That was true. 'Let me show you it, then you can decide.'

I put on my thick winter boots and followed Lochijon in his socks and plastic sandals outside. We walked over to the wagon with a stove pipe coming out of the roof. There was a rickety, homemade ladder angled up to the raised doorway at the front end. Lochijon ran up the rungs two at a time. I wobbled behind taking cautious steps; there was no rail to hold onto. It was as he had said. There was a bed, and it was warm. I slept there that night.

The next morning I returned to the cafe for breakfast of *plov*, a pilau rice with chopped onions and carrots.

'This is real *plov* like it is made in Samarkhand. It's not made the same anywhere else, but Samarkhand *plov* is the best,' Lochijon said to me when he handed me my second plateful. It did taste good.

The hills rising up ahead from the cafe did not present as difficult a task as I had thought. I had a pleasant ride winding along the river valley. The ice road was smooth; even the gravelly, hilly sections were well-maintained.

There was an inverted rainbow perfectly haloed around the sun. As it dipped below the hills, I remembered the one I had seen near Uluu before my birthday. Was it another sign? Was this going to be another lucky day? Every day since my birthday, my luck had continued; kindness had been thrust upon me at every turn. What was in store at the next village? It was only around a few more bends.

When I saw Razvilka, I thought my luck had finally run out. The village looked deserted. There was no sign of movement among the scattered houses. It was only the tall smokestack churning out black fumes that made me think there must be some people around. I turned off the road.

On one porch, a bare lightbulb was switched on. I went to the door and knocked. A lady opened it. When I enquired about a shop, she said I must come in for some food. She was having lunch.

We sat at the table in the kitchen. In the corner there was a small tortoise in a plastic tray. Until then, I'd thought every Russian had a pet cat – house cats that never went outside in winter. Alina reckoned that tortoises were easier to look after. She also had several tropical plants covering the fridge top and window sill. Every home had a tropical pot plant; they thrived in the over-heated Russian home environment.

Alina told me that Razvilka was once much busier. Now there were only thirty inhabitants. Alina's children had all left to study in the cities of Kazan, Krasnoyarsk and Moscow. The children always left. Those who stayed worked in the factory because it paid well. It had to pay well for people to live here, a long way from anywhere. The nearest real shops were in Khandyga, 160 kilometres away. If you could save up enough money for a 4x4, life got easier, she said.

Alina wanted to know what I needed to buy. There wasn't a big shop now, she said; there wasn't even any bread. I didn't need anything. I had gone to the village because it was the only distraction until Kyubeme. The 'shop' was in the entrance hall of one woman's house. There was a chair and narrow shelf with an array of random biscuits and chocolates and other packaged consumables. I bought chocolate. The chocolate came with free accommodation for the night. Once again, I had been showered with kindness and wonderful hospitality.

20.

On my ride along the Kolyma Highway, the only time I was disturbed by people in the night while camping was during the night before I reached Kyubeme.

It had been another slow, steady day under sunny skies. The road hugged the hillside and wound in and out of the gullies, formed by streams that cascade down the rock faces in the spring thaw. I had decided to push on up towards the plateau where the Kyubeme River begins, even though it was late in the afternoon.

The cliff faces were sheer on my right and the ground fell away on my left into the milky blue frozen river, rich in minerals.

If I could have stopped sooner I would have, but the road was narrow with no places to pitch a tent. Twenty-five kilometres later the ground levelled out, but the snow was deep. When a truck lay-by came into view at dusk, I knew I'd found my camp-spot for the night. That it was almost 800 metres higher in altitude than where I'd started the day and on a wide plateau that would be open to the elements, namely the wind that whipped across the plain, was irrelevant. There was no alternative.

At the time I pitched my tent, I was still warm from the uphill slog, and the wind was absent. Trucks were few and far between now. I hadn't seen one all afternoon. That didn't mean one wouldn't come past in the night, driver fuelled up on vodka, and run over me. Stranger things have happened. To avoid the risk of being run over, I dug out a path off the parking area and cleared a space for sleeping by digging deep and stomping down the snow.

The snow was thick with a surface crust that almost took my weight. It would crack into sheets when I stepped on it, but always there was one step where I'd break through and sink deep into the soft snow beneath. In an attempt to reduce tent pitching time, I used the outer shell only. When the inner tent was connected, there was no risk of it blowing away whilst I was inside acting as an anchor. It was only once efforts were well underway that I realised I would have to secure the tent using only the guy ropes. Fixing the guys in the loose, powdery snow was a challenge. Even the large snow stakes would not hold fast. Instead, I shovelled snow into the dry bags and used them as anchors.

By the time the tent was secure and attempts to light my stove had failed, my fingers were numb. I crawled into my sleeping bag, clamped my hands between my thighs and waited for my fingers to thaw out. I decided to fix the stove in the morning and make do with eating a few cold snacks for dinner. It would be another thirsty night. I rolled over and closed my eyes.

A vehicle pulled up, engine running, lights shining towards my tent. I extracted an ear from my hats and bag and heard voices, then the slamming of doors. The vehicle remained. I ignored it, thrust my head back in the bag and tried to go back to sleep.

'Hello?' came a muffled voice in English. I ignored it. 'Hello?' I heard the crunching of footsteps on snow. Reluctantly, I reached for the zip and popped my head out of the tent. 'Do you want coffee in the car?'

'I'm OK, thanks.'

'Come have coffee. It will warm you up. Then you will sleep well tonight.'

It was still early; I didn't really need to sleep yet. *Why the hell not?* 'OK.'

'OK, good. Where are you from?'

'England.'

'Ah, England. We like England.' The voice laughed; the body rose from where it had been crouching and walked back to the 4x4. 'Come. It's cold out.' I wriggled out of my sleeping bag, put on my down jacket and boots, and followed in my thermal leggings.

Inside the 4x4 was Vladimir the driver and Sergei (another one) in the front passenger seat. Andrei (another one) finished his cigarette outside and climbed onto the back seat with me. Now, with the light on, I could see that Andrei was large, even beneath his thick jacket. His stubbly round face shone with a friendly smile and kind blue eyes. He spoke a little English and was the interlocutor once my understanding of Russian was exhausted. Sergei had the look of a man who had served in the army. Tall and muscular with shaved head, he could have looked intimidating. Instead, his eyes beamed, perhaps reflecting a vodka glaze, which would also explain his semi-permanent smile that showed the dimples in his cheeks. Vladimir, the driver, was the quiet one. They had stopped so he could sleep. He had one foot up on the dashboard and was leaning back into the chair with head resting against the window and his hat folded down over his eyes; his arms were folded tight across his chest as if he were cold. He raised his hat and looked up as I entered, said hello, and quietly returned to doze. He wasn't the talkative type.

'I only went out to have a cigarette and piss. That's when I saw you,' said Andrei. 'I came back, and Sergei said I should come and invite whoever was in the tent for a drink.'

'You spoke English,' I commented. 'How did you know?'

'Know you were English? I didn't. I only knew you were not Russian. No Russian would be camping out here tonight. It's forty.' He meant minus forty.

153

'It's not that cold,' I said. I was getting good at telling the temperature without looking at the thermometer.

'No, it's thirty-five now. Later it will be forty.'

'Respect.' Sergei called and reached to shake my hand. 'You're a strong girl. I wouldn't camp in this weather. Do you want a vodka?' he asked as he poured a drink for himself and Andrei.

'Not a good idea,' I commented.

He poured more coffee into the thermos mug and passed it back to me. 'If you have one drink, you must have three.' Sergei said. 'Whether coffee or vodka. Now eat.'

In the middle of the 4x4 was a wooden board laid out with a variety of food: cheese and meat, *pelmeni* Andrei's mother had made, and a large tupperware of the ubiquitous *plov*. The vodka was washed down with segments of clementine.

'Vodka is a good idea,' Andrei commented. 'It will warm you up inside. That is why we drink it,' he laughed.

I couldn't argue with that. Of course, if I drank one vodka, which I did, I had to have three. Russian tradition. As I failed to keep count and downed a fourth, then the total increased to six. Someone always keeps count.

'Have another coffee,' Sergei said as he refilled the mug.

'No, no, I'll never sleep.'

'You'll sleep. That's what the vodka was for.'

'No, no. I'll just have to get up to pee in the night.'

'Pee before you get in your tent.'

'Trust us. We know about the winter here. Now drink.'

After more laughs and jokes and with the empty bottle cluttering the footwell, it was time to be on our separate ways. It was with some reluctance that I clambered out of the 4x4 and into the cold, dark night. Now, though, I was radiating heat. That was the first night I wasn't only not cold, but positively aglow in my sleeping bag. At least, I was until I woke up in the early hours desperate to pee. It was harder to get to sleep the second time. The wind had picked up and was blowing fine snow under the tent, which was flapping wildly with the gusts.

As I burrowed deep into my sleeping bag, feeling the cold, it was as though the 4x4 and the vodka and Andrei and Sergei had all been a dream.

21.

The next morning, as I had a full thermos of coffee, albeit tepid by then, I didn't bother trying to start the stove. Kyubeme didn't seem far, now that I'd had a decent night's sleep and plenty of food. As I was trying to fold up and pack away the tent, which was flapping in the wind, a truck pulled up and stopped. The driver got out to give me a hand. He was curious to know what I was doing. There was no chance of setting off without breakfast with him first. And a photo.

It was a glorious day and not cold by Siberian standards either. That was the difference between March and February. In March, it was warm enough to stand around outside and simply marvel at the sights. And what a sight to behold! Up there, on the high plateau between two river valleys, everything was snow-covered in a perfect blanket, touched only by the wind. The relentless stream of air rushing over the land had brushed every crevice and ridge in the snow until it was polished. Even the trees were covered tip to root in white. It was all so sweet and smooth and unblemished like the icing on a Christmas cake. I was riding through a white world touched by the gentle rays of the sun. Life, right then, was pure innocent joy.

And that's why, when I arrived at Kyubeme, I was overcome by a sinking feeling like I was falling to the bottom of a deep well, down and down and down. I had been floating high on a cloud, my bike carrying me effortlessly through the air. And now I had fallen from grace.

Kyubeme wasn't a town. It was barely a trailer park, little more than a piece of land upon which a few people eked out an existence. Scattered around the site were a handful of tin-top container houses. Oil drums lay discarded with only the tops peeking through the snow, which was probably hiding all manner of discarded junk. The only reason to stop was to refuel.

Kyubeme was neither alive nor dead; it was purgatory – an obligatory stopover people make between wherever their journey begins and their final destination. It was as if Kyubeme lay between the pure whiteness of heaven and the freezing cold of hell. Although, it was hard to tell whether I had been in heaven or hell. After all, winter in Siberia is a paradox: a dreamlike white wonderland with a nightmarish icy grip.

Thankfully, there was a small cafe. It consisted of one room split into the dark kitchen area and the brighter eating area with a couple of tables covered in plastic cloths and benches pulled up beside them. Of course, it had a TV too; a cafe in Siberia is not complete without a TV.

I entered the cafe and asked where there was a guesthouse. I faintly hoped that the real Kyubeme was situated out of sight somewhere off the main road, and I only needed to be directed towards it. There was no guesthouse, the lady cooking and serving food told me. That sinking feeling returned. There was no shop either. *You're kidding me!* This was not good news.

'You mean, there is nowhere to buy food anywhere in Kyubeme?' I hoped I had misunderstood the lady.

'No. There is only what you see here,' she pointed up at the shelf behind her stocked with a box of Choco-pies and a couple of chocolate bars.

'That's it? You've absolutely nothing else?' I was thinking about

157

the 275 kilometres to the next town and what little food I had in my panniers. *What the hell made me think Kyubeme was a proper town? Too late now …*

The lady opened a cupboard door, took out some bags of instant mash and showed me. 'This is everything. They are for us to use, but I can sell you some if you need.' *Oh, well, in that case, everything's going to work out fine.* Even the chefs on *Ready, Steady, Cook* couldn't create much with instant mash, Choco-pies, peanut M&Ms and a Bounty bar.

I ordered *plov* and sat down. There was not much else I could do. While I was eating my second plate of *plov* and washing it down with my second weak coffee, the young girl who was working at the cafe spoke to me. If I wanted, I could stay with her and her husband. I was not going to refuse.

Katya and Andrei (another one) convinced me to stay another day in Kyubeme. If I did, I could have a *banya*, they said. I didn't take any convincing. It was a relief. Another rest day was most welcome. As for the banya …

There is no doubt that when travelling in winter, it is far easier to keep clean than in the sweaty, sultry summer months where dust and dirt accumulates thick and fast. The cold, however, offers no incentive to strip down to a minimum and have a proper wash with water when camping. I had no desire to strip off my thermal base layers. So I ended up wearing the same clothes twenty-four hours a day. No one would have denied I could do with a wash. *Yes, a banya would be lovely.* My face lit up.

My first experience of a Russian banya was during the previous summer. I had crossed back into Russia from western Mongolia the day before and spent the afternoon riding along the upper section of the Chuysky Trakt, the road that runs from Novosibirsk through the mountainous Altai region to the border. I had found a beautiful campsite beside the Chuya River. Typical of a Russian campsite, it was unofficial and free with several pitches demarcated through use, each with a circle of stones for a fire, now blackened and with a few empty beer cans or a vodka bottle thrown in. It was early in the afternoon, but I was happy to stop cycling early to sit out and enjoy the summer sun while drinking Medvyed beer from a can with an image of a bear on the front of it. I had the campsite to myself. I picked the furthest, most secluded spot to pitch my tent. Everything was perfect. I could see the burnt red rock faces towering up the left bank. The sound of shallow water flowing over the rocks was relaxing. The cool beer was soothing as it trickled down my throat.

It wasn't until late at night after the stars had come out, and I had already gone to sleep, that the peace was shattered. Three cars came speeding through the area, engines revving, and stopped outside my tent. *Seriously, why stop outside my tent? This place is huge. You could go anywhere.* Car doors opened and loud music filled the air. I didn't know the songs, only the type of music. It was that god-awful techno shit, which so many young Russians love, with a heavy beat that they think if played loud enough will compensate for the lack of any rhythm, tune or meaningful lyrics.

I lay in my tent trying to work out who these late-night revellers were, and whether I ought to be concerned for my safety. I hoped if I stayed quiet, they'd ignore me and be on their way quickly. They ignored me all right. They certainly never paid me any attention when I crawled out of my tent, stood up into the headlights of one of the cars lighting up the arena they'd formed and stared at them for a long time. They were just kids who had driven out from Kosh Agach for a late-night party. They were oblivious, too absorbed in their own lives to be concerned about anything other than themselves. I got back in my tent and tried to sleep. They couldn't stay much longer, I presumed.

I presumed wrong. At three in the morning, I dragged my bike and tent through the campground looking for another place to lodge for the remainder of the night. To my surprise, many available spaces were now taken, large cars parked, tents pitched, families blissfully asleep, unaware and ignorant of the happenings at my end of the site. Eventually, I found a space beside the river.

I woke late the next morning. It was while I was finishing my cup of coffee, having packed up my gear, that I saw a woman and two teenage boys walking over to me. As was so often the case, now that I was ready to leave, someone took that moment to strike up a conversation.

'Hello. This is my mother and brother. My mother wants to know if you would like to join us for breakfast?' the older boy asked in English.

'Thanks, but I was just about to leave.'

'We also have a banya beside the river. She says you can have a bath too. Do you know the Russian banya?'

'I know it, but I haven't had one yet,' I replied.

'Well, come on then, if you don't mind. We won't keep you long. Everyone who visits Russia must try a banya.'

And that was where I was initiated into the Russian experience of hot steamy saunas beside the Chuya River in a portable tent with a wood-burning stove to provide the heat and hot water, a bucket of river water to provide the cold water, and a layer of birch wood on the floor to prevent a muddy quagmire. That was probably the most scenic sauna I shall ever have. It certainly helped sweat away the memories of the sleepless night.

So, when Andrei mentioned a banya, back in Kyubeme – a place I had initially thought devoid of any delights – memories of the summer came flooding back, and I jumped at the chance. Not a portable, hiker's banya but the real deal.

'Do you have any clean clothes?' Katya asked me when Andrei returned and said the water was hot enough.

'Not really,' I replied.

Katya rummaged through her wardrobe for some trousers and a baggy T-shirt. 'Here. See if these fit. For afterwards,' she said. Then she passed me her dressing gown. Katya was only twenty-two. She was a similar height to me with blond hair, but whereas I am all hips, she was all tits. The T-shirt fit loosely. I squeezed into the jogging bottoms and hoped my cyclist's thighs wouldn't split through the seams. I heard a little rip; the stitching pinged apart on my inner thigh. 'They are old. Don't worry about stretching them,' Katya commented, seemingly unawares to the alterations I had inadvertently already made. *Better not sit down.*

I followed Katya outside. Donned in her dressing gown against the cold night air, I shuffled along in Andrei's large *valenkis* (fur boots) down the icy paths. Katya showed me to the banya, made sure I could find my way back and left me to it. It was a stand-alone wooden building, raised above the ground. Up three steps, I opened the first wooden door into a small room. On one side were a bench and several hooks on which to hang clothes. It was cold. I took off Katya's clothes and stepped out of Andrei's valenkis onto the hard wooden floor. My feet curled at the icy touch so that only my heels and toe tips touched anything. Standing naked, my muscles tensed automatically against the chill. *Quick now. Don't hang around.* My heart was beating fast.

I grabbed my shampoo and opened the second wooden door. A blast of hot air shot out and a cloud of steam filled the room. I tiptoed in and shut the door behind me. It was hot and humid and hard to breathe in the heavy air. Almost instantly, I began to feel beads of sweat on my forehead. I looked around and saw a two-tiered bench along the back wall. Little plastic bowls lay on the side with half-used bits of soap. In the corner was the stove and next to it a large metal urn of hot water ready to ladle out into a bowl and wash with. It was far too hot for me, so I used mostly cold water with a little hot added to take off the chill. Even so, the heat was overwhelming, the benches too hot to sit on without a towel. I opened the door and stepped back into the other room. The rush of cold air was equally refreshing and shocking. I stood there until I began to shiver, then rushed back into the steaming sauna room.

When I finally emerged, clean and rosy-cheeked, I was overcome with immense tiredness – that good state of well-earned relaxation after a long day's exercise. I returned to Katya's home under a sky awash with stars.

'Look out of the window,' Katya said when I got back to the cabin. There was a hint of mischief in her eyes, trickery behind her smile. She was kneeling on the sofa with her arms folded on the windowsill behind. I narrowed my eyes slightly and tilted my head sceptically. 'Come on. Take a look,' she encouraged. 'It's fine.' Her hand beckoned.

I turned round and knelt up on the sofa beside her. She pushed the window open wide, called something into the chilling night air and moved out of the way. I leaned over and peered out …

'Holy Shit!' I exclaimed and jumped straight back. *Seriously, what is that?* Katya laughed. I cautiously leaned forward again to take another look. Staring me in the face out of the dark was a shaggy black head with two giant paws up on the ledge.

Then I laughed too.

'*Medvyed*,' was all Katya said. Bear.

'Yeah, it's like a bear,' I agreed. *Is that thing real?*

The breed of dog, I discovered later, was probably the Russian Caucasian. Bred for their size and strength, they are incredibly loyal and protective, excellent for protecting homes and farms and livestock from intruders – human or animal – and can be very vicious in their duty. They are the largest breed of dog; to say it was more akin to the stature of a bear is no hyperbole.

The next morning, ready to wheel my bike to the cafe for breakfast before leaving, I went to get my bike from the lean-to. I had forgotten all about the bear-dog until I cast a passing glance through the chicken-wire and wooden wall of the makeshift shed and saw that shaggy beast standing next to my bike. My bike looked like a child's toy.

Er ... Um ... Shit. I looked around. Katya and Andrei had gone to work; I could see no one else. *Well, if I'm going to leave this morning, I need my bike. And if I'm going to get my bike, I'm gonna have to get some guts, open that shed door and go in to get it ... It's just a big dog.*

Very slowly, and quietly, and as calmly as possible considering the rate my heart was pumping, I slid the latch across. *There, there ... Good pup.* The bear-dog took two steps towards the door. *Good God!* The lean-to was only big enough for the bear-dog to take two steps. The lean-to was actually a very adequate size; it was the dog that was disproportionate.

It was like the world had been turned on its head and what should have been big was small and small was big. Time could have been flowing backwards and apples rising from the floor and floating back up to the tree with gravity all askew. I was Alice in Wonderland. Except this was no wonderland. This was some hellish place of existence, neither living nor dead, real nor imaginary, where you could only buy Choco-pies and instant potatoes. And it was guarded by a giant bear-dog. *What kind of fucked up place is this!*

22.

If I was going to get by cycling for the next three days on a diet primarily consisting of Choco-pies and instant mash, I needed a filling, nutritious breakfast to start me off that morning. It was while I was scoffing down my second plate of *plov* that Andrei (yet another one) walked into the cafe and into my life. He was an electrician on his way to a small village past Ust-Nera. Dressed in *valenkis* and blue overalls, he stood tall with his chin up and a permanent smile on his face. He had seen my bike outside; he was talking animatedly about it and asking lots of questions.

'Oh no, sorry, don't answer. Eat, before your food goes cold. One thing – can I have my photo taken with you and the bike after you've eaten?'

I liked this guy from the start. He hadn't lost his enthusiasm for life. Nothing, I thought, would ever get him down. When I'd finished the *plov*, Andrei's food had arrived. I sat down opposite him and said I was in no rush to leave. He passed me his unopened can of coke and a clementine.

You should have seen my eyes light up at that. Fresh fruit! My mouth watered at the thought of the tiny segments and sweet juicy taste. Besides drinking juice in Yakutsk and the few segments of clementine to wash down vodka, my supply of vitamins had been severely lacking.

Fresh fruit was not a good food for carrying in my pannier freezer.

Andrei saw the look on my face. 'Wait one minute.' He pushed back the bench and walked outside, then returned with a bag full of apples and clementines, which he gave to me.

'They're from China,' he said apologetically, 'but they do taste good.' Most fresh produce came from China to this region. People never failed to mention this and always seemed slightly disgusted by it.

'It's too much,' I said. Too much as a gift; too much to carry; too much to eat before it would freeze.

'You're right,' he took back the bag and gave me two apples and five clementines, then called the lady at the cafe to give me two chocolate bars. 'That's better. Eat some now. The rest you can wrap up in your jacket. These oranges make good snacks on the road.' That fruit was the best tasting fruit I had in Russia. The Russian food I'd had was not gourmet cuisine and too bland for my taste. Biting those segments of clementine was like a sensory explosion in my mouth, my taste buds bursting like fireworks. Who'd have thought a little clementine could give such pleasure? I thanked Andrei profusely. Then we went outside and took some photos posing with the bike in front of his 4x4.

My spirits had been lifted. I collected my gear and set off immediately before this high was sucked out of me and absorbed into the Kyubeme air. It was another gloriously crisp, sunny day. The cycling was slow and steady.

I had reached the point between the initial morning enthusiasm and being in a relaxed hypnotic rhythm where the pedals rotate almost of their own accord, but where boredom can set in. Then, as I rounded a bend, I saw a sign on the metal crash barrier, written on a piece of cardboard and tied to a post. I squinted to read it as I flew past down the hill.

No way! I slammed on the brakes as hard as I dared and slid to a halt, back wheel skidding on the ice. I put the bike down and ran back to it.

'HELEN. I LOVE YOU. Andrei,' was scribbled in blue biro with a little bicycle scrawled in the corner. That made me smile. And smiling made my day. You see, it doesn't take much to bring real pleasure into someone's life. A little thought and a piece of scrap cardboard can do it. Remembering about a note Lars had left me on a dirt track in West Africa a few years ago, I turned over the cardboard to make sure there was no additional message on the back.

I was still smiling late in the afternoon when I saw a track carved out down towards the river. I pushed my bike along it to an old quarry, veiled in snow. Quarries had been a favourite camping spot in West Africa. With shovel in hand, I stomped off the track and into the snow, which came up to my knees. Once I had shovelled out my tent grave, I stomped around some more to flatten the snow, then dug a trench back out to the track in order to pull my bike through more easily. Then I pitched the tent. Finally, a night of winter camping and everything was as it should be. Almost.

OK, so my hands got freezing cold putting up the tent, and I had to run and run and run to warm them up. That only helped a little, so I got into my sleeping bag. OK, so my stove wouldn't work again, this time because the shaker needle had fallen out somewhere and got lost. It was probably at the bottom of my bag, but it was easier to get out the maintenance and repair kit and use the replacement. OK, so the large bin liner I was using as a vapour barrier liner split during the night, as did the second spare I had, so that my feet stuck out of it and got very cold, but that was nothing unusual. Before Yakutsk I had been using an emergency bivvy bag as the liner, as this had worked well in Scandinavia. That had split the first time I used it in Siberia, and the duct tape repairs were a failure. Instead I had bought a supply of large bin liners in Yakutsk. These, too, split in the cold. But a vapour barrier liner is not essential. It only adds some warmth and keeps your bag dry of sweat. OK, so in the morning, the lid of my Nalgene water bottle was frozen shut, and when I gave it a little tap to try and break the icy seal, the plastic bottle itself shattered into fragments, but I still had my thermos flask for tea. OK, so I say all this like it wasn't a big deal. Frankly, though, when so many things don't work as they should in just one night of camping, it starts to piss you off.

The next day, I had only one litre to drink all day because my Nalgene was broken beyond repair. I couldn't be bothered to get the stove out and melt more snow while on the road, so I was severely dehydrated by the time I made camp down a side road.

Now I was getting the hang of winter camping again. Nothing broke. It was almost enjoyable. I say almost; it was still too damn cold. The thermometer hovered around minus forty degrees Celsius. But those two nights were not simply about surviving. To counter my dehydration, I drank cup after cup of sweet hot chocolate. It was similar to when cycling in extreme heat – then, it doesn't seem to matter how much liquid I take on during the day, I can still drink two litres in the evening.

The best part of those two days of cycling was that a grand total of four trucks went past and none stopped. That meant no photos, no explaining what I was doing, and no standing around getting cold feet. It meant I spent the majority of each day cycling. With little food or drink to snack on, I had few reasons to stop. Following a river downstream, the cycling was easy. There were no steep hills where I would sweat a lot going uphill and then get cold from the windchill while freewheeling downhill. The gradual slope was barely noticeable, but it still required me to pedal gently to overcome the friction from the bike. This all meant I cycled eighty-five kilometres each day. And that meant I would reach Ust-Nera in three days, not four. Or two nights of winter camping, not three.

That meant I had overestimated the amount of Choco-pies I would need. If, when I arrived in Ust-Nera, someone had checked my panniers, they would have thought I had come only to trade in fake Wagon Wheels. These Choco-pies, which aren't entirely a biscuit, or a cake, or all chocolate, are really rather gross. Why anyone – other than food-deprived cyclists passing through Kyubeme where there is no real shop – should ever consider buying them, let alone eating them, is beyond me. Cardboard has more flavour than the chocolate coating and biscuit layers. The marshmallow part has the texture, consistency and taste of foam.

Luckily, I had plenty of oats for porridge. Breakfast, now that I remembered to sleep with the stove fuel pump to keep it warm, was the best part of the day. While still encased in the warmth of my sleeping bag, I could drink coffee overdosed with sugar and eat a filling meal of porridge, which was delicious as long as I devoured it quickly (not a challenge) in the short interval between it being piping hot and stone cold.

Then followed the trauma of trying to clean the pan. No end of scrubbing and scraping could remove the last frozen morsels cemented to it. If you are considering winter camping, you have to get used to the idea of porridge remains reappearing in every subsequent drink or meal made in the same pan, until you can thaw it out and attack it in a warm kitchen armed with a wire scrubbing brush and washing-up liquid.

At least you know that when you get a chewy bit in your tea, it is only a thawed out, rehydrated piece of oat, and not some unsavoury bug that inadvertently crawled or flew into your mug. The absence of bugs is one benefit of winter camping. No ants. No termites. No flying, buzzing, biting, crawling, creeping, scuttling or scurrying insects that are the bane of camping throughout Africa and other tropical (even temperate) climes.

The third day to Ust-Nera was much like the previous two. The same clear blue skies. The same kind of cold that gradually warmed throughout the afternoon before plummeting when the sun went down. The same monochrome Siberian scenery of forest and snow. The same, except for the hill where the road deviated from the Elgi River to skirt around the northern edge of the mountains before returning to follow the Indigirka River into Ust-Nera. I stopped, back at river level, to warm up my hands and feet and drink some tea, and saw a little bird dart across the road and land on a branch. When I pulled down the hood of my jacket, I could hear it chirping a sweet song of spring. It went on chattering and twittering until I almost believed it too. Certainly, it was warmer during the day now. But don't believe everything the little birdie sings. Sometimes, the prettiest things whisper the biggest lies. At least the ubiquitous black crow cawed and squawked that winter was here to stay for a long time to come. That was easier to believe, although I'd have preferred it to be wrong.

23.

Any interesting account of a solo, long-distance cycle ride is bound to be misleading. It will undoubtedly give a warped impression of how the vast majority of the cyclist's time is spent. It is the people we meet that bring the stories to life, not the endless hours in the saddle. For me, it is the times I'm not cycling that are often the most memorable parts of cycle-touring. Don't get me wrong, I love the cycling part: travelling slowly enough to take in all the details of the surroundings, both vulnerable to and reliant upon the forces of nature is, I think, the best way to see a country. But there needs to be a balance.

What I may have failed to portray in this Siberian Winter's Tale are the prolonged periods of time with no one but myself for company. When drivers stopped, the conversation was brief and uninspiring, each one much like the last. The usual questions could be answered without thought. Sure, they will leave the carload of people with plenty to talk about and a good over-dinner story of the time they met this strange girl from England cycling through Yakutia in winter. From my point of view, I learned very little; the encounter sparked little curiosity or food for thought during the long periods I was alone. As the days and weeks progressed, even those encounters became rare.

For the most part, I was alone, just me and nature. And that's fine; I like it that way. The natural world is a marvellous place, full of beauty and colour and wonder, with so many scents and sounds and sensations. Except when the whole of nature is in hibernation beneath a thick layer of pure white snow. There are no signs of life, no colours, few sounds, no smells. There is little to stimulate the senses and you're left in a state of perceptual isolation. It leaves a large void in the mind. The only way to fill that void is with your own thoughts. But when there are no inputs or boundaries, anything is possible. The mind is a curious thing, and people by nature are social creatures. We are not designed for solitude. Without the extreme temperature to contend with after Yakutsk, my mind was free to wander, rather than being focussed entirely on survival. I may have been physically confined to the road, but my mind could escape and roam beholden to no one.

Perhaps one of the reasons I have been happy cycle-touring for so long is my ability to think of nothing. I always assumed that this was normal, something everyone could do. Apparently not. My friends look at me weirdly when they ask what I'm thinking, and I reply 'nothing' in all honesty. But you must be thinking of something, they say. However, thinking of nothing is not an action that can be commanded. If I try to think of nothing, the neurons in my brain go into overdrive, so that I am constantly fighting off thoughts. Thinking of nothing is staring blankly ahead with an empty head and a free mind. Cycle-touring is my meditation.

After you empty your head of all thoughts and concerns, so that your mind is as free as an eagle soaring over the steppe, imagination takes over. New thoughts and ideas overflow into your reality. The real world and the one you've created begin to overlap, entwine and merge, until it's hard to perceive where one world ends and the other begins. And out there, alone in the Siberian wilderness, so far removed from my life back home that the wintry, icy reality seemed like a dream, there was no reality check. There was nothing to pull me back in.

Everyone moves through life connected in some way. Most people have short, strong bonds connecting them closely to their friends and family and the place they call home. Others of us have stretched those bonds until we can wander almost free, but we are still connected loosely and can be reeled in any time. Perhaps one bond may break and another one form, but there's always something holding us together. But what if your mind travels so far that the last bond finally snaps and frees you forever to wander as far from your reality as you dare? Are they the crazy ones? The ones that got away.

The daily distraction of calculating distances and times to the next town or hotel or cafe was part of my routine. It's something to think about when cycling. It uses a part of my brain that is sadly neglected when I am travelling. The analytical and mathematical left side of my brain was trained for years at school and university, then put to work whenever I earn my living as an engineer. It is only more recently, since I began travelling for long periods of time that the creative right side of my brain has had a chance to thrive.

I had too much time to think. So when there was nothing left to calculate, I thought about home and my family and friends; I thought about my life of freedom and insecurity on the road, and how it differs from my life of routine and familiarity back home; I thought about whether I should take the route to Chersky or Magadan – that debate was still raging in my mind; I considered whether I would make another such extreme winter journey, and I dreamed once more of returning to the warmth of Africa. I wondered whether my next journey would be alone because I am getting tired of my own company.

I thought about the past and the present and the future, the future of this planet and the people on it. There are too many possibilities, too many uncertainties, too many reasons to be pessimistic with outcomes I cannot change. If I look hard enough, there are also many reasons to be optimistic. There is hope.

I have debated all these things before. My views have not changed. I am not going to save a world that has been shaped by violence. I am too much of a pacifist, too apolitical, for that. For too long I have stood by and watched things evolve around me. Yet I can do my part to make the lives of people around me better.

I can enjoy my short time on earth the best way I know, by seeing and learning and trying to understand and make sense of it all. And I can write about it because I enjoy it and it makes me happy, even though better books have been written, and worse ones. If I write a good book, it may even bring joy or happiness or inspiration to someone else.

I decided, there and then, to write *A Siberian Winter's Tale*. Sometimes it is only when the words are indelibly marked in print that it's possible to see clearly the thoughts that are so jumbled in my mind. Only when the naked words are staring you in the face can you begin to understand what you have seen and done or why you have done it. In this case, it might confirm my suspicions that this journey was an entirely absurd endeavour.

I stared out across the white wilderness – a blank page full of possibility – and I listened, waiting for the first word to come to me. Any word. But the blanketed snow absorbed all sound and the trees echoed back a deathly silence.

I pedalled on, my tyres leaving a trail in the snow. Slowly, those tracks turned to thoughts that later became the ink trails scrawled in my journal.

Stifled by the Siberian silence surrounding me, I strained to listen. I heard a faint sound – words – a strong, powerful voice shouting to be heard. But it wasn't coming from the south through the vast taiga wilderness carried along frozen river arteries, or from the north

173

across the tundra wasteland and the Arctic coast, or from the distant towns I had already passed further west, or from Magadan in the east. Could it be coming from the ghosts of people sent to the gulags whose bones are the foundations of the road along which I'd been travelling? I wondered whether that would be a thousand screams or one common, indistinct voice as though death mirrored life and the individual did not exist?

The words did not come from the stars either; although, they were quietened as if coming from a distant space beyond our universe, travelling light years across galaxies and muffled by dark matter. They came from my very core, somewhere unreachable deep inside me, as if locked in at the far end of a black hole that can never be reached because the harder you try, the further it stretches into oblivion. The more intensely I listened, the further the voice retreated until it was a faint whisper and then nothing more than a tiny ripple of the air. And then there was silence. Except for the snow crackling under the tyres.

I wondered how to tell this Siberian Winter's Tale. There are only so many ways you can say that it was cold and that does not make a story. People make a story. But as I have said, although I had met a few, I never had the chance to know them well. My journey was full of fleeting encounters on the ice road. To bring characters to life, so the reader loves them or loathes them, I thought I would have to embellish. Perhaps, I thought, the only way to tell this story would be to write it as fiction, set in a fantasy world – Siberia – full of fictional characters that would leap out of the page, grab the reader and drag them deep into the fold.

If I was ever to write a fictional book, I would like it to be a Kafkaesque creation inspired by some of my favourite writers: with the surrealism of Murakami, a fantasy–realism blend of Bulgakov laced with Vonnegut's satirical wit and Kingsolver's flowing prose. I mention such great writers because they inspire me, not that I compare. I suppose, if I am to set a benchmark, it should be suitably unattainable. Achievable goals never lead to greatness. They are for schoolchildren to boast perfect scores. But life is not perfect, even if it is one long lesson. It is human nature to strive, and drive and determination will get you further than you could ever imagine. Cruising along in the slow lane will get you to your destination eventually, but I am more interested in the twists and turns, the unexpected highs and lows. Success often follows failure. For too long I have simply been cruising, scared of failure; perhaps, even, scared of success.

I let my imagination run wild in a world without borders or boundaries, unbound by the laws of nature and rules by which we live. A world where anything was possible.

From this world, all manner of strange characters – fictional friends – emerged. Their stories unfolded. But then their stories and my life began to merge and twist and combine until a talking turbaned cat appeared in my memories of travelling as a sixteen-year-old in India, and Sarala my four-hoofed Kyrgyz companion could convey his thoughts to me as we traversed his country.

From the blank white snow-covered canvas, characters emerged for a Siberian story that one day I might write. I took traits and features from the people I had met and combined them into larger than life characters. I conjured stories and backgrounds for each of them until they became something more complete, more real. There were Masha and Tatiana, Bogdan, Andrei and Misha. And these characters merged into my present. I was freed from my cold reality and released into a fictional world that held no bounds.

Occasionally, I regained consciousness to realise I had only travelled a kilometre or two down the road. Not much had changed. I was still cycling, the pedals rotating, the warmth slowly leaching out of my toes, with the road going on and on and on along the river, hemmed in by the valley that shut me off from the world. I was still alone. The hypnotic monotony sent me drifting back to my dreams, which seemed more real and colourful and full of life, where so much more was going on. Time became meaningless as it distorted and stretched, so that an hour or a day or a whole decade might have passed, but each time I awoke to reality, I was still only a kilometre or two further down the road.

This was how the hours passed, until one time I noticed that the temperature was dropping, signalling the setting of the sun. My countdown to find a camping spot had begun. As the minutes ticked by, I imagined Bogdan shaking his salt-and-pepper head from side to side. How I wished he would appear with his truck and invite me in for hot tea, bread and *salo*, and try to convince me to stay in the truck for the night because it was too cold outside.

The next day, as I stood at the top of the pass, donning my down jacket ready for the long, freezing downhill, a young Masha appeared from a bus that had brought some schoolchildren on an excursion from Ust-Nera to this viewpoint. She came bounding over, excited about my bike, asking if she could have a ride. She leapt onto the back of my bike with gymnastic agility, and we freewheeled around and down the hillsides together. Masha's blonde hair was streaming out from under her hat and waving wildly in the wind; a wide, open, uninhibited smile of joy and freedom spread across her face. Although, of course, when I stopped at the bottom of the hill to stomp and warm my feet, Masha was no longer there, her image swept away on the wings of the little birdie that flew across my path into the trees where it chirped that spring was just around the corner.

I remembered, years ago, reading a book set in Russia with a character called Misha. *Death and the Penguin* was the book. Misha was the penguin. On long stretches of uphill, I imagined Misha shuffling along beside me, a silent black and white companion who blended perfectly with the quietness of the white Siberian wilderness. Of course, penguins don't really live in Siberia. But if I wanted a pet penguin called Misha, then I could easily conjure him up. The perfect travelling companion, he never answered back and never complained. He just kept shuffling along at the same slow, steady pace as me.

You might think I sound unhinged. But trust me, at the time, this was the stuff that was keeping me sane as I neared Ust-Nera.

24.

Ust-Nera was surrounded by steep-sided white hills like the walls of a fortress. Along the ridge tops, the snow-covered rocks looked like battlements. It felt safe and well protected, yet at the same time as if the town was trapped under siege and escape would be impossible.

I had finally made a decision: to go to Magadan. It had been exhausting. Now I was drowning in the tides of two opposing emotions: relief that a decision had been made, and regret that I wouldn't be going to Chersky … this time, at any rate. That I could return and make the journey another time was the only thought that made the decision bearable. It eats away at you to want something so badly for so long and be so close, yet unable to have it.

To know that the only thing stopping me was myself was hard to accept. I had found my limit. I'd been standing on a desolate beach, my toes digging into the sand, feeling the shallow water of indecision lap around my feet too long. The tides had come in and gone out, washing over me for days. Should I dive into the sea and swim for Chersky, risk the rip tides dragging me out, leaving me without the strength to weather the storms and raging seas and ride the rise and fall of the ocean's swell? Or should I simply turn my back and return over the beach and walk the more familiar path to Magadan?

In my heart, I knew the answer: I must turn back if I wished to return home. I didn't have the strength for a fight. Physically, I would recover. Mentally, I wasn't so sure. I know we're all a little messed up in our own ways, some more than others. I'd generally consider myself weighted on the level-headed side of the scale. But over the last days, I would definitely say I'd been unbalanced. Everyone has their tipping point, a critical mass or trigger that will turn even the most calm, reasonable person to perform acts of irrational insanity. Thankfully, most of us go through our lives in a stable state, or the world would be one hell of a cuckoo's nest. But I felt the scales tipping. I was slowly sliding and curious about how far I could go. But I was scared I wouldn't be able to pull myself back. Freeing the mind might ultimately lead to being trapped by it, unable to escape. It was like a drug, full of allure, yet carrying a heavy risk. It's why I won't ever take hard drugs – not because I don't want to try out of curiosity but because I don't think I could stop.

I hadn't realised how mentally strong I would need to be for the Siberian winter. After six months on the summer journey across Asia, I was physically fit, but travelling alone all that time had drained me mentally. The solitude of Siberia was pushing me close to an edge I wasn't prepared to go over.

The one question above all others that I get asked once people realise that I travel alone is, 'Don't you get lonely?' When I say that I rarely get lonely, they express surprise. They look at me, furrowed brow, with a heavy dose of scepticism, as though it's not possible to be content in one's own company. I add that the occasional times I feel lonely, I'm as likely to be in a room full of people. But I think what people were really asking was whether I got bored with my own company. Many people are not comfortable left alone with their own thoughts.

In my younger years when I travelled alone, I was rarely on my own because I sought company. I stayed in hostels and surrounded myself with other young people. These were fleeting meetings; we would travel together for a few days, even a few weeks, when our paths followed a similar route. Ultimately, though, we were on our own journeys looking for answers and knowledge. I suppose we were all a little lost and searching for something; although, none of us knew what.

The older I got, the more I found myself seeking solitude. It was not something I lived with because there was no other choice. I chose to be alone. Not everyone needs close relationships or companions for fulfilment all of the time. Happiness can be found through thought and creativity. But I was beginning to realise that solitude, like other good things when taken in excess, can be detrimental to your health.

Perhaps it would have been a calm crossing to Chersky, but I could not take that risk. It was the right decision. I needed to rest. I needed to get a grip. It didn't mean I had to like it.

Now I'd made the decision, I needed to book the flight home. That wasn't simple. I spent the best part of a day trawling the town for an internet connection. Sent from one building to another, all to no avail, I eventually ended up back where I'd started. Use a travel agent? Easy, if you had enough cash to pay for the tickets because the agent won't accept credit cards. Go to the bank and get cash? Well, of course, that is what I did. That would have been simple if I could have withdrawn enough money in one transaction, but then the machine devoured my card. Even entering the bank was confusing. There was no sign indicating there was a bank in the building. The large insignia on the outer wall suggested it was the headquarters for a football club. I entered through the main door and was faced with a second door straight ahead as was common in Siberia. I opened that too. There was a narrow unlit corridor running to my left and right, and in front of me were two doors. It seemed like a labyrinthine choice: take the dark corridor and risk getting lost in an inescapable maze, or risk taking the wrong door and be faced with an eternity of doors to be opened ahead of me. I almost turned back. It was all too much. When one of the doors opened ahead of me and a person came out, I was so stunned I didn't even notice whether it was a man or a woman. They took one glance at me as if they expected me to be there and opened the door ahead of them, the one I'd just come through. I felt like Josef K in Kafka's *The Trial*.

The agency was closed by the time I returned to the travel agent armed with cash that had taken two days to obtain. There was no such thing as opening hours listed. One helpful local suggested I go to the other travel agent at the far end of town. This other travel agency was open. It had a queue. It also had the opening times listed, which helpfully informed me that the agency closed at midday on a Friday for the weekend. It was half past eleven on Friday. I waited my turn, restraining the fidget within.

When my time came, the agent informed me that she couldn't book any tickets because the connection was not working. I insisted she persist. Reluctantly she did. Midday came and the agent looked up at the clock. As she did, the computer rang into action. I could see the loathing written over the agent's face as she looked at me, that awkward customer at the end of the day.

'Shall I book the tickets?' she asked me again. I could have said yes, but the price she quoted was more than the other agent and a lot more than I could buy online myself. If only I could get online. To have taken so long and with the tickets virtually in sight. I'd been going round and round the town as if on a never-ending Escher staircase. Here was my escape.

'No,' I replied. *Oh, I'm such a cheapskate.*

And so the trial continued.

I tried phoning a travel agent in Magadan. It was a convoluted conversation lost in translation that left only confusion, no booking.

There was one solution left. It lay outside this crazy world I was trapped in. Phone home. That wasn't simple either. The hotel phone could not make international calls; the post office had telephone booths, but no telephones. I ended up calling on my mobile at an extortionate rate. It connected, then the line went dead. Out of credit. I walked over to the mobile phone shop. The girls in the shop were incredibly helpful. Finally, it felt like my problems would be solved. They registered a new SIM card, the best one for my needs, and topped it up with credit.

'Hi Dad, I can't talk long. Can you help? I need you to book me some flight tickets online.'

'Of course.' Well, of course he could. Good old Dad. 'Um … where are you? Are you OK?'

'I'm fine. I'm in Ust-Nera. But I need to book flights from Magadan. I'm going to Magadan now.'

'So, how are you?' Clearly, he didn't comprehend my opening gambit about being unable to talk for long.

'I'm fine. Dad. I haven't got much airtime. Can you book me a flight with Aeroflot on the …'.

Beeeeeeeeep. *Bugger.*

I returned to the phone shop to top up with more credit. I complained to the girls about the lack of internet access. They proceeded to tell me that occasionally there was mobile internet connection in the early hours of the morning. That evening, I composed a comprehensive email to my dad, then set my alarm at hourly intervals throughout the night. Eventually, at 4 a.m., I got connected for a brief five minutes, long enough for the email to send. In the early hours of the following morning, I received electronic tickets by email from the airline companies. Good old Dad. He'd booked my return journey to England from Magadan via Khabarovsk, Vladivostock, Moscow and St Petersburg with three different airlines.

Focusing for two days entirely on booking tickets, however frustrating, was a much-needed distraction from thinking about the damn decision I had made to not go to Chersky.

25.

The morning I left Ust-Nera was another glorious day in Yakutia. There was not a cloud in sight. I could even feel a slight warmth on my cheeks from the sun burning in the bright blue sky. Compared to a fierce bite at minus forty, minus fifteen is a gentle touch, a light brush. It fools you into thinking that the real cold is not so bad, and when the sun goes down, you'll be able to cope as the temperature plummets. It's like a wild animal waiting for you to let your guard down before striking mercilessly.

The road hugged the shaded hillside on the south side of the Nera River. I looked longingly at the valley bathed in light and warmth. The cycling was hard work; my legs were lethargic. My mind fought with the idea that somehow I had failed; cycling to Magadan was a poor consolation. I tried to convince myself again that I didn't have the time to reach Chersky, and that there'd be plenty more adventures whichever way I rode.

I drowned my thoughts in music turned up full blast on my iPod. Music can shine a light on even the dreariest outlook. The day passed uneventfully, cycling and singing and stopping to drink tea and snack where the sun's rays reached the road. I had set my sights on Burustakh, a small village on the map, for the day's end. I could camp there or, with some luck, find a warm place to reside for the night.

I wasn't that lucky. There were only a couple of buildings, inaccessible through deep, untouched snow. This was where the *zimnik* or winter road for Chersky left the Kolyma Highway and followed a small river east and then north. This was the road I should have taken. The sign read only 187 kilometres to the next settlement, Sasyr, and 1,483 kilometres to Chersky. *That sounds doable, perhaps I do have time. It's easier now it's not so cold. I could always cancel my flight from Magadan.* I calculated how much food I would need to reach Sasyr. I didn't have enough.

Still I was being torn in a mental tug of war between the tough, risky challenge and what was beginning to feel like the easy, uneventful way out. Undertaking challenge and striving for success is like a drug; to reach Chersky was my fix. By turning away, I was going cold turkey on my addiction.

If I had had food, I might well have taken that *zimnik*. Instead, I pedalled on along the Kolyma Highway in search of a place to camp for the night. If I still felt the same when I reached Artik, the next settlement, the following morning, I could always stock up on supplies and head back. Those are the thoughts made before the sun sets and the chill takes control.

I pedalled on, low on energy, until finally I found a place to get off the road. My hands and feet were soon cold from traipsing through the snow and putting up the tent. A few hill repeats on the track to the river got the heart pumping. Then it was time for dinner.

Would you believe it? The damn stove wouldn't work again. Taking it apart, checking the seals and testing it in Ust-Nera had been a pointless endeavour. The metal cup had come apart in my bag and the fuel screw was frozen shut. Once I had fixed it, the pump wouldn't pressurise the fuel bottle, nor would the spare. I shoved one pump down my jacket and the other inside my sleeping bag. Hungry, I munched on cold snacks and chocolate and sipped the last dregs of the tea before curling up in my bag.

185

Another stove failure convinced me of one thing: I was fed up with the problems caused by the cold. Forget about Chersky. I'd be quite content with the easy ride to Magadan. This decision was final.

With a shorter road to Magadan, I was carrying more supplies than I needed. The packs of chemical hand warmers I'd been saving for an emergency could now be used whenever I wanted. And I wanted warm feet all night. Peace of mind and feeling in your big toes, helped by being so dehydrated that you don't need to get up and pee, is the perfect combination for twelve hours of deep, dreamless sleep.

With less than forty kilometres to Artik, I expected to make it in time for a late morning coffee. Despite weeks of slow winter cycling, my mind still estimated speeds according to a summer ride. I had also not learnt that going without dinner meant tired legs the next day. Hell, those forty kilometres seemed to take forever, even with a tailwind following the river downstream.

Beside that river was the first time I stopped and felt uncomfortable being by myself. I couldn't help feeling that I wasn't alone. I looked back up the road, half expecting to see someone come round the bend. But most Russians, it was clear by now, stayed indoors or in their vehicles in winter. It was a feeling of being followed down a dark alley, but when you look back over your shoulder no one is there.

It was a dull, overcast day. There was only the wind. And suddenly I realised it was the first time in weeks that I noticed any sound emanating from the wilderness. This invisible companion had shattered the Siberian silence. It's low, ghostly whispers on a long, drawn out sigh had made me uneasy. The wind had brushed away the fine snow, so that parts of the frozen river gave a milky turquoise tint to an otherwise dreary, monochrome picture. Where snow had hardened, the wind had sculpted it into ripples and waves, smooth arcs and sublime curves. Cracking sounds erupted as the river ice broke and shifted. The bitter wind cut deep through my not-so-windproof jacket. I pedalled on.

Finally, Artik came into view. Mesmerised by the thought of coffee, I sped up and strained to pick out the cafe. I was so focused on the dilapidated buildings, I failed to see the soft snow in the road. I careered through the snow onto a patch of glistening ice and then full pelt towards the metal barrier alongside the road. To avoid plummeting head first over the embankment or becoming a twisted entangled mess of bike, body and barrier, I took evasive action by leaping voluntarily from the bike. I ended up spreadeagled, face down, kissing the icy road beside the barrier, with the bike mounted on top of me, wondering if that perhaps wasn't the best avoidance manoeuvre and hoping no one saw my epic fall.

Spitting ice and grit, checking my teeth and rubbing my bad knee, which must have twisted somehow, I rose slowly. Slightly shaky, because I really needed a sugar hit and the cafe of my dreams was not getting closer at that moment, I heaved up the bike and pedalled off. At least, I tried. The wheel was misaligned, the handlebars twisted, the brake pads rubbed on the back wheel and the chain had slipped off. I bodged it into a rideable state and went in search of this cafe, which was rapidly becoming a unicorn of the catering trade in my mind.

Then I saw it. *Oh God! You've got to be kidding me.* It was closed – permanently – crumbling walls, windows without glass, boarded up. How my heart sank. A little flutter of hope tried to surface that there'd be another, but it was soon drowned by the overwhelming evidence that this place was a shit-hole with nothing to offer. It was Kyubeme's big brother.

26.

By the time I reached the far end of town, I was resigned to being entirely self-sufficient and outside at all times for 270 kilometres until Susuman, the next town. No cafes, no coffee. That wasn't so bad. I could ride out of town until I found a pleasant site to camp and rest for the remainder of the day in peace and quiet. I could read during the day, fire up the stove (once I'd warmed up the pump) and drink tea instead. If I got chilly, I'd go for a brisk walk or wriggle into my sleeping bag and use another of the chemical hand warmers. It seemed like a great idea in my head.

On the far side of the village, I stopped by a man walking down the road. I couldn't resist; I had to ask if there was an open cafe. His reply was a decisive 'no'. While we discussed what possible reason I could have for being here, on a bike, right now, in winter, a van screeched to a halt beside us.

'You OK? Any problem?' asked the young, blonde-haired driver leaning out of the window.

'No, all's fine. I was asking if there's a cafe here.'

'There's not, but if you need to eat, there's a *stolovaya* I can take you to. What's your name? I'm Sasha. Aren't you cold?'

A canteen? Oh, I am so weak-willed. 'OK.'

Sasha (another one) had a bright spark in his eyes that I hadn't seen in many others working in these mining towns. He was friendly and energetic, although I couldn't work out whether his behaviour was down to his blood-alcohol level or base nature.

'Come, come then. Let's go, it's cold,' Sasha motioned as he leapt out of the van. In a whirlwind of frenzied activity, my bike and bags were piled into the back. I squeezed onto the back seat beside two less charismatic characters. I tried to look beyond the unwashed clothes and stale, smoky breath.

'That's Vyacheslav and Rurik,' Sasha indicated with his eyes through the rear-view mirror as he spun the car round.

Vyacheslav turned and moved closer as he handed me an apple and banana as a gift, talking all the while with his repulsive breath, forcing me to edge away until I was pinned against the window. His lecherous gaze was marginally less disconcerting than Sasha's driving.

Sasha had his foot pinned to the floor. With a wheel spin, he set off racing down the main road in a less than straight line until, suddenly, he jammed on the brakes. We slowed rapidly, skidded, and got traction again just as Sasha spun the wheel and we turned down a narrow side road. God knows how we made that turn. That white-knuckled seat grasp, foot-stomping-on-imaginary-brake, pale-faced look my Dad makes whenever I'm driving too fast for his liking was suddenly understood.

The canteen was inside what appeared to be an old people's home or hospice. Soon we were all sitting at a long table, decorated as though it were someone's birthday. My eyes lit up at the sight of so much food. One lady put a bowl of borscht in front of me. 'Eat, eat,' she commanded. 'Do you want bread? Try the salad. Take a samosa. And fruit.' I dug in.

Then the vodka appeared. I'd seen the bottles. I'd seen empty ones get replaced by full ones. I hoped they'd stay at the far end of the table.

'Pass the vodka here,' Sasha called out. It got passed to him.

'You'll have a drink?' he asked me.

'No, I need water, tea.' I was very dehydrated.

'Babushka, water for the girl,' Sasha commanded one of the women. 'OK, but you have a vodka too.' He filled my glass.

'Drink! To your health.' How could I refuse that? I took a sip.

'You must drink all of it.' I reluctantly emptied the glass. It was promptly refilled by Vyacheslav.

'If you drink one vodka, you must drink three,' Sasha said. 'Russian tradition!' He laughed.

'Yes, yes, I know.' I'd heard that before. I resigned myself to three vodkas. I shovelled in bread to line my stomach and set to the borsch with renewed determination.

'You have a lovely body,' Vyacheslav whispered as he leant closer, wafting foul breath my way. *Ugh.* I ignored him and reached for the rice and fish. 'Doesn't she have a lovely body,' he said, louder, to no one in particular. He made a curvy hourglass figure wave with his hands, clearly not the shape of my body, although I'm sure that's what he was trying to insinuate.

I started to work on my escape plan. It was getting late in the afternoon; I'd need to leave soon if I were going to wild camp.

'Excuse me,' I said to the lady opposite, who I'd picked out as the most authoritative yet friendly person there, 'is there a guesthouse here? Or somewhere I could stay tonight? Otherwise I need to leave very soon.'

'No,' she replied abruptly. *That's that, then.*

Sasha added, 'I know a hostel, a place you can stay.' He and Vyacheslav were talking. It turned out they were scheming. I knew it when we were all back in the van and Sasha mentioned 'Vyacheslav's Hostel'.

On guard, but keeping an open mind because I trusted Sasha at least, we arrived at Vyacheslav's hostel: a tall, wooden building on the outskirts of Artik. I would have assumed it to be derelict, but appearances can be deceptive, none more so than when it comes to houses in remote parts of Siberia. Admittedly, the interior decor was in need of a personal touch. The paint of the steel blue walls and radiators and pipes was flaking. Upstairs, in one of the rooms were several empty metal frame beds. One bed had a duffel bag on it. A young Uzbek man was in the tiny kitchen. The other room was Vyacheslav's.

We hung out my clothes and sleeping bag on the hot water pipes to dry. I was so tired, all I could think of was collapsing into one of the empty beds and sleeping until the next morning.

Sleep was not what Vyacheslav had in mind. When we were alone in his room, he turned his attention to me. Hands wandered. Voices were raised. Even with a language barrier, it was clear what he wanted. My verbal tirade was understandable globally. Vyacheslav apologised and told me to sleep if I wanted as he had to go out. He returned with a bottle of vodka and a heart-shaped chocolate. He gave me the chocolate. *Now, this is awkward.* With another firm rebuff from me, he left and joined Sasha in the kitchen with the vodka. And that should've been that. But Vyacheslav couldn't let it go. When Sasha left, he tried his luck again. Now, I don't know much about Russian chat-up lines and pulling techniques, but it seemed to me that persistence was the name of Vyacheslav's game.

'I love you. Can we have sex?' He tried to put his hand on my leg. I pushed it away.

'No.'

'You have a beautiful body. Let's have sex.' He made a curvy hourglass wave with his hands again.

I pulled a face of disgust. 'No.'

'Why not? Let's have sex.' *Ugh.*

'No.'

'Sex?' he slurred as his hand made another reach for my leg. *Enough.*

I instantly stood up and towered over him. 'No sex.' Then I walked out to gather my belongings and leave. It was clear I would never be comfortable and able to rest here. It looked like I'd be camping after all. I should have left sooner, but with it being on the chilly side of thirty – you know, minus thirty – I was not overly inclined to venture back outside unless necessary. Now, it was necessary. Although, it was Vyacheslav who needed to cool down.

As I was shoving clothes into my panniers and trying to pack away the sleeping bag, Vyacheslav grabbed me from behind me. 'Helen, Helen, don't leave. I love you.' *Oh God. Please. Don't give me this shit.*

'You don't love me. You don't *know* me. We've only just met. And you're drunk. You have no idea about love. You see a girl and all you can think about is sex. Why do you say "I love you"? It's ridiculous. You're ridiculous. Get out of my way.' Upset and pissed off, I gathered everything into my arms and headed for the door.

'OK. OK. No sex. Don't leave.'

The only things I knew for sure were that there would be no sex and that I was leaving immediately.

This was not the first time that I had been told 'I love you' by a man who had only just met me. In Central Asia, the declaration of love was usually superseded by a grope for my tits or bum, or grab of my hips to pull me closer. A stern 'no' in these cases was usually interpreted as a 'yes, just playing hard to get'. In Africa, men asked straight up if we could have sex, no pretence at 'I love you'. It was blunt and unsubtle, but there was no lecherous groping. An equally blunt and unsubtle rejection was enough. Everyone knew where they stood. It was a simple question and answer exchange. The rejection was usually followed with, 'Shall we have a beer then?' And that was that; we'd be platonic friends from there on. The way it should be. No more talk of sex, or wandering hands, or awkwardness, or being made to feel like a piece of property.

I stumbled outside into the frigid air. 'Where the ...?'

Sasha's van, along with my bike and other baggage, was gone. Not here. Disappeared. Vanished. OK, so Sasha had driven off somewhere and likely not very far. But I had no idea where. I dropped my bags on the floor and stood there, staring blankly ahead, thinking only that I had really screwed up this time. *What to do? What to do!* I wanted to leave. I wanted to cycle away. *Where the hell is my bike?*

I looked up at the building and imagined Vyacheslav was either sitting on his bed with head in hands or at the kitchen table pouring another vodka, drowning his sorrows. I did not want to go back up there. There was nobody about to ask. I looked in the garage and another open building; they were deserted. *Where is everybody?*

I started walking. There was no one strolling down the footpaths, no cars on the road, no children playing on the swings in the park, no lights on in windows or smoke coming from chimneys of buildings that had seen better days. Everything was covered in white. It was a post-apocalyptic scene with me wandering aimlessly in search of survivors.

I traipsed through the deserted town with two overloaded panniers in one hand, unravelled sleeping bag in the other and roll mat trailing behind, sobbing as I went, towards the only place I knew: the canteen.

Outside the concrete building and thick metal door, I ditched my bags, wiped away the tears, composed myself and pulled the door handle. The damn thing wouldn't budge. I yanked harder, knocked loudly and swore profusely. Still it remained locked. I walked around the side, but there were no other doors, so I took a seat on the bench outside and started blubbering uncontrollably. *Good God, what is wrong with me! Get a grip. Think.* I just needed to find someone, anyone, to speak with.

Then I heard the fumbling of keys. Four ladies wrapped head-to-toe in fur poured out, all talking at once.

'Ah, we heard something. Are you OK?'

'What's wrong?'

'It's OK, tell us the problem. There's no need to cry.' I wiped the tears from my face.

'Where's your bike?'

'I don't know. That's the problem,' I sobbed.

'What? I don't understand.'

And then I blurted out the whole ridiculous, sad story of how I got into this mess. My lack of Russian meant it sounded like this: 'I to Vyacheslav's house with Sasha. Say hotel. Not true. Vyacheslav drunk and wants sex. I don't want sex. But he say sex. Sex. Sex. Not good. Now I want to go. But bicycle in van. No van. No Sasha. I come here.'

'Drunk Russian man sees young girl and wants sex. Typical,' said one lady, and the others shook their heads knowingly.

'The vodka. It's bad,' said another, and the other ladies shook their heads knowingly.

'Don't you worry, you're safe. You come inside now.'

Motioned to wait in the corridor, I watched an old man shuffle slowly by, holding out a frail hand to the wall for balance. A woman in a white dressing gown walked past in slippers, varicose veins on view for anyone tired enough to be crouching down against the wall because there were no chairs. I stood up.

Minutes later, one of the fur-coated ladies came back. 'It's OK. We've found your bike. It will be here soon. Then I will take you to the *Administratsiya*. They have said you can sleep at the hospital tonight. You will be safe there.'

That wasn't the first time I'd stayed in a hospital on a bike tour. It wasn't to be the last either. The following week, I was again directed to the hospital as a substitute for a guesthouse. Neither of these Russian hospitals lacked for cleanliness. The starched linen on the beds, the bathroom that doubled as a laundry room and the excellent canteen all seemed underused. The lack of patients suggested one of two things: either the population of Artik was incredibly healthy or they preferred to self-medicate. From what I'd seen, their choice cure was vodka.

I had let the whole Vyacheslav episode get way out of control. I hoped I hadn't gotten him into too much trouble. If he hadn't been drunk; if I hadn't been so tired and hadn't drunk any vodka, I'm sure I could have handled the situation much better.

That was the low point of the trip. The next day, though, was a good day. A long one, too. It always surprises me how the best of times follow the worst of times. It shouldn't. After all, it's precisely because you hit an all-time low that the following things take on such a positive glow. Why exactly I enjoyed the next day so much, I cannot say. What I can say is that I was perfectly content, despite things not going entirely to plan.

27.

Six months later and enjoying the lingering end of the British summer, Yakutia and that cycle ride are but a distant memory. My experiences there are so far removed from my present reality, I could be convinced that it was all a dream. I have photos of myself there as proof. But I look at these now and see another person staring back at me. I look at that person and wonder what made her yearn to go there. If, while on my travels, I had looked at a photo of myself at my desk in an open-plan characterless office or staring blankly ahead at the car in front while stuck in a traffic jam, I would have had an equally hard time assimilating it as my own reality, not someone else's life.

You see, I am living two incompatible lives, destined never to be entirely satisfied with what only one can offer. One provides safety and security, long-term friendships and family for support, a regular income and comforts of an easy life. The other offers challenges and adventures, new friends and independence and, ultimately, freedom. I enjoy both lifestyles, but there always comes a time when I crave the other. The only times of total satisfaction are when life is rushing past like a freight train and I am racing to catch up and jump on board; when there is no time to think, just act. The problem is when I get a seat on that train and my world slows down to one of a rhythmic trundling of wheels down an inescapable track with scheduled stops, I tire of the routine and stability and look out of the window and see my other life. It looks so exhilarating and exciting, and all I need do is leap from the carriage to have all those things I don't have on board.

As the days passed in Yakutia, I began questioning a few of the things I was seeing. When I saw an aeroplane smoke trail the day before I reached Artik, it was as though the white line cutting the clear blue sky in half had been painted there just to break the monotony. A plane seemed out of place so far from civilisation. As I looked up at it, fascinated because it was so out of the ordinary, it made me feel less alone, more connected. Hell, did I imagine that plane just to feel less isolated and more normal? No, *that* would be crazy.

And what about the morning I woke up to the sound of the *vargan*? I call it a vargan because that's what Nikolai called it. It's the local Siberian name for the Jew's harp or mouth harp. I had gotten talking to Nikolai in Khuzir on Olkhon Island weeks earlier when I was still at Lake Baikal. We were waiting for a ride back to Irkutsk. A tall, lean young guy, pale like a true local with black, scruffy hair and the first growth of an attempted beard, his jeans needed a wash and his thick roll-neck woollen jumper was of the kind made by a babushka. He had no designer outdoor gear. His fingerless mitts had holes even where the fingers didn't go.

Nikolai said he liked to play music and asked whether I minded if he played a tune. Well, of course not, I said. He took out a little box; I thought it might be a harmonica. Instead, it looked like a wooden key. Nikolai put the vargan to his mouth, clasping it between his hands as if it were a fragile bird, then leaned back against the chair, closed his eyes and began to play.

He strummed his thumb against the metal pin, which vibrated while the air passed through the wooden key and hummed a soft, strange tone. Warming up slowly, it was a hypnotising, mesmerising sound that filled the room so there was only us and the music. Nikolai used circular breathing; the music was never interrupted. Gradually the tempo increased, the beat grew louder, and he rocked back and forth in time. Then right at the climax, he stopped.

Silence.

A few moments passed before either one of us spoke.

'You'll hear that sound again in Yakutia,' Nikolai foretold. 'They call the vargan a *khomus* there. It's the only instrument native to this region. We're too poor to have guitars.' And he laughed – at himself, at Siberia, at Russia. I laughed with him. On my travels so far, it is only the Siberians who can laugh at themselves in the way we Brits understand – in that self-deprecating, mocking way.

I remember thinking of Nikolai when I woke one morning in my sleeping bag. I'd camped out in my bivvy bag rather than putting up the tent. It was still dusky when I roused, hearing a soft sound emanating faintly through the wilderness. The vargan, I thought. *But it can't be.* I had no idea where the nearest settlement was, except that it wasn't close. I listened harder, lifting the hats from my ears and holding my breath and remaining motionless; the sound continued. It sounded like panpipes in the background too.

To this day, I wonder if I imagined that music. I doubt it. It was more beautiful than anything I could create and more complex than the sound of the wind through the trees. It was as beautiful as the first rays of sun reaching me as I lay in my sleeping bag, even though I was wedged in the rut of old tyre tracks that had since been covered in snow.

The music, like the aeroplane, was as foreign to the Siberian wilderness as I was. They proved the presence of other people. And that was why I questioned them. Even animal prints in the snow could be a figment of my imagination, another thing to convince myself I was not entirely alone. Until Ust-Nera, I'd not seen a single animal besides the hardy Yakut horses and the ubiquitous black crow in weeks. I recognised some footprints as hare and others as small cats. I even spotted massive ones in the distance running parallel to the road that, by their size, I presumed must be bear. I pedalled faster. I really hoped I wouldn't see a bear; I could live with crazy.

So, what was real and what was imagined? When I could no longer trust my own mind, who could I trust?

The wheels turned freely, aided by a gentle decline and tailwind. Fine snow snaked along the road in wispy tails like sand in the Sahara. When a lorry passed, the snow whipped up into a cloud and sprinkled over me. The dusty specks melted at the touch of my warm face – such a delicate, ephemeral existence – and, as with my frosty breaths, I watched as they were swallowed into oblivion by the immense Siberian atmosphere.

At the opposite side of the windswept plain, I rounded a bend and began pedalling uphill. Gradually, warmth returned to my body. I stopped to delve into the bag of individually wrapped chocolates I had been given by one of the nurses. Some had velvety caramel inside, others were rich truffle or soft fudge. All were now rock solid and cold, so as to barely register any taste. Still, it was energy that I needed, and I was sick of the trail mix I'd been eating for weeks. I'd singled out and scoffed the M&M's a long time ago; now the mix was a cluster of peanuts with the odd cashew or raisin outcast. As my aching jaws were straining to chew yet another chocolate, an old truck passed. I took that as my cue to start moving again.

Minutes later, as I reached the top of the hill, I spotted the old truck parked up at the roadside. The driver leant out of the window and invited me in for tea. I climbed up and squeezed in next to his wife, who was along for the ride. They had a family-run business buying and selling goods between Magadan and Ust-Nera. We sat in the cabin, shared our food and made small talk. They offered me a lift. I said no. They didn't insist. It was mid-March now, and spending time outside was not such an incomprehensible endeavour.

On the map, two villages were nearby on my route. I expected to pass them that day. They offered hope of human contact and conversation, perhaps a cup of tea and somewhere to relax for a while. I was optimistic about finding something, as the lady who worked for the Artik *Administratsiya* had mentioned these villages.

I'd learnt not to expect a village because it was marked on the map. Unlike European maps, maps of remote areas of Asia and Africa are more like guidelines, subject to the whims and artistic creativity of the map maker, never mind the changing landscape due to famine and war and other such population-changing disasters that so rarely affect Europe in such a dramatic way.

Delyankir was little more than a check point. A group of workmen were congregated on the bridge clearing snow. Snow ploughs made easy work of clearing the roads, but bridges, being narrower and uneven, had to be cleared by less industrial means. Shovels in mittened hands, high-vis jackets buttoned up to the chin, trapper hats pulled low over their ears, their eyes followed me as I passed, mouths agape in stunned silence.

Ozernoe resembled a village structurally, but it was a shell of a former community. I stopped where the trees thinned out on the raised bank above the frozen flood plain and looked towards the houses. The outer walls were crumbling or tilting drunkenly, one stage before collapse. The only sign that people might live there was that the track off the road looked compacted and clear of fresh snow. I considered going to look, but the effort required overwhelmed my curiosity.

28.

I was in a good mood. The cycling was easy as I sang along to music. Apart from the couple of trucks that had passed earlier in the morning, I'd had this little piece of Yakutia all to myself. I rather liked it.

All day it had been overcast, the landscape dulled in the half-light. Devoid of shadows, it appeared lifeless. The valley had widened, the hills receding from the road. Now, the only trees appeared as stubbly five o'clock shadow on the shrunken hillsides.

I descended the embankment and crossed undulating terrain, a never-ending series of gradual rises and falls going on and on to the unreachable horizon, until, what seemed to be hours later, I crossed a river. There was nothing to see on either side. All around, it was a white world. There was no one and nothing there. If the end of the world were a place, this is how I imagined it would be.

The silence was deafening.

I needed to hear something. Anything. Another voice, to know I wasn't alone. Perhaps I should have shouted out. At least I would have heard my own voice. But I thought that would be a crazy thing to do. Instead, I stayed silent and listened to the voices rattling on inside my head.

So this is the End of the World.

'The end of the road, you mean,' sighed Andrei.

'No, I mean the End of the World. I keep telling you,' I insisted.

'Look, it's not the end of the road or the end of the world. You're in the middle of nowhere, talking to yourself again.'

'Yeah, I know I'm fucking crazy.'

'Too right. It could be worse, you could be sane.'

'Hell, I wouldn't know. We're crazy and free.'

'And this is the best place to be that. No one cares what you do out here. Siberia's the last great wilderness; here we live by our own rules. So, you gonna stand here for the rest of time and die of cold? Or shall we go find the end of the road?'

'Yeah, let's go see what lies beyond the End of the World.'

You know who I bumped into beyond the End of the World? Not Bogdan; although, that wouldn't have surprised me. It was Sasha (another one).

This Sasha was a truck driver (another one). He stopped in the middle of the road, wound down the window and asked (I'm sure you can guess) if I would like a cup of tea. (I'm sure you can guess my answer too.)

Sasha, like Bogdan, didn't fit the mould of a truck driver. He was quiet and caring, his character more suited to nursing an injured animal back to health than driving vast distances across frozen wastes. But man must make ends meet any way he can. Truck driving is as honest a living as any, even if it's not a glamorous one. Besides, parts of the job must appeal to someone of a contemplative nature – all those hours alone, with nothing but the changing lay of the land and gradual transition of daylight from morning to night to distract. Then I wonder, is it these things that attract a certain kind of person or do they transform them?

As my grasp of the Russian language had advanced as slowly as my progress along the Road of Bones, rather than discussing the finer points of Russian culture or the deeper meaning of life, we instead limited our talk to the state of the road ahead and the day's temperature: currently a balmy fifteen – that's minus fifteen. Sasha wasn't the talkative type, but sometimes another person's presence is company enough.

Sasha reckoned it was thirty kilometres over a pass to the next village. He said there was a shop there. Now, I don't know if it was his Russian blue eyes shining brightly in the dull light, pulling me in as though they were portholes to his soul, that made me believe him. Probably, I heard the word 'shop', imagined food and warmth and people, and decided I must reach there by nightfall. It was a completely irrational thought. Thirty kilometres and a big hill to climb with little remaining of the day on tired legs from the ninety kilometres I'd already pedalled since breakfast. Any one of those things should have been enough to convince me that I would not make the village that day.

Still, with a smile, I set off from Sasha's truck that remained parked in the middle of nowhere. Wonderful scenarios of how my day would end whirled around in my mind like autumn leaves kicked up and spun around on the breeze. Mostly those images involved a warm, dry place. They were to be swept away with a forceful gust, leaving only the bare-branched reality of winter.

The sun had set by the time I reached the top of the pass. All the while, as I had pushed my bike ever onwards, ever upwards, the setting sun and darkening sky and first stars appearing all told me I should stop and camp. But I was perfectly content plodding steadily along. Besides, the road to the pass wound up a steep-sided valley. The rocky edges rising up on my left and a steep drop looming to my right forced me onwards.

I freewheeled fast down the other side of the pass. Wrapped up in all my layers and warmed only by my hopes of what lay ahead, I looked over my shoulder to watch the last glimmers of light change to a luminous cerise and, too quickly, darken to black. Then, as the road flattened out, I pedalled furiously. I hadn't cycled this fast the entire trip. I ignored the possibility of hitting some unseen object in the road and focused on the faint distant lights flickering through the darkness, which kept alive my dream of a shop and a warm place.

Those damn lights never seemed to get closer. Kilometres passed. I kept on pedalling, perfectly content except for the hunger gnawing at my stomach. Every so often I would think that I was getting closer, but then the road would swerve away from the river and the lights would disappear from view. So I pedalled on, optimism fading, until I thought that I must have reached those lights by now, only to notice that they had now reappeared, transported to the other side of the river. To be so close to them, yet further away than ever. With reluctance, I turned my head away from the lights. No good would come from dwelling on what would never be. The lights were behind me now. Instead, I looked at what lay ahead. And would you believe that I saw another faint light in the distance! It was so faint – fainter than the stars – and when I blinked, I lost sight of it and then stared and strained and searched the black space beyond until my hopes were rekindled with a flicker. But there comes a time when your body needs real food for energy. Hopes and dreams will only fuel you for so long. I endured the burning muscles in my legs because the pain meant that I was still warm. Once that stopped, I would feel the cold instead.

I stopped to turn on my GPS. My margins of safety and sensibility had dwindled; now it was going to be a fine calculation. The question was no longer about when I would reach this village Sasha had talked about – which, by the way, was definitely further than thirty kilometres away – the question was could I reach this village today? According to the GPS, it was five kilometres further. *I can do that.*

Eventually, the 'village' came into view. It was a large collection of buildings spread along the river, hemmed in by the silhouette of a hillside rising up behind it. Those buildings were decrepit, crumbling, rusted skeletons. Another abandoned village? *Sasha, you lying bastard! What now?*

Then I spotted a light in a small wooden house and was instinctively drawn towards it.

I knocked on the door. And waited. A dog barked viciously.

I knocked again. And heard noises.

I waited for whatever was going to happen next. I mean, this was clearly not a shop. *Who the hell lives out here, alone, anyway? Peaceful hermits or psycho cyclist-killers?*

The door creaked open and a tall, tough-looking man stepped out. *Not the hermit type.* I spotted the chopped wood piles beside the house. *So he knows how to wield an axe.* Suddenly, it struck me that camping far from here was the better option. *Come on, now. There can't be much passing trade for psycho cyclist-killers. Get a grip.*

The psycho cyclist-killer stood there in silence staring at me. Thinking about it later, I suppose he too was weighing me up: foolish tourist or murderous psycho-tramp? Either way, we both thought the other had a screw loose. I mean, what other reason was there to explain our both being out there, in some frozen hell beyond the End of the World?

'Er ... um ... Hi, how are you? I'm looking for the shop.'

'Shop? What?'

'I'm looking for a shop.' *I can't believe I'm having this conversation.* Of course there was no shop. But at that moment, I couldn't think of anything else to say that might explain my being stood on his doorstep. Except that I was a psycho-tramp.

'There's no shop here,' he replied gruffly. He sounded heartless. He stood on the boundary of his house like a guard. His stiff shoulders and braced stance said he would defend his home to the death. *Sod this. Let's get the hell out of here.*

'How far to the next village with a shop?'

205

'Fifteen kilometres.' *Fifteen!*

I cycled those fifteen kilometres that evening. And more. Because after fifteen kilometres there was no village. Or shop. The lying bastard. There were lights. They were what had kept me going. Lights and hope. While I was cycling, I was warm. Well, not so cold as if I stopped. *If only I could keep cycling right through to sunrise.* I didn't want to stop and camp because I didn't want to stop and be cold.

I'd persevered because of the lights in the distance. And you know what was at those lights? Some industrial site guarded by ferocious, rabid-sounding dogs. I didn't dare enter the grounds for fear of being mauled to pieces. So I pedalled on.

And that's when I saw yet more lights. But this time they were moving. Moving towards me. Like headlights. Only bigger. And so high above the ground that they couldn't possibly be a vehicle. At least, not a vehicle I'd seen before.

Out of the Siberian night silence came a distant rumbling. I stopped to listen and decipher the sound. *What is it?* The noise got louder and louder until it filled the air, and I couldn't tell from which direction it was coming. It was as if the very bowels of the earth were grumbling in discontent. Then I saw the outline that was moving with the lights. It thundered towards me, growing larger and larger. The lights grew brighter and nearer, and the great rumbling sound filled the air until I couldn't have heard my own shouts if I had bothered to call out. The monstrous, earth-moving, ground-shaking, thundering beast bore down on me on a collision course. Blinded by the lights, I could not tell how wide it was. Would I be run over and the driver never know his roadkill? I stopped and looked around frantically for an escape route. The high-sided snow walls blocking in the road left few options. I would have to ditch the bike and all my belongings and dive into the snow.

Then it was upon me. I edged closer to the side of the road and watched. It was the wheels I saw first, rolling past, towering above my height. I looked up just in time to see a microscopic insect of a man at the controls inside the machine's cabin. How could such a small creature as man control such a giant, lumbering, rumbling mammoth? The machine never slowed. It was gone from view before the last sound of its existence left my world.

So, beyond the End of the World, there are no shops. It's guarded by a psycho cyclist-killer, giant rabid dogs and an army of mammoth machines. Yeah, more of the machines passed me that night. Images of Judgment Day from *Terminator* flickered through my mind. The mining industry stops for no man. Dissection and disembowelling of the earth for its mineral riches will not stop until every last drop of life has been extracted.

In a peaceful interlude, I stopped to investigate my surroundings and look for a place to camp. I fumbled blindly in my pannier for my head torch and turned it on. The snow sparkled like diamonds and the ice in the air shimmered and flickered like glitter. The torch lit only the steamy heat emanating from me, which was as thick as smoke. I couldn't see a damn thing through it. I turned off the torch and pedalled out into the dark, clear air.

Eventually I came to a river. On the far side of the bridge, a track ran down to it. I pulled off the road and finally, twelve hours and 155 kilometres after leaving Artik, I found my place to sleep that night: on a bed of snow with the stars my blanket. Before that, I ate noodles for dinner followed by the remaining rich chocolates for dessert. Then I leant back and watched the moon rise. It was magical and dreamlike. It was the first night that it felt warm enough to sit outside, relax and read my book. The thermometer read minus thirty-five degrees when I finally rolled over and closed my eyes.

29.

When I woke, the thermometer still read minus thirty-five degrees, but the sun was already rising. I fired up the stove, read my book and wondered what today would have in store. A shop, I hoped.

It was not far to Kadykchan. There was a shop there, the psycho cyclist-killer had told me. What he had failed to mention was that it was three kilometres from the main road. Three kilometres each way seemed an inordinately long detour for my tired legs, when I couldn't be sure of the reward at the end. I pedalled on, content enough. There was a cafe further on, I was told by a passing driver.

Not another lying bastard! At the crossroads, which appeared in the middle of nowhere, with side roads going to who knows where, several trucks were pulled over in a lay-by. There was a derelict building. Probably, at one time, there was a cafe. Now, however, you had to make your own coffee and snacks. I pulled out my thermos and looked longingly at the truck drivers. It wasn't even the idea of food and hot drink inside a heated vehicle that was so tempting. I just wanted someone real to talk to. Shamelessly, I went and asked for a top-up of water, knowing full well I'd be invited to join them.

We sat and talked and ate, and we watched the buses come down from Kadykchan further north, and up from the south from I've no idea where, and turn off left and right down the side roads. People on their way to work, silent and glum, stared blankly ahead or out of the windows. They looked haggard and tired. Tired of life; tired of living. The truck drivers, though, were a different breed. We laughed and joked. Then we said goodbye and went our separate ways.

The natural lie of the land had been disturbed here. By the river, the earth had been moved and quarried into ridges. With the snow covering, there was something beautiful about it, like a landscaped garden. In summer, the bare earth and damage would be exposed, the raw wilderness transformed, never to return to the way it was.

Crumbling, empty, concrete high-rises littered the land. The wooden remains of a gulag, collapsing with age and under the weight of the snow, hinted of harsher times. The snow clung to the trees in clumps like cotton candy, but the trunks' tall shadows reached across the road like prison bars. This road is a museum through time; winter has freeze-framed each episode of history. The snow, like the Russians' memories and the Road of Bones, tries to hide it all, but it is all there under the surface, never to be entirely erased or forgotten.

After the previous day's massive effort, Susuman was now only 115 kilometres away. My legs were still tired and needed rest, but I decided to push on to Susuman. This was a major town according to Bolot's hand-drawn map. Visions of hotels, busy restaurants, a plethora of convenience stores and the hubbub of city life spurred me on. I should have known better.

The outskirts of the town were only derelict buildings. Then I rounded the bend and the city vista opened up in front of me. *Ugh. No!* A towering, blackened smokestack loomed over the city. Thick smoke rose from it and spread outwards, defacing the subdued pink sky. The rest of the buildings appeared diminished in the shadow of that colossal eyesore. They looked dull and lifeless. The streets were empty.

My heart sank into the pitiless depths of the well it had fallen into at the similarly depressing sight of Kyubeme. Too many times in the last days had my hopes been dashed. No, dashed doesn't come close to describing it. They were battered, bruised and squeezed, slung against the wall, picked up and ripped to shreds, and the fallen remains trampled over to finish them off. Those hopes, however small or seemingly unimportant looking back now, were what had kept me going. I had found that my body could keep going, even when it was beyond tired and aching, as long as my mind willed it to.

I stopped and leant over the handlebars, staring out across the urban wasteland. My mind drifted. It didn't drift off to another time or place, to memories or imaginations. I was too tired to create anything. I was nowhere. It was as though I had been transported back to the End of the World where nothing existed. Everything, quite simply, ceased to be.

I was snapped out of my trance by the cold nipping at my toes. I ignored it.

'Find a hotel, get warm and get food. Then you can rest,' Tatiana whispered with her hand on my shoulder.

'I know,' I sighed, seeing my present depressing reality.

'Then you can sleep as long as you like. But not out here. Not now.'

'I know,' I replied and pedalled off in search of a hotel. Pedalling and looking for hotels didn't require any thought, only action.

Could I find the hotel? No.

Could I find the hotel when a passer-by gave directions and pointed out a building? No.

Could I find the hotel when I turned on my GPS, which gave the exact location? No. Because the hotel looked like every other building: anonymous. There was no sign indicating it was a hotel. Nothing.

I asked three locals, 'Are you sure this is the hotel?'

They confirmed that the building I was circling was the hotel.

I circled it again, looking for the entrance. Could I find the way in? No.

The doors were locked.

I asked the three locals again, 'Are you sure this is the hotel?'

They pointed the way. All the doors except one were locked. The unlocked one looked like every other. I had given up by then and assumed the hotel must be closed down.

I entered through the unlocked door. There were more doors, but they were all locked, except one. I opened it into an empty, high-ceilinged, wooden-floored room resembling a school sports hall. I closed the door. The concrete stairwell looked straight from a 1960s failed inner-city housing project. I exited the building.

I asked the three locals again, 'Are you sure this is the hotel?'

They indicated I must go up the stairs.

I entered again through the door and went up the several flights of concrete stairs. I don't recall exactly how many flights there were, except that it was too many for my tired legs. At the top of the stairs, there was a door. It was open and had a small sign indicating that this was a hotel.

I walked over to reception, asked for a bed, was handed a key and shown the room. Then I went back down all the stairs, collected some bags, walked back up the stairs, and repeated this twice more for my other bags and then the bike. Finally, I could take off my heavy winter boots and hats and gloves and jacket, collapse on the bed and close my eyes.

'You need food before you sleep. And you'll feel better if you have a shower,' Tatiana whispered.

'I know.'

I opened my eyes.

I got up off the bed and walked to reception and asked about a restaurant. The lady said there was no restaurant in the hotel; I had no difficulty believing that. She also said there was no restaurant in the town. The whole town! I expressed mild surprise, mainly because the overwhelming tiredness I was feeling did not allow for anything other than the slightest of gestures. She said that there were several convenience stores where I could buy food.

I went back to my room and put on my boots and jacket and hat and gloves, walked back down the stairs, exited the nameless hotel, walked through the icy streets under the light of the moon until I found a corner shop where I bought instant noodles and beer and chocolate, then returned the way I had come, along the street, into the nameless hotel, up the stairs and into my room where I took off my boots and jacket and hat and gloves. I went and asked the receptionist for hot water to soak the noodles in. Then I returned to my room and dug out my penknife to pop the top off the beer bottle. I sat down on the bed and leant against the wall, took one long, deep swig of cold Sibirskaya Corona and shut my eyes.

'Your hot water,' a voice whispered from the doorway. It was not Tatiana. It was the receptionist. I didn't know her name.

I opened my eyes.

I finished the beer while the noodles were cooking in the hot water, then scoffed the noodles, devoured the chocolate and lay back down on the bed. The shower could wait until the morning. I had more pressing needs.

I closed my eyes. And I disappeared into a world of utter darkness where all was silent and peaceful.

When I woke, I felt refreshed. It's amazing what a good night's sleep can do. Like a computer that has crashed and been rebooted, I now functioned as I was designed to. My mind was alert. My body, however, was still exhausted.

I stayed two more nights. I read and ate during the day, and slept deeply and dreamlessly during the night like an innocent newborn. I would have stayed to rest longer, but I couldn't justify the expense. I needed a proper meal too; instant noodles were not going to restore my strength. Besides, there would be time to rest later. There are things I still want to do, and I couldn't do them in Susuman.

My body wanted to stay put and never move from that hotel again, regardless of the cost, but my mind was frantic, banging on the walls, searching to escape. I tried to sit back and read, but my eyes only scanned the words on the page. My mind wasn't taking in a single sentence; it was off elsewhere, darting to and fro like a hyperactive child, relentless. *Come on, come on, get up, let's go do stuff.* My body screamed, 'Leave me alone!' But my mind kept pestering, poking and prodding. Inside, my nerves twitched electrically. When I'm on edge like that, there is no peace.

I reluctantly forced my body to move. Without thought, I packed my bags, got kitted up, carried everything down the stairs and attached the panniers to the bike, lifted my tired leg over the crossbar of the bike frame and, with a wobble, started pedalling.

It felt good to be breathing in the sharp, icy cold air. Being cooped up indoors in a hot and stuffy hotel room, surrounded by the mess that accumulates when tightly packed panniers explode and stinking clothes fester and rubbish piles up in the bin, is not a good way to live. Gradually it weighs you down, so that you don't notice the slide into filth and despondency until you manage to escape it.

As I cleared the shadow of the hotel, the blinding brightness of the late morning sun caused my eyes to fill with tears. It was the pain. Every time I blinked, it felt like sand grinding in my eyes, hundreds of tiny pinpricks jabbing into the cornea. I knew if I closed my eyes, the pain would subside. But I could not cycle with my eyes closed. The sunlight, reflecting off the buildings and snow and icy road, was blinding me. It was a relief when I rounded the bend and into shadow as the sun disappeared behind the hills.

This wasn't the first time I had felt the early effects of snow-blindness. I'd suffered the same searing pain other days, though it was becoming worse. As winter drew to a close, the sun strengthened and the days lengthened. My ski goggles, although offering UV protection, were not dark-tinted. They were better suited to the low winter sun and long dusky hours. Now they didn't block out enough light. Or, perhaps, I hadn't been wearing them enough. Back when it was really cold during the daytime, the goggles always misted up and froze over, and I couldn't clear the ice until I got into a warm dry place. I cycled without goggles because I had to see where I was going. I didn't suffer with snow blindness then; the sun was not strong enough. Instead, the freezing wind dried my eyes out, and the moisture from my breath froze onto my eyelashes. When I blinked, they would sometimes get frozen together, my eyelids impossible to prise apart. I would stick a finger over the frozen eyelid until some warmth seeped through the glove and melted the ice.

Now, it was so warm that I sweated profusely; the foam seal around the goggles became saturated and felt slimy. Under the goggles, beads of sweat formed and, unable to evaporate, rolled down my forehead, stinging my eyes. The urge to wipe away the sweat was overwhelming. It was impossible to raise the goggles, wipe my face and replace them without them steaming up and freezing unless I stopped cycling. On the other hand, my sunglasses fogged up instantly because they didn't create a seal around my face. It was fine when I was walking, but as soon as I resumed a cycling position and began pedalling, the steam from my body and breath steamed up the glasses and instantly froze.

It was one hundred kilometres to Yagodnoe, the next town. My map informed me it had a hotel and cafe. I could spend two easy days getting there, then rest again, satiated on a hearty filling meal.

I started thinking about heaped plates of *plov*, bowls of borscht thick with chunky meat and vegetables, and side dishes of *pirozhki*. Of course, this was not what I would actually get, even if there was a cafe to be found. Undoubtedly, there would be a long menu suggesting all manner of wonderful dishes. But this would not resemble reality; availability would be limited to one or two standard meals on the list. Yes, there would be *plov*, but it would be a fraction of a meal-sized portion. I would have to order three plates to be close to satisfied. The borscht would be watery soup with only one or two pieces of meat. The *pirozhki* would not be the meat-filled ones available further west, but bland-tasting potato-filled or barely palatable cabbage-filled ones. Still, better than instant noodles. Or Choco-pies.

Someone waving from a pulled-over vehicle broke my concentration. I pedalled over to say hello. I hadn't met anyone to have a friendly conversation with in a while. I'd spoken with people in Susuman, but these were practical exchanges: paying for the room, asking directions, buying food.

The man with the shaved head was all smiles. 'Would you like a drink?' he called out from the passenger seat.

I peered in and saw the driver and two others in the back. They were all jovial. I suspected vodka. I definitely didn't want vodka. I wanted conversation.

'We have tea. Come on. Drink some tea. We can give you a lift if you want. Where are you going?' I didn't want a lift. I began reeling off my well-honed explanation as to why I was here, cycling in winter.

Vadim the driver interrupted, 'Come and get in while we're talking. It's warmer in here.'

The bald guy got out of the passenger seat and into the back. I leant my bike against the vehicle and climbed in to take his place. The banter was good medicine for my fatigue.

'Why didn't you want to get in the vehicle with us?' one of the guys asked.

'Oh, I … um …' I stuttered. 'I thought you were drinking vodka.'

Vadim interrupted, 'Oh, no, not now. We're on the way to work.' It seemed to me that work was as much a reason to drink as to abstain out here. 'And yes, you need to be careful. You're a woman travelling alone. It's probably safer if you don't get involved with men drinking vodka.'

'You're right about that. I've learnt that lesson.'

'But you're safe here. We're all good guys.' Vadim smiled broadly again.

After tea, we went our separate ways. I had needed that inconsequential conversation, not just for the social interaction; it reminded me that most people in this world are good. I should not let one negative experience taint my view.

30.

I knew the Tatiana I encountered in Susuman was a figment of my imagination; it was the same with Bogdan, Masha, Misha the penguin, and Andrei. Yet, somehow, Tatiana's gentle touch, which had helped me to find the strength to do what I needed at the end of the day, felt very real. More real than feeling nothing at all.

The slide into unreality had been as imperceptible with each passing day as was my progress along the Kolyma Highway. It was only when I stopped and looked back down the road that I noticed how far I had descended. My concern was that I liked it. This new world I was creating around me that merged reality with my imagination was fascinating. I still knew what was real and what was not, but I wanted to go further. Something was pulling me in.

Curiosity can be dangerous, especially when you don't understand what it is you are playing with. The mind, like the oceans, is vast and deep; only part of the surface has been explored. Fathoms of a dark, mysterious, unknown world remain untouched. I wanted to know what else my unconscious, dreaming mind was capable of. But what would happen if I continued to be drawn into this new world? Would reality subside and slowly melt away until all that was left was my own imagination? The idea intrigued me. And scared me. I wanted to get as near as I dare without going that step too far. I wanted to walk right up to the cliff and wriggle my toes over the edge. The risk was that once you've gone over the edge of insanity, there's no way back. However strong the pull, I knew I had too much to live for in the real world. I was not ready to lose touch.

It was Sasha (yet another one) who finally dragged me back to reality. Still, I was sad that my experimental trials into the realm of unreality came to an end, my fictional world destroyed. Try as I might over the next week, I couldn't conjure up Tatiana, Bogdan, Masha, Misha the penguin, or Andrei. I didn't need them anymore, so my mind carelessly discarded them like empty bottles. It was for the best, for my sanity. It didn't stop me thinking about what might become of them. I could continue their stories, even if they weren't a part of mine.

This Sasha was not Sasha who was my almost-twin or Sasha who was Vyacheslav's co-conspirator or Sasha the truck driver whom I met beyond the End of the World. This was Sasha the truck driver from Yagodnoe who signalled to me like an incoming plane.

He had passed me in his truck, stopped, wound down the window and asked me where I was going, what I was doing, where I was from and what I did for work. *Rabotat*, work, was a common word in the Russian language. What a person did for a living was important. It was not that any one job was more important than another, only that every person fulfilled a different role in life, and that was in some way explained by the work they did. It was no use saying I was an engineer; the reply was always, 'What sort?' It's hard enough to explain what sort of engineer I am in English, and I didn't know the word for ejection seat in Russian. Instead, I said I was an aerospace engineer, which is what I studied.

So, when Sasha had stopped again further down the road and saw me catching him up, that's why he signalled me to stop as if I were a plane, calling out: 'Why do you cycle? You're an aviation engineer;

you must know it's quicker to fly!'

Yes, I had been the butt of that joke before. I laughed. It's surprising how easy it is to laugh along with another person. It's the same with smiles. If I'm having a bad day, the best solution is to smile at a stranger. They will invariably smile back and that makes the world a brighter, happier place.

Sasha had poured a mug of tea for me, which was balanced on the truck's front bumper. A row of *confetti*, individually wrapped chocolates, was laid out alongside. 'Please,' Sasha said, 'these are for you.'

This Sasha seemed like a guy who would get on amicably with anyone, who judged no one, who accepted everyone for who they were. There are not many people in the world like that. A lively character in a large body, he was closer to what I had imagined a stereotypical trucker to be. Although by then, I knew that for every stereotype, there are countless counter-examples.

Sasha wrote his phone number neatly onto a scrap of paper while I chewed laboriously on frozen toffees. 'I live in Yagodnoe. When you get there, call me. You can come and stay with me. There's no need for camping or hotels. Please, phone me.'

'OK,' I replied, although I wasn't sure if I would. The distasteful memory of Vyacheslav in Artik still made me wary. My instinct told me Sasha was a genuinely good guy; I reminded myself that most people are. It wasn't that I'd lost faith in other people; I had lost faith in my own judgement. Besides, I hate making phone calls, especially with a major language barrier; though, I can be very resourceful when necessary. Back in Tommot, when I'd been given the phone number of (the real) Tatiana's friend, I'd had no problem explaining my predicament to a waitress and getting her to phone on my behalf. The difference now was that the daytime temperature was closer to minus fifteen than minus forty. The idea of camping was not dreadful but appealing.

It turned out to be a wonderful day for cycling. The gently descending road as it followed the river provided respite for my tired legs. I cycled in silence beneath the towering icy rock faces, scared that the slightest whisper might cause a terrible cascade of snow and rock. Road signs warned of avalanches. Bolot had warned me of the risk of avalanches in this area, showing me photos of one that had wiped out one of the vehicles in the group he was driving with. Fortunately, the vehicle was towed out, and the passengers were unhurt. 'It's dangerous,' he warned. 'You should probably get a lift.'

I didn't get a lift.

I was alone. There was no lift to get. It was hours since I'd left Sasha; I'd seen no traffic since. And I was glad of that. I was enjoying the cycling too much. If a vehicle had passed, I would have felt compelled to flag it down. Instead, I pedalled faster; my heart beat faster, gripped by fear again: like the fear of lions in Botswana and that of falling through the ice of Lake Baikal.

As I neared Yagodnoe, knowing I wouldn't have to camp if I didn't want to, I began making plans for my arrival. I was famished; my first stop would be a cafe.

In the last few kilometres, the volume of traffic had increased dramatically, as had the number of times I was stopped and asked the usual questions. I'd forgotten about the curiosity I aroused. Unfortunately, my empty stomach made me impatient.

Five kilometres before Yagodnoe, an approaching car, with the driver's window wound down, slowed as it passed. I didn't stop. The driver spoke quickly. I couldn't understand him. He smiled as though he knew me. His face did look familiar. *Where do I know this person from?* I smiled back and waved; although, by then he had already passed. It was a fleeting encounter. I looked back to get another glimpse of the car. Had I seen it before? It was slowing down. *Oh no, don't turn around.*

It turned around. The car pulled up alongside me. This time I stopped. There was a woman in the passenger seat. I bent down, pulled my jacket hood and headband down to hear better and peered through the window.

'Hi,' I said. I still hadn't the first clue who it was, but I could tell they knew me.

'This is my woman, Talia. I told her I met this young woman on a bicycle and had invited her to stay. We've been hoping you would call and have been trying to work out when you would arrive. Well, Talia suggested we come and look for you. You couldn't be far away, we thought. And here you are.' *Sasha!*

The reason I hadn't recognised him was that without his truck, a part of his identity was missing. It always surprises me how little of the world around us we actually register and take in. Big bold Sasha in his *valenkis*, thick padded jacket and fur trapper's hat, standing tall outside his truck, was a different-looking man to the one in the shirt, crouched in the rusted car with a woman on his arm. I had failed to look at the person underneath the accessories.

'Talia thought it better she came along too. You know, so you can see I'm not some strange man. She thought you might be scared of a man inviting you to his home. But here, you can see now, it is safe. I want you to feel welcome in our country.'

I laughed; my fears and suspicions vanished.

'OK, come on. We can talk more later. It will be dark and cold soon. Follow us. We will drive slowly.'

'Er … how far is it?'

'Not far. Don't worry, you'll be fine. We live on the far side of town, but it's only two or three kilometres away. It's all downhill.'

It was all downhill except for the last 500 metres, which were very much uphill.

Sasha and Talia lived in a modest pink cottage on the outskirts of town. It was quaint and picturesque with a snow-covered roof and long, glassy icicles of longsword proportions hanging off the eaves. Where the snow had built up and not been cleared, it surrounded the cottage like a hedge. Inside, the cottage was bright and clean and homely.

'Don't worry about taking your boots off,' Sasha said. I did worry about my boots. They were my only boots, worn always when outdoors, also worn when frequenting the Siberian public outhouses. The filth on the soles didn't bear thinking about. I also worried about the stench of sweaty, festering feet. At least the socks were clean on that morning. I took my boots off. By a margin, it was the lesser of two evils.

It was a lovely evening that passed too quickly. Most of the time was spent sitting at the kitchen table. There was no shortage of food. Or drink. I opted for beer. Sasha and Talia drank vodka. Despite my being very dehydrated, beer was at least a safer option than vodka. Oh, how naive! Sasha, like every Russian I'd seen drink vodka besides Baba Liliya, made a toast, knocked back the glass in one and promptly refilled it. Talia took a small sip. I swigged my beer.

'OK, enjoy the beer, but you must have one vodka,' Sasha said as he reached into the cupboard for another glass.

'No, no, I'm fine, really,' I stammered. Sasha ignored my protestations, filled up the glass and passed it to me. *Oh, I'm so weak-willed.* When he made another toast, I accepted my fate and necked the shot.

'You know, there is a Russian tradition …' Sasha said as he reached for my empty glass to refill it.

'I know, I know,' I interrupted. 'If I drink one vodka, I must drink three.'

'Hah!' Sasha exclaimed loudly. 'You know Russia well. You have drunk vodka the Russian way before! Do you know this?' he said as he flicked his finger against his neck, suggesting we get drunk.

'Yeah, I understand,' I replied.

'Sasha!' Talia scolded and gave him a firm nudge on his arm. 'Leave her in peace. Let her drink beer if she wants to drink beer. We don't have to get drunk.'

She looked at me and said, 'Don't listen to him. You don't have to drink it.'

'It's OK,' I replied. 'Can I have some more water though?'

'See, it's OK,' Sasha said, smiling. 'You must come again in the summer. This is a lovely country in the summer. We go fishing on the river, not just for a day but for whole weeks. You'd love it. If you like the countryside and camping, there is no better place.' Sasha was not telling me anything I hadn't already been told many times before. Each story filled me with a longing to stay – a week, a month, longer. I knew that was impossible. Instead, a hungry yearning filled me: the urge to return. It is hard to leave a place when you feel an attachment like that.

The more I travel, the more people say to me there can't be many places I haven't been. That is not true; a lifetime is not long enough to see even a fraction of all the places I would like. It's true that the list of places I want to visit is getting shorter. But the list of places I wish to return to is expanding. Siberia is on that list.

It was cloudy the next morning. The land had taken on a dreary aspect; the snow appeared less white, the trees less dark, the defining lines blurred. Any shred of enthusiasm for cycling faded into the dull atmosphere.

Sasha, however, would never let a lack of sunlight dampen his spirits. He pulled back the curtain to reveal a thermometer outside the window. 'It is twenty,' he informed me. He meant minus twenty. 'That is normal for nine o'clock. Cold,' he laughed, 'but not cold for you. You have been cycling in much colder.' I couldn't deny that; besides, like it or not, I couldn't change the weather.

We parted ways. Sasha smiled, Talia waved, and I wobbled down the snow-packed driveway laden with more gifts. I was leaving with

223

more than what fitted into my panniers, though. Sasha and Talia had given me something intangible, yet much more important: human companionship.

31.

I shouldn't have been surprised when it started snowing. Sasha had predicted it; the clouds signalled it. Back home it snows so rarely that when it does we think it a wonderful thing. Even the most miserable grump will take immeasurable pleasure in complaining about the chaos reigning on the icy roads. Here in Siberia, endlessly surrounded by the stuff, the novelty had worn off long ago.

The road signs counted down the kilometres to the next town, Debin. It didn't take long for me to decide I would stay there for the night. On arrival, two women informed me that there was no guesthouse. Instead, they directed me to the hospital. There I spent another night, cosy under starched white sheets, oblivious to the weather outside.

When I peered out of the window in the morning, fresh snow covered everything. My boots were the first to leave footprints down the tree-lined path. The snow was soft and light, not like the heavy packed crust I had to break when searching for places to camp off the road. The painted buildings gave the illusion that it was brighter than it really was. Back on the road, the whiteout was almost total.

I did see the bridge over the Kolyma River. What I didn't see was the pile of shovelled snow filling one side of the road. I cycled right into it. *Oops!* And because there were some workmen on the bridge (presumably the ones who had created this unintended roadblock), I pretended as though I had stopped of my own accord. As if I was fooling anyone. I reached into my handlebar bag, pulled out the map and inspected it closely to see how much further to the next town. Then I steered my bike round the snow and continued on my way.

Early in the afternoon, I turned off the road and freewheeled down to a cafe in Orotukan. Practise and repetition had made my routine slick. There wasn't a single cafe along the Kolyma Highway that I hadn't stopped at.

I parked my bike close to the door, removed the front pannier containing my down jacket, thermos, water bottle and snacks, and lifted off my handlebar bag containing my valuables. I had previously kept the thermos in one of the bottle holders on the bike frame, but these had broken long ago like almost every other plastic item. Half the pannier hooks had also snapped. My bags were secured to the racks with wire and spare straps.

Inside the cafe, I took a free table near the radiator. Radiators had been uncommon earlier in the journey, where rooms were kept warm by the thick hot water pipes running around the walls. As I had several hours before needing to look for a place to camp, I settled down to write my journal. It had been sadly neglected. It gave me great pleasure to be able to write with a pen. Outside, in the cold, only a pencil would work.

Occasionally I looked up and watched different people coming in. This roadside cafe was a popular stop, not dominated by truck drivers and mine workers like cafes before, but by regular couples and families travelling between cities. Leather jackets and jeans for the men and fashionable fur coats for the women were more common than heavy parka jackets and *valenkis*. So many people. People coming, people going, people chatting and laughing.

I'd been in the cafe a couple of hours when one of the young women who worked there came over. She cleared away the plate and empty glass, then returned.

'Excuse me,' she said timidly.

'Yes?' I looked up from my book.

'I hope you don't mind, but me and my colleagues were wondering …' she hesitated, partly out of shyness, partly because she and her colleagues were wondering a lot of things, and she didn't know where to start, 'where have you cycled from?'

I explained. 'From Neryungri.' She gave me a puzzled look like everyone else when I mentioned this town. 'From Neryungri,' I repeated, 'to Yakutsk, then Ust-Nera, Susuman, now here.' As I reeled off the names of the towns along the way, her eyes widened with comprehension.

'But how did you get here?'

'I cycled.'

'No. How did you get to Neryungri?'

'Oh, well, um …' This was the part of the story that always caused great confusion. 'Well, I actually flew to Irkutsk and cycled near Lake Baikal. Then I took the train from Irkutsk to Neryungri.' I waited for the inevitable question.

'But there's no train from Yakutsk.'

'No, I took the train from Irkutsk.'

'But there is no train from Yakutsk. How did you get to Neryungri?' I sighed. I always had this problem. No one could tell the difference between Irkutsk and Yakutsk the way I said them. It was as though Irkutsk, over 3,000 kilometres away, did not exist. Out here, beyond the End of the World, I suppose it didn't. Yakutsk was like the moon, towns beyond that were distant stars, and Moscow – that was always spoken of in a hushed tone like a magic word – was a galaxy on the edge of the universe, invisible to the naked eye, that most people could only dream of.

'Not Ya-kutsk. Ear-rrr-kutsk.' I tried my best to roll my r's. And failed.

'Ah, Irkutsk.' *Yes, that's what I said.* 'Now I understand. But that's so far!' She didn't understand. She stood in silence for a while and then asked, 'Do you make this bicycle journey every year?'

I laughed a grotesque, snort-loudly-and-choke-on-your-drink kind of laugh. That was the funniest thing I'd heard in Russia. She really didn't understand. 'I think once is enough,' I chortled. But that wasn't true. I wanted to come back in the summer. And I still wanted to cycle north to Chersky.

'OK, thank you. I won't disturb you any longer.' She turned to leave.

This was my moment. 'Excuse me. I was wondering …' I was wondering only one thing, 'do you think I could camp here tonight?'

'Of course,' she replied and wandered back to the canteen.

A few minutes later one of the other women walked up to me, 'My colleague said you wanted to camp here.'

'Yes. Is that a problem?'

'No. You can sleep in the cafe. It's open twenty-four hours. There's no need to camp. It's cold outside.'

I'd never slept actually inside a cafe beside other customers before; it felt ludicrous. Have you ever seen someone bunking down with a sleeping bag on the floor of Starbucks? Still, when winter cycling in Siberia, anything goes. I didn't mind the cold, but I couldn't be bothered with putting up the tent, and bivvying out would have surely attracted attention. 'Oh, OK then. Thanks. Where should I sleep?'

'Anywhere you like.' The lady looked around the room. 'Perhaps by the radiator. You will be warm and shouldn't be disturbed too much.'

So that's how, at midnight, I rolled out my Thermarest, laid my sleeping bag on top and crawled into bed. To say I was warm is an understatement. Polar-rated sleeping bags are meant for sleeping outside in extremely cold environments, not for use next to radiators in overheated cafes while wearing thermals because your British reserve prevents you from stripping naked. Come to think of it, unwillingness to strip naked in a cafe has nothing to do with British prudishness. There are times when it's only sensible or sensitive to cover up, like in Muslim countries ... and Siberian cafes. It was too hot and noisy to sleep well.

The next night, I slept significantly better. It had been another wonderful day. The cycling was easy, although my tired legs screamed for a rest. The weather had improved. The snow had stopped. The thick clouds had cleared leaving only a milky veil of cirrostratus for the sun to shine through. It was mid-afternoon when I cycled down to a frozen river. In this area, it was common for temporary tracks to appear on the ice of the frozen rivers; the bridges remained unused in winter, snow piling up and making them dangerous to cross. There was a lot of snow everywhere since the recent fresh fall.

I considered camping at the river crossing, but the appealing flat areas were frozen riverbed where I would spend the night worrying about the ice breaking. The solid land, covered with trees and shrubs under the snow, was definitely not flat. I dismissed the idea of camping there. Instead, I checked my map and identified a track leading off from the main road not much further along. If that didn't lead to a place to camp, there was the village of Myakit beyond.

I should have learnt that Siberia in winter was not the place to be fussy about where to sleep. There was no sign of the track when I passed where the junction should have been. *Damn it*. I checked the distance to Myakit: fifteen kilometres. *Is it really that far?*

I stopped at the top of a rise and could see the road leading down the hill and out over the flat plain straight ahead of me. From this viewpoint, I wasn't optimistic. There were a few buildings in the distance, but something wasn't quite right.

The problem with long straight roads is that the horizon never seems to get nearer. The problem with this specific straight road was that the nearer to the buildings I got, the clearer they became and the greater the dread they caused in me. Myakit began to look less like a village and more like scattered, abandoned buildings. It didn't help that my legs were tired and stomach was empty. Still, there's no point getting too disappointed with the things you can't change. The engineer in me said to stop seeing problems and look for answers. *I'll be able to camp there anyway. Look out for a track leading to one of the buildings. Maybe I can even camp inside one of them.*

Or maybe not. The buildings hadn't been lived in for over a decade. The whole area was covered in over three feet of snow. Rather than expend an inordinate amount of energy shovelling a path for myself and the bike, I continued cycling. *There'll be a place to camp eventually.*

I was so happy when I saw a lay-by up ahead. There was a truck parked there already; hopefully, it would leave soon. There was not a chance in hell that I was going to cycle any further until the next day.

It didn't leave soon.

Instead, the driver invited me to rest in his truck, while he worked on his repairs. When his workmate arrived with the spare parts, we chatted, drank tea and then, when they had finished, they apologised because now they were going to have to leave me stranded in the cold.

I couldn't help but like these guys. We were each on our own journeys through life, but where our paths had crossed, we had decided our lives would be better if we stopped and exchanged stories and showed some kindness to one another. It would be unlikely to alter our destinies, but it made a great difference at that moment. I don't remember their names; I only remember their faces because we took photos before parting ways. I've no idea what we talked about, but I remember clearly that we were all at ease and laughed a lot.

The sky was turning lilac by the time I started digging a place to lay out my bivvy bag. Sleeping out without the tent had worked so well the last time, it didn't seem worth the bother now. By the time I was in my sleeping bag, the thin film of cloud had gone. I lay staring up at the stars.

When I opened my eyes, it was morning. I saw a crow fly high overhead across the blue sky. In the shade of the trees, dug deep into the snow, I'd slept peacefully straight through sunrise. That was my best night's sleep of the trip. How I hoped for more of those. And then I realised there would be only two more nights until I reached Magadan. Suddenly, the trip was nearing an end, and I didn't want it to. I was starting to truly enjoy the winter cycling again.

As if I needed more convincing, the day turned out to be fantastic. Not only were there clear skies, but the temperature was in single figures – that's minus ones, admittedly, but single figures! The road followed the frozen, milky turquoise river, which glistened in the sunlight as though the surface was liquid. There was a smoke trail in the sky from an aeroplane. I didn't question whether it was real or not. I no longer questioned my sanity. And I met lots more people who stopped to talk with me. There were those who asked questions and those who gave me gifts. I finished the day with about five kilograms of extra luggage.

I was given a two-litre bottle of grandma's homemade fruit compote by a good-looking young man on his way home from visiting her 600 kilometres away.

The director of a Kolyma gold mining company stopped in his shiny black 4x4. Once his crew had filmed a short interview with me, he gave me a photo book chronicling his exploits in the industry. The director's photo book weighed about two kilograms and was too big to fit in my panniers. His crew handed me a couple of Kit Kats, which were wholly better conceived gifts, being consumable and calorie intense.

I even had lots of time to stop and take photos. Not that there was anything new to take photos of. I already had hundreds of photos with a repetitive theme. Flicking back through them was monotonous ... Snow. Forest. Snow. The road. Trees. Snow. More snow. The bike. Snow. More trees. Snow on trees. Snow on trees with the bike in the foreground. Icicles. And the odd selfie, in some of which there were icicles hanging off my face mask. Whenever I arrived in town, I took hundreds of photos of buildings instead ... Soviet-style concrete apartment blocks. Abandoned buildings. Falling down buildings. And a few shoddy wooden shacks. But on this day, I took photos simply because I was trying hard to slow down the journey. The nearer I got to Magadan, the further away I wished it was.

If I'd known that this was to be the last good day, I would have slowed down even more. It's not that the next days weren't full of surprises; only that I never had the same feeling of peaceful contentment, that I was where I was meant to be – where everything made sense. Sense was one thing that had been notably absent recently.

32.

It was late afternoon by the time I arrived in Atka, which was a real town with people living there. The town had clearly seen livelier days, though. There used to be 2,000 inhabitants; now there were 200. There appeared little hope of revival; it looked destined to become yet another deserted town along the Kolyma Highway.

It was in the Atka cafe that I met Vova. Vova walked in with blue checked flannel shirt fitted tightly over his stout paunch, which his camouflage army jacket failed to hide. He was a gruff looking guy with an unwashed look and thick stubble covering his double chin. He spoke loudly. It was a tiny cafe, and his rough rasping voice filled the room. It was immediately clear that he liked to talk. There was no possibility of concentrating on reading a book or writing my journal. When he asked if he could sit at my table, I was less than enthralled.

It turned out that Vova owned a spare apartment that he rented out. It was currently empty; I was welcome to stay there.

I followed Vova in his car through the streets of Atka. Like so many towns in this region, it was built on a grid structure and hard to identify the inhabited apartment blocks from the deserted ones.

When Vova had said the apartment was empty, he really meant that the usual occupants were currently out of town. I don't know how long they had been gone for, but it looked like they had just popped out for the day. It felt as if I was intruding. Vova waved away my concerns and told me to make myself at home. He carried my bike up the two floors and deposited it in the narrow hallway adorned with posters of Avril Lavigne, next to a baby buggy. The obligatory tropical pot plant, with long leaves drooping over the sides, stood guard on the sideboard below the mirror.

I wandered through the flat, wondering who lived here. The toilet was without a door, at the far end of the hallway, facing the front entrance. I peed quickly, hoping Vova wouldn't wander back in without knocking. The kitchen was tidy with well-stocked cupboards, but the living room decor had not been updated since the flat was built. Thin, worn carpet in swirling shades of turquoise was laid out on the floor. The copper-coloured curtains didn't match the carpet or the flowery wallpaper; the sofa was yet another mismatched colour. The only consistency came from the tiger picture on the wall and the tiger blanket covering the sofa. The TV was huge and old, as deep as it was wide, with twisty dials to change channels. I was going to plug it in and turn it on, but the electricity socket had burn marks around it. Burning down the apartment would not be the best way to show my appreciation.

Vova invited me up to his apartment for dinner. Despite his rough appearance, he was a polite, intelligent, insightful man. He talked for hours over dinner. It didn't perturb him at all that I understood only a fraction of what he was telling me. I was thankful he didn't expect me to talk. It was exhausting trying to understand, without having to structure responses in my limited Russian as well.

He talked about the town and how things used to be. There were those who moved away from this region in search of a better life, he said, and those who stayed, realising that this was the better life. He stayed in this region because he loved it. He loved the nature. He liked to be left alone to live his life the way he wanted. Politics did not interest him. The government and Moscow were half a world away. They had forgotten about him and he cared nothing for them. He might not be wealthy in rubles, but he had all he needed and was content, and that made him a rich man.

People who think this way are a minority back home in England. Our culture encourages us to spend, spend, spend. Spend money on things we don't need with money we don't have, which means we must work, work, work. What Vova said about Moscow, by which he meant all of western, European Russia, was true of much of England. People who live there are either burdened by debt or burdened by wealth. It is far better to live a happy, healthy life, a burden to nothing and no one. Out here, you could be free. There is no price on that.

After a parting shot of vodka (surprisingly, and thankfully, not followed by two more), I returned to the apartment. There, I sprawled out on the sofa, pulled up the furry polyester blanket with a tiger on it, and promptly fell into a deep sleep.

The disadvantage of Vova's generous hospitality was that I was awake a couple of hours before I wanted because he had prepared breakfast for me. He made tea, fried some eggs and cut up a loaf of white bread the way Russians do, by roughly slicing it into thick chunks and then cutting them all lengthways down the middle. I would have loved to go back to sleep after breakfast, but Vova insisted on guiding me to the far end of town. I waved goodbye to him at the Atka town sign, watched as his car returned up the icy street, then looked to the hills I was about to ascend.

At the top of the pass, I stopped. The hill climb had made me ravenous, despite Vova's breakfast. I scoffed more cheese, biscuits and chocolate while putting on my down jacket ready for the long downhill. As I was setting off, a lorry pulled up, and the driver wound down the window.

It was Sasha – the Sasha with the alluring soulful blue eyes I met near the End of the World. He invited me to have breakfast.

'I've just eaten,' I explained. 'Maybe a cup of tea?'

'Come on, get in.' I climbed into the truck and proceeded to take off several layers. Clothes on, clothes off: this was a regular feature of my cycling days again now that the traffic, and with it the number of people I met, had increased.

Sasha was quiet. That was his way. He offered me bread and boiled eggs and lots of fruit. My eyes lit up at the sight of clementines. 'Have as many as you want. I'm sorry, they are from China,' he said apologetically.

I wanted to laugh and joke with him and call him a lying bastard and tell him about the rest of the day after I'd last seen him – that day when there was no shop, but there was a psycho cyclist-killer and behemoth earth-moving machines coming to run me down in the darkness of night. Instead, I quietly took a clementine, peeled it and savoured the juicy segments.

It was an uneventful day after I left Sasha's truck. By the time I reached Karamken, the next village, late in the afternoon, it was snowing heavily. I stopped at the cafe. The ladies working there were wonderfully friendly. I felt relaxed, wrote my journal and watched the news on TV. When evening came, I intended to camp outside. But that was before Vova walked in.

Induced by a vodka haze, the man who had been my host the previous night stumbled loudly through the door. His shirt had come untucked, and his hairy pot belly was hanging out. He couldn't walk in a straight line, but had managed to drive one hundred kilometres down the ice road without hitting anything or damaging his vehicle.

He spoke loudly when sober; now he was overbearing and vulgar. He sat himself at my table, thrust my journal to one side and called out for glasses and a bottle of vodka to be brought over. I thought back to Vyacheslav in Artik and how the women had shaken their heads knowingly when they realised alcohol was involved.

'Leave her alone. Can't you see she's tired?' one of the women pleaded with Vova. Besides feeding me and giving me unlimited free tea, they were now doing their best to protect me.

Eventually Vova left. I really was tired and would have liked to go and pitch my tent and sleep. I didn't dare, though, because an unkempt ginger-haired man in ragged clothes had been lingering outside. He'd come in earlier looking for leftovers and had checked the empty beer cans on the table hoping there was a sip or two left. The women had thrown him out. When I had gone to check my bike and bags a while later, he asked me for money. He was finishing the dregs of a vodka bottle. I didn't trust him. It was too late to cycle far, and based on past experience, the chances of finding a place to camp were remote.

It was just then that a slim, immaculately dressed lady walked into the cafe. She spoke with the women, walked over and asked if she could sit with me. *Oh please, can't I just be left in peace? You could sit anywhere; why here?* 'Of course,' I replied politely.

'Where are you from?' the lady asked.

'England.'

'And you cycled from there?'

'No,' I sighed, 'from Yakutsk.' I expected the usual flurry of questions, but they didn't follow.

She wasn't interested in small talk. She cut straight to what she wanted to say. 'I'm a teacher and live here in Karamken. Would you like to stay at my home tonight?' *Oh hell yeah! How's that for a change of luck. You're my hero.*

'That's very kind. Are you sure?' I replied quite calmly.

'Come then. Let's go.' And with that she stood up and motioned for me to follow her. 'You're safe here.'

I didn't hesitate to pick up my journal and book and bags and follow her out of the cafe. I thanked the women, who I suspected had something to do with my change of fortune. As I passed, one woman winked and said to me quietly, 'You'll be safe with Kate. She's a good woman.'

Indeed she was.

33.

Melancholy.

That's what I felt on my last day riding the Kolyma Highway. I didn't want to reach Magadan because I had wanted to reach Chersky. I didn't want to reach Magadan because that would mean the end of the road and the end of the journey, and I was just beginning to enjoy myself. It had taken so much time and effort and difficulty just to become comfortable with winter cycling in Siberia, although the nearing of spring and warmer days certainly helped. And now it was nearly over. I didn't want it to end. It seemed so unfair. I also didn't want to reach Magadan because I couldn't decide where to stay.

Two weeks earlier, when thinking about the day I would reach Magadan, I had wondered where I would stay. If all went well, it was possible I would have a week to spend there before my flight. With no affordable hotels, my lodging options were limited. Since then, however, the problem had reversed itself.

Denis and Nastya had stopped me a week earlier when the weather was bad to see if I needed help. We'd sat in their 4x4 drinking coffee and homemade fruit juice laced with vodka. They'd given me a flask full of coffee to take with me. 'Give the flask back to us when you reach Magadan,' Denis said as he wrote his number on a scrap of paper. 'You can come and stay with us, and then we can eat lots and get drunk. It'll be great.'

A truck driver had also given me the number of a friend to call in case I got stuck. And a road worker, who I interrupted to get water, had asked if I had a place to stay in Magadan because, if I didn't, he could help. When he asked how I was leaving Magadan, I said it would be by plane. He offered to drive me and the bike to the airport sixty kilometres away because taxis are expensive. Then Kate, from Karamken, had phoned a teacher friend in Magadan who had also said I could stay with her.

I began to reminisce about the last couple of months: the challenges of cycling in such extreme temperatures and the kindness and hospitality I had been afforded. I thought about all the people who had helped me, and who I will always remember. I thought back to the days when I'd talked to no one at all. I thought about how the journey had been so different from what I'd expected.

And then I tried to recreate the unreality that had unfolded as I reached the End of the World. I wanted to bring back Tatiana and Misha and ... But I couldn't. They had vanished, along with the Siberian solitude. I missed it. I was no longer travelling through a pure white world untouched by man. Now, the ice had melted from the road and cars streamed past, tyres splashing up the slush and dyeing the snow black. Everything was dirty and contaminated in this imperfect reality.

A car sped past and seconds later the brake lights went on. It pulled onto the hard shoulder. I was sure they had stopped for me. The passengers got out and stood behind the car smiling at me. I strained to make out their faces, but even when I reached them and shook their hands, I hadn't the faintest clue who they were.

The lady spoke quickly. 'You probably don't remember us. We saw you at the cafe in Orotukan. I came and said hello and asked where you were going.' *Maybe I vaguely remember.* 'I had been talking with my husband ... This is my husband, Pyotr.'

'Hello,' I said and shook his hand. He said hello quietly back. It was clear already that he left his wife to do the talking. He didn't have a choice.

'And I'm Polina,' Polina continued. I shook her hand. 'Yes, we have been talking a lot about you.' By 'we' she meant 'I'. 'We wondered where you would stay in Magadan. And then we saw you cycling on the road, so close to Magadan, and I said to my husband that it must be a sign. That's what I said, isn't it?' Polina turned to Pyotr. Pyotr nodded but Polina had already turned back to me and was continuing the story. 'I said, we have to stop. It's a sign from God.' *One thing I know is it's not a sign from God.* 'So I said to my husband that we must stop for you. Where are you staying in Magadan?'

'Er … I'm not sure.'

'You must come and stay with us. Mustn't she?' Polina turned to Pyotr again. Pyotr nodded obediently. It didn't matter whether Pyotr nodded or not. The decision had been made. 'Would you like to stay with us? You're very welcome.'

'Er … the thing is that I have a week before my flight.'

'Then you shall stay for a week. You're welcome to stay for longer: two weeks, a month …'.

'OK.' This was the kindest answer; it silenced Polina and let her take a breath.

'Oh, wonderful!' Polina beamed. Pyotr smiled a resigned smile. 'I will give you my number. Pyotr! Find a pen and paper.'

'It's OK, I have one.' I rummaged in my handlebar bag and pulled out the pencil and my journal, flicking through the pages to find a blank space.

'Call us when you get to Magadan. Pyotr will come and fetch you.'

I figured it would be better to agree the plan while I could aid the conversation with hand gestures. 'Where in Magadan shall I meet you?' I asked.

Polina first gave an address that meant nothing to me; then she tried explaining the location giving convoluted directions that baffled me.

Seeing the confusion on my face, Pyotr spoke up. 'Take the road into town, continue up the main street. Phone us when you reach the station. It's on the left. You can't miss it. I will come and get you.' It sounded so simple; I was convinced I'd get lost. Still, I had plenty of backup options. I'd never yet, in all my years of travelling, failed to find a place to sleep for the night.

Swept up in Polina's enthusiasm and with renewed energy, the next fifteen kilometres were a breeze. I stopped only to take a photo of my bike at the 'Magadan' sign, which had a few stickers from overlanders stuck on it. Then the road climbed uphill. It began to snow. It wasn't snow with big, soft, delicate flakes like up on the plateau. It was cold, wet, miserable sleet. It was hardly a glamorous grande finale. It was just another day on the road.

Magadan was the endpoint of my Siberian Winter Trail, but it was not the End of the World as I had supposed it would be. Magadan lies beyond that, beholden to no one and living according to its own laws. It is an island of life, surrounded by nothing and connected to the real world by only a narrow causeway called the Road of Bones – a lifeline whose foundations are built of the dead.

My journey across Siberia had turned out very differently to what I'd planned and expected. In cycling to Magadan, my route was undoubtedly easier than it would have been had I gone north to Chersky. But when it came to making the decision on the route, I was wrong in thinking I knew what lay ahead on the Road of Bones. The road had unexpected secrets in store for me – not so much secrets it held, waiting for me to unearth, but secrets it exposed within me. Those deepest, darkest secrets that are within all of us. Most we never know are there; others we do our best to keep buried. But out there, alone in the stark naked winter, there was nothing to hide behind, and I was unable to hide from myself.

I had a wonderful week in Magadan under the care of Polina and Pyotr. Every day they took me to see new sights with their friends from church, Sveta and Losha. If I had stayed in a hotel and relied on a guidebook to direct me, I would have visited the regional museum and the Mask of Sorrow sculpture that stands tall on the hill overlooking the town, nothing else.

I would not have known that it was Sveta's father giving a talk at the regional museum on the local traditional art of bone carving. He stood behind a small table covered in samples of the material from which he worked: whale bone, walrus tusk and the cheaper, more common, reindeer horn. In the display cases around the room were samples of his and other local artists' work: miniature mammoths, bears, whales and walrus, owls and ravens, and Chukchi people fishing and dog-sledding and kayaking.

The most intriguing of all the carvings were the paunchy characters with pointed heads, slit eyes and wide mischievous smiles. All Sveta could tell me was that these *peliken* were Chukchi good luck charms. Subsequent research into these curious figurines revealed that *peliken* is the Russified word for a billiken, a character created by an American artist from Missouri that became an international phenomenon in the early twentieth century. It seems that one billiken figurine made its way to Alaska, where native carvers recreated the billiken, simplifying its features so they could be carved into tusk and bone with their basic tools. The billiken then travelled from Alaska to Uelen in Siberia and into Chukchi folklore, where it's believed hunters originally hung the figures on their hunting gear, so that everything bad would pass from them into the idol.

That a Chukchi good luck charm should have its origins in the American Midwest does not seem unbelievable; in Magadan I saw more evidence of cultural connections with Alaska and the rest of the US than with Moscow. Transport connections from this region to the US are much less direct these days, when all flights go via Moscow, and there are no passenger ship services out of Magadan. Historically, movement was across the Bering Strait to Alaska. It wasn't until the Russian conquest of Siberia in the sixteenth and seventeenth centuries that connections were made with the west. Culturally, the indigenous ethnic groups of the Russian Far East are more closely linked to Alaska.

Like Sveta's father, Losha was a carver too. One afternoon I went to their workplace. It was a small room in a basement in the city centre. This was no gallery for prospective buyers, simply the ordered chaos that many artists require to be creative. The room, with work benches around the edges, was covered in carvings, half-finished sculptures, and pieces of tusk and bone and tooth that were yet to be touched by tools. Finished pieces, some damaged and of no saleable value, were stacked gathering dust on shelves along the walls and piled into overflowing display cabinets. An electric dentist's drill lay on one workbench with a cable connecting it to a power supply. An angled lamp was clamped to the desk.

Losha opened a second door to a recessed cupboard. Through the gloom, I saw a pile of large bones and tusks heaped on the floor. After some rummaging around, Losha emerged holding a massive mammoth tusk about one and a half metres in length. As he passed it to me, he said I'd need both hands to hold it. My biceps ached while I stood, smiling, waiting for Sveta to capture the moment on camera.

Mammoth remains, I learned, are frequently found in Siberia. One well-preserved carcass of a male baby mammoth, named Dima, was found near Magadan in 1977. Dima was six to twelve months old when he died around 40,000 years ago. He now lies in a museum in St Petersburg, tufts of woolly hair still intact on his lower legs. A cast replica hangs on the wall of the museum in Magadan. His emaciated body, with ribs protruding and skin pulled taut, is only about one metre high. It looked like a baby elephant, except for the diminutive ears.

There has been some speculation that woolly mammoths could be recreated using DNA from specimens preserved in the ice, though little useable DNA has ever been extracted. Even if feasible, the ethics and costs make such an undertaking questionable. For now, there is a life-sized mammoth sculpture made from scrap metal that stands facing the town on the shore of Nagayeva Bay.

Nagayeva was the name of the nearby settlement that existed before Magadan was founded. The main port is in this bay. Today, it is used by the fishing industry and for transport of goods into the city. Once, it was where prisoners were brought by ship and then sent to work in the gulags.

On the hill above the bay stands the Mask of Sorrow, a tall concrete statue of a face with tears in the shape of small masks rolling down one cheek. Behind, a young woman kneels with hands over her face. On the ground are stone markers, some with names of the labour camps, others with religious and political symbols associated with those who, indiscriminately, were sent here and suffered.

Standing on the hill at the Mask of Sorrow, there is a good view of the town spreading inland from Nagayeva Bay. The old wooden houses still stand, clinging to the hillside beside the port. Although the houses are very basic, people still live in them. Most who can afford it now prefer to live in the centre in the tall modern apartment blocks that tower over the rest of the city sprawl.

Sveta explained how Magadan had expanded and grown over the last fifty years. She pointed out beyond the hill to the left. 'That's Ola. We'll take you there one day this week. The children are on school holiday, so we can all go,' she explained. 'The bay there is a popular place in the summer when people go to the beach for a barbecue. But it will still be nice now.'

245

On another day, she took me to her children's school, where her mother, Tamara, ran the library. Showcases displayed pictures and the work of prominent people who lived in Magadan and went to the school, many of them writers and actors. One cabinet was dedicated entirely to the cosmonaut Pavel Vinogradov, who had revisited the school in recent years. The walls were covered in posters detailing the history of the school and those who attended it, especially during the early years, before and during the Second World War (or Great Patriotic War as Russians refer to it). Here was one of the few places where people who suffered in the Gulag system and during Stalin's purges were remembered.

Before I left, Tamara searched around the library. 'You must take something as a gift.' She spoke all the while she was looking, talking to herself more than anyone else. 'Ah, yes. This,' she said and picked up what she considered an appropriate present.

It fit snugly into the palm of her hand, which she held out to me. She uncurled her fingers from around the small object to reveal a painted, wooden *matroyoshka*.

'Not one gift but many gifts,' she smiled. With her other hand, she separated the Russian doll into two halves to reveal another doll inside. She split that doll too. There were more inside that, each smaller than the last. 'See, five gifts for you.'

It's Tatiana, Bogdan, Masha, Misha and Andrei, I thought.

The following day we – Polina, Pyotr, Sveta and Losha and their children, and I – drove over to Ola in the next bay. I wandered down to the shoreline where thick ice marked the boundaries of high and low tide. I stood, hands in pockets, and looked out. *So here I am at the end of the road, beyond the End of the World.* And I closed my hand around the small object in my pocket. It was Tamara's gift: the Russian doll.

'You know, you're still crazy!' a voice whispered.

Yeah, and I'm still alive, I thought. Alive, crazy and free.

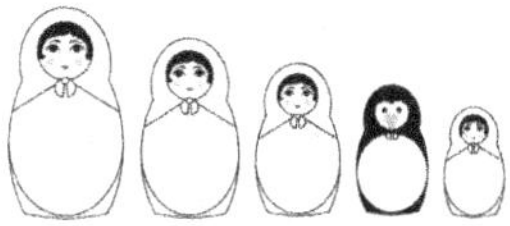

Epilogue

A couple of weeks before I first flew to Russia in the summer, I went to an art exhibition at Houghton Hall in Norfolk.

Houghton Hall was built in the 1720s for Sir Robert Walpole, who is considered to be Britain's first Prime Minister. He was an art collector and wanted somewhere to house his collection. But he and his heirs, like so many, spent more money than they had. Eventually, to pay their debts, the fabulous collection was sold off.

It was Catherine II of Russia who bought much of it – including magnificent paintings from Rubens to Rembrandt and Velázquez to Van Dyck – as a job lot to add to her already prolific collection of art from around the world. She had always been a lover of the arts and wanted to decorate the Hermitage, her name for an extension of the Winter Palace in St Petersburg.

Through a collaboration between the UK and Russia, the art originally owned by Sir Robert Walpole was loaned from the Hermitage Museum and brought back to Norfolk. The art I saw at Houghton Hall, exhibited as it had been when Walpole was alive, was impressive. Learning about the connection with Russia made me want to visit the Hermitage museum and see Catherine II's even grander collection.

The advantage of cycling to Magadan rather than Chersky was that it took less time; I had a week spare in which to also visit St Petersburg. After the cultural vacuum that exists when you spend the winter alone in the Siberian taiga, St Petersburg was the perfect antidote. It was like being reborn into another world; the world I had left behind three months ago.

Culture shock. St Petersburg was an assault on the senses. It was bright and colourful. Oh, the noise! And the smells.

I stared, mesmerised, out of the taxi window at the wide highways from the airport. Then I stepped out into the city centre. The traffic was deafening. The hustle and bustle of people going to and from work and shops with dawdling tourists mingling amongst them was bewildering. I didn't know where to look. The massive buildings were so grand and beautiful and colourful. I kept looking upwards as they reached for the sky, but then I bumped into people or walked off the curb. And as I breathed in, I smelt the overpowering exhaust fumes and strong odours wafting from cafes and restaurants and rubbish where a bin lay discarded. It was all too much, coming from the Siberian winter where there had been so little to trigger and stimulate the senses.

I spent my first full day in St Petersburg in the Hermitage Museum, enthralled with the vast array of art and sculptures from all ages on display. I walked through the British collection and saw, hanging on the walls, paintings that I'd seen in Norfolk a year ago. I was surprised; I had seen so many things during the year that had passed, I had forgotten about the day I'd seen them at Houghton Hall. It was as though I had come full circle.

After this journey, I found it harder than usual to integrate back into my other life of office work and routine. My thoughts kept going back to Siberia and everything I had experienced there. After three months in the region, I am more bewildered than ever as to what Siberia is. Every insight and hint of an explanation are pieces of a jigsaw that I failed to put together into one complete image. The fragments, piled high, have exacerbated my conviction that I do not understand the region at all.

I have left this book as a shaken and stirred cocktail of images and impressions and feelings. I hope that you, the reader, make better sense of it than me.

One day, I hope to return to Siberia. Perhaps, it is that I understand it so little that it fascinates me so much.

Acknowledgements

I thank all the people I met on the road for watching out for me. And I thank you, the reader, for listening to me. I am humbled for I received so much and am able to offer so little.

As with all my adventures, I funded this journey by working and saving up. With limited finances, I am therefore grateful to those companies who sponsored me by supplying equipment and clothing suitable for the Siberian winter conditions: to Cumulus for the down sleeping bag and Thermarest, Alpkit for the down jacket, Schwalbe for the bike tyres, Dogwood Designs for the bike pogies and Airtrim for the filter mask.

Thanks also to Jennifer Barclay, my editor, for correcting all my mistakes and contradictions. And to Jimmy Howe, who patiently listened to all my questions for improving the draft manuscript and willingly gave considered responses knowing that I was only voicing my concerns, probably knew the answers already, and would ignore his suggestions anyway.

Finally, thanks to mum and dad – always there in the background, the solid foundation upon which everything I have done and created is built.

Lightning Source UK Ltd.
Milton Keynes UK
UKOW04f0616201117
313023UK00001B/359/P